D0849772

COMPUTER-BASED
TRAINING

COMPUTER-BASED

TRAINING

A GUIDE TO SELECTION AND IMPLEMENTATION

GREG KEARSLEY
HumRRO

ADDISON-WESLEY PUBLISHING COMPANY
Reading, Massachusetts / Menlo Park, California
London / Amsterdam / Don Mills, Ontario / Sydney

Library of Congress Cataloging in Publication Data

Kearsley, Greg, 1951–
  Computer-based training.

  Bibliography: p.
  Includes index.
  1. Employees, Training of—Computer-assisted
instruction.   I. Title.
HF5549.5.T7K33 1983   658.3′124′02854   82-16411
ISBN 0-201-10333-8

ISBN 0-201-10333-8
ABCDEFGHIJ-AL-89876543

Preface

This book attempts to meet two needs. First, it is meant to serve as a guide for training professionals who have responsibilities for selecting, implementing, managing, or evaluating a Computer-Based Training (CBT) system. Second, it is intended to be a comprehensive and up-to-date source of information on the use of computers in business, industrial, military, and government training for those involved in the CBT field.

Even though computers have been used for training purposes since the early 1960s, their application has been relatively limited until quite recently. There are many reasons for this long acceptance period, but the delay is primarily due to economic, technical, or socio-political obstacles. Only with the emergence of microprocessors have the costs of CBT dropped into the range of "tolerable costs" for most training budgets. At the same time, the costs of conventional training approaches have become intolerable. Thus, cost is no longer a major obstacle holding back CBT.

The kinds of instructional capabilities possible with CBT have improved to the point where computers can now provide very sophisticated learning experiences sometimes rivaling those provided by the best human instructors. The hardware and software involved have become very powerful, reliable, and usable. Most of the things that have caused technical problems in the past are now well understood (although not necessarily solved).

As far as socio-political obstacles are concerned, CBT has established sufficient credibility by virtue of a diverse range of successful applications that it can now challenge the inertia of "traditional" training approaches (i.e., text and classroom lectures). The results of hundreds of experimental studies and operational projects show that CBT is practical, effective, and often results in cost savings. CBT is no longer perceived as a novelty or a risky gamble. There are, however, still problems integrating it into a "lock-step" and "chalk and talk" training world.

There can be little doubt that CBT will play a very important role in future training systems. It is estimated that almost 50 percent of all U.S. workers currently interact with a computer system in their daily jobs. As more and more occupations become computer based, CBT will become well accepted and quite cost effective. The legacy of more than two decades of CBT research and development provides a good framework to guide current and future applications. This book attempts to document this framework in a manner useful to training practitioners.

A few words about the organization of the book are in order. It is divided into a series of chapters that correspond to the major steps associated with a CBT project.

- Understanding the Rationale for, and Nature of, CBT (Chapters 1 and 2)

- Conducting a CBT Feasibility Study (Chapter 3)

- Selecting a CBT System (Chapters 4 and 5)

- Developing CBT Materials (Chapter 6)

- Implementing and Managing CBT (Chapter 7)

- Evaluating CBT (Chapter 8)

- Current Limits and Future Potential of CBT (Chapter 9)

Although each chapter deals with a particular aspect of CBT, the chapters are not self-contained. Every chapter contains information needed for the other chapters. For example, while Chapter 3 discusses how to conduct a CBT feasibility study, there are important considerations relating to feasibility in all of the chapters. Thus it is recommended that you read the entire book even if you are only interested in a particular aspect of CBT covered in one chapter. On the other hand, once you have read the entire book, you should find that the contents of a single chapter will be sufficient to guide you in a specific CBT activity (e.g., developing materials, evaluation, etc.).

It is important to understand that this is not a book about computers, but their application to training. This book does not require any computer background to read, nor will it teach you anything new about computers, and it avoids all but the most general and essential computer terminology. The fact is that in today's computer society, you do not need to know about "bits, bytes, and bauds"—just how to use computers as a tool.

Finally, let me deal with an objection that is bound to arise from some readers: "If CBT is so great, how come I'm reading a book about it?" CBT represents one of many alternative instructional approaches. It is well suited to certain kinds of training applications, as the first two chapters discuss. Traditional instructional delivery methods, such as print and classroom lectures, have a number of virtues (i.e., inexpensive, quick, flexible) and are likely to prevail for many years to come. At present, there is no way that the information contained in this book could be created and delivered to you in electronic and interactive form as conveniently or for the same price as you paid for this book. However, some day in the not too distant future when paper is very expensive and cheap desktop or hand-held computers are owned by everyone, the story will be quite different. In the meantime, we should focus on the many applications where CBT (in conjunction with other instructional media) results in significant improvements in training effectiveness and efficiency.

I owe many people debts of gratitude for their help in completing this book. First of all, I would like to acknowledge Steve Hunka, Eugene Romaniuk, and Craig Montgomerie of the University of Alberta, Fred O'Neal and Victor Bunderson of WICAT, and Robert Seidel, Michael Hillelsohn, and Beverly Hunter of HumRRO for their influential contributions to my thinking about CBT. I would also like to thank Judy Pumphrey and Doris Stein for their diligent efforts in typing the manuscript, as well as Rudy Manuel, Ginger Harper, and Alice Thompson for the artwork. Wendy Ebersberger provided editorial assistance and the index. Finally, I am grateful to HumRRO for its support in completing this book.

Alexandria, Virginia   G. P. K.

Contents

COMPUTER-BASED
TRAINING

1

Why Use Computers
for Training?

In this first chapter, we will look at the major reasons underlying the use of computers for training. To help make the discussion more concrete, illustrative examples from actual CBT applications will be used. When you have finished this chapter, you should have a good grasp of the *why* of CBT and be able to identify possible opportunities for CBT in your own or other organizations. A checklist is provided at the end of the chapter to help you do this.

At the outset, you should understand that it is the interactive nature of CBT which underlies virtually all of its benefits and outcomes. CBT is an inherently *active* mode of learning. The learner must continually do something—answer a question, select a topic, ask for a review, and so on. This contrasts with the inherently passive instructional approach involved in classroom lectures, videotape, or textbooks. To the extent that these other approaches can be made interactive (e.g., increasing the amount of discussion in a class, computer-controlled videotape, programmed instruction), they can accrue some of the natural advantages of CBT.[1] In fact, adding computers to an already existing curriculum or media is one way of turning passive learning into active learning.

Almost all CBT applications are driven by the need to improve the efficiency or effectiveness of a particular training system or situation. Increased

---

[1]Note that it is possible (through ignorance or oversight) to create relatively passive CBT and, hence, eliminate the most important aspect of the medium.

efficiency means achieving the same training outcomes with fewer resources (i.e., people, equipment, facilities, materials, travel expenses, etc.). In short, increased efficiency means reducing costs and saving money somehow. Increased effectiveness means getting better training results (i.e., improved student achievement or job performance), usually for the same level of resources although sometimes additional costs are acceptable. Increasing both efficiency (reducing costs) and effectiveness (improved outcomes) at the same time corresponds to the goal of improving productivity—more for less.

While increasing efficiency and/or effectiveness are the general goals of CBT, they normally manifest themselves in terms of more specific objectives. Some of the major ones are:

- Increased Control

- Reduced Resource Requirements

- Individualization

- Timeliness and Availability

- Reduced Training Time

- Improved Job Performance

- Convenience

- Change Agent

- Increased Learning Satisfaction

- Reduced Development Time

The rest of this chapter discusses each of these possible outcomes of CBT. Later in the book (Chapter 8), the cost/benefits of CBT based upon these considerations will be examined. The details of the CBT systems used in the applications mentioned, as well as the types of CBT involved, will be discussed in subsequent chapters.

INCREASED CONTROL

One of the biggest failings in training systems is not the lack of good instructors or instructional materials, but simply the lack of control over training activities. For example, it is not uncommon to visit a field office or military post where training materials are kept and find an inch of dust covering everything. Perfectly good (and needed) instructional materials may simply be unused due to poor instructional management. Alternatively, a corporation may spend a considerable amount of time and money developing an instructional course which is then distributed to different training centers to be taught; however, instructors at each center may modify the course such that it produces different outcomes than were originally intended. In organizations where the uniformity of training is important (e.g., the military, banks and insurance companies, government agencies), lack of training standardization is a costly weakness. Finally, consider the case of a maintenance training course that requires trainees to spend a certain number of hours practicing actual equipment repair tasks. If their performance is measured only by successful repair of the equipment at the end of the session (or worse yet, by simply spending the requisite numbers of hours), there is no way of knowing if trainees have learned good troubleshooting or diagnostic skills. In other words, there is no real control over the learning process—only certain checkpoints.

CBT allows increased control in terms of improving utilization or completion of learning materials, increasing standardization of instruction, or monitoring of student progress. The use of computers to generate and score tests that indicate student progress or completion of training units can provide as fine a level of control over training as is desired or necessary. By using the computer to deliver instruction, each student receives the same uniform training (even though it may be delivered in different places at different times) and a high degree of standardization can be achieved. If the task to be learned is a complex one involving many subtasks (e.g., equipment maintenance), the computer can be used to test the mastery of each subtask at a level of detail that would be difficult or impractical to do otherwise.

The most common way of using computers to improve control in a training system is Computer-Managed Instruction (CMI) in which the computer is used to register students, assign training schedules, generate and score tests, and produce reports on student progress and utilization of training resources. One of the largest CMI systems in use today has been developed by the U.S. Navy (Davis 1978; Van Matre 1978). This system manages the daily instruction of about 10,000 students in twenty-four courses at nine schools, representing about 28 percent of Navy technical training. It generates detailed reports on student progress (see Figure 1–1), which indicate where the student currently is, how long it will be before they are finished, and an assessment of their learning progress.

Another large CMI system is used by IBM to train its field engineering staff who are responsible for maintenance of customer equipment. The system involves approximately 400 remote terminals located in IBM offices throughout the United States, and is used by about 10,000 employees (Branscomb 1980). In this system, the training materials are usually in print form (e.g., technical manuals), and the CMI system is used to ensure that the employees have mastered these materials via online testing.

Many insurance companies and banks now provide their basic claims processing and teller training via computers (Rahmlow 1978). This means that the same training program is provided at all branch locations; hence, each

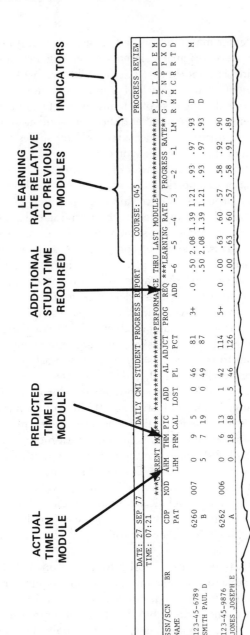

Figure 1-1 Navy CMI Report

claims processing clerk or bank teller receives identical training nation-wide. The use of uniform procedures as a consequence of standardized training can make significant contributions to a smoothly running organization.

REDUCED RESOURCE REQUIREMENTS

CBT can reduce resource requirements in a number of ways. By providing instruction at branch offices or field sites, the need for central training facilities and personnel can be reduced. Because of the reduction in training duration possible with CBT due to individualized instruction, it is often the case that fewer instructors or facilities are needed for a given number of students.

Alternatively, instead of reduced staff or facilities, it is possible to achieve higher student throughput using CBT for the same level of resources. Because training durations are reduced, the same number of instructors or classrooms can handle a greater number of students over time. CBT also can be used to achieve higher instructor-to-student ratios, since the "routine" aspects of the instruction can take place by online or offline self-study and the instructor is needed only to help students with problems. Thus, whereas a single instructor might have only been able to supervise two or three trainees at one time (a typical situation in apprenticeship training), with CBT the instructor may be able to supervise five or six trainees with no loss in the quality of the instruction. In fact, since the system is able to pinpoint the specific problems encountered by the trainee, and the instructor can deal with these on a one-on-one basis, it is quite possible for the instruction to be much better even though the class size has been increased.

The most significant reduction in training resources due to CBT is the use of computer-based simulators and trainers to displace the need for actual equipment. A large number of civilian and military occupations involve the operation or maintenance of complex equipment such as aircraft, manufacturing machines, weapons systems, nuclear propulsion plants, and oil rigs. The best example is probably the use of CBT for pilot training. Major airlines and the military use CBT in conjunction with simulators to reduce the amount of actual flying time required for training. American Airlines estimates that it has reduced training time by 50 percent at its Flight Academy and saved $30 million per year in fuel costs. Whereas it cost the airline $48,000 to train a pilot in 1966, with the use of CBT it now costs $11,600. The Navy has reduced pilot training costs from $5,000 per hour to $400 per hour in one of its programs through the use of computer-based simulation. United Airlines is planning to do all of its flight training for the Boeing 767 via a CBT system, eliminating the need for any special-purpose trainers or actual flying time.

The use of CBT instead of actual equipment is one of the most compelling and cost-effective reasons for the use of computers in military and industrial training. Hands-on practice with equipment is often recognized as a critical as-

Figure 1-2 Use of TICCIT® for Hands-On Electronics Training (Courtesy, Hazeltine Corporation)

pect of a training program; however, the actual equipment is typically unavailable for training purposes and, therefore, hands-on training is minimized or omitted. The use of computer-based simulators and trainers can provide the kind of practice needed without the costs (and risks) associated with the actual equipment. Furthermore, through the use of graphics, it is often possible to provide the trainee with a better understanding of the equipment via computer-based simulation than is possible with just practice on the actual equipment (see Figure 1-2).

INDIVIDUALIZATION

Individualization—allowing each student to learn at a speed and in a fashion most suited to his or her particular learning style—has always been one of the central goals of CBT. Simply allowing students to learn at their own pace produces significant time savings over conventional classroom training, since classroom instruction tends to be geared to the pace of the slowest students. However, CBT can do far more than allow students to control their rate of learning. Most CBT systems allow students some control over the order in which they learn topics, i.e., the sequencing of instruction. Moreover, students are usually free to practice things they find difficult as much as they want, and to skip over things they understand.

Apart from the humanistic value of individualization, what are the practical benefits in training? One major problem in most training programs is that many students are either under- or overqualified for what they are to be taught. As a consequence, they are either overwhelmed or bored by the training. A real benefit of CBT is that the skill and knowledge levels of students can be assessed at the beginning of training, and individualized learning programs (either online or offline) can be created to match their entry level. A second area where individualization becomes important is remedial instruction during or after training. Because of differences in past experiences and knowledge, different students tend to have problems with different aspects of a training program. CBT can provide the specific type of help needed to ensure that each student finishes training with the same acceptable level of competence or mastery.

For example, IBM uses CBT as part of its basic and advanced sales training programs to ensure that all trainees have the appropriate entry level skills for classroom-based training courses. Sales representatives are provided with pretraining materials in their branch offices and must pass computer-administered tests on these materials to qualify for classroom training. The tests and pretraining materials make sure that all students taking a particular class have the appropriate entry level skills; in fact, students cannot attend the classes until they have demonstrated their readiness.

Another realm of training where individualization is becoming important is customer education in the computer systems domain. In earlier times, computer systems were sufficiently expensive that computer manufacturers were able to provide a high level of educational support to almost all customers; however, as computer systems have gotten smaller and less expensive, this level of customer education support has become impossible. Thus, most computer manufacturers have turned to providing "self-study" customer training. A major problem in providing effective self-study materials is the great deal of variation that exists in what customers need to know because of the differences in applications, configurations, and their level of computer sophistication. Hence, there is a great need for the type of individualized instruction that can be provided by CBT. Digital Equipment Corporation was one of the first computer companies to recognize the value of CBT for this situation and to develop computer-based education packages for customers (e.g., Heines 1978).

TIMELINESS AND AVAILABILITY

A major problem in training is to be able to provide instruction when and where it is needed, i.e., at the right time and right place for the student. Due to a lack of instructors or scheduling considerations, employees must often wait considerable lengths of time for training vital to their jobs. In the meantime, they are in a "training" mode and relatively unproductive. Alternatively, training may be given to employees because it is available (or they are) even though it may not be needed or relevant to their present jobs. This leads to the problem of "cold storage" training—teaching things that may be needed in the future but are likely to be forgotten.

The transportation and scheduling considerations associated with a central training facility represent a major obstacle to providing timely and inexpensive training. Travel expenses often represent 30 to 40 percent of an organization's training costs. The use of CBT to provide field-based training can drastically reduce such travel costs. Even after the costs of the equipment and development are accounted for, the savings can be appreciable (see Chapter 8).

Clearly, CBT has tremendous advantages in terms of providing instruction "on demand." Once CBT materials have been developed, they can be made available whenever and wherever needed, provided that the terminals are available (see Figure 1-3). For example, the Bell system conducts a tremendous amount of technical training related to new equipment that must be installed, operated, and maintained. The cold storage problem is significant (Davis 1981). The use of classroom instruction for such equipment training means that most employees will get this training either too early or too late. Since there are thousands to be trained and only a small proportion can be accommodated at a central training facility at one time, the training must be spread over many months prior to and after the equipment is available. In contrast, with the use of CBT, all employees can be trained simultaneously in the field at the time the equipment is put into service. Furthermore, the use of simulation allows employees to get hands-on training before the equipment even arrives. This means that they can be fairly proficient at installing, operating, and servicing the equipment from the first day they work with it—instead of many weeks or months later.

The shortage of certain types of employees and the instructors to train them is another aspect of the availability problem that CBT can address. For example, because of the growth in the electronics industry during the past years, there is a great dearth of suitably trained electronics engineers. Large corporations that depend heavily on electronics are using CBT to train individuals with appropriate backgrounds or upgrade the skills of existing employees (Modesitt 1981). Similarly, the energy boom of the past decade has created a high demand for skilled workers in the oil and gas drilling industry. Not only is there a need to train many new people, there is also a need for training that can be given close to the remote sites where oil and gas exploration take place. Having to bring an employee from a drilling rig in the high Arctic or hundreds of miles offshore for training is an expensive activity that CBT can eliminate. It is not surprising that the oil and gas industries have a very high level of interest in CBT (e.g., Rebstock 1980).

Figure 1-3   SCHOLAR/TEACH 3® Providing "On-Demand" Training
(Courtesy, Boeing Computer Services Company)

REDUCED TRAINING TIME

The capability of CBT to reduce training time is one of the most well documented and impressive outcomes. While the time savings possible with CBT
varies considerably, a median value is about 30 percent over conventional
training approaches (Orlansky and String 1979). Actually, this time savings
with CBT is almost completely due to the individualization of instruction,
not the use of the computer itself. However, it is virtually impossible to run
a large individualized instructional program without the use of a computer
to manage the activity. (See the discussion of CMI in the next chapter.)
Thus, in principle the time savings could be achieved through any form of
individualized training, but in practice it is only likely to be achieved in the
context of CBT.

There are many cost savings associated with reduced training time. Since most employees are paid their full salaries during training, reduced training durations reduce the amount of money spent on training. In those cases where training is held away from the work location (e.g., at a central training facility), per diem costs can be reduced. The most important benefit, however, is that employees can be back to their jobs faster, thus providing services or performing their role in achieving the mission of the organization. Essentially, training is employee and organizational "down time," which can be reduced through CBT.

It should be noted that taking advantage of the time savings made possible by CBT often requires significant changes to the training system and the organization. Training systems that have been built around fixed schedule, classroom type instruction must undergo considerable change to accommodate variable schedule CBT. Students not only begin and end training at different times, but also take different amounts of time to complete their training. This means that the organization must often change its work assignment or personnel policies and procedures to take advantage of this situation. For example, when CMI was first implemented in the Navy, the duty assignments were still left on a fixed schedule basis as per the duration of the old fixed schedule training. This meant that trainees who finished their assigned training early (as most did) had nothing to do; consequently, they were often given temporary assignments (e.g., guard or recruitment duty) while waiting. The word soon got around that it was not a good idea to finish training early, and training completion times suddenly increased! Once the Navy changed to a continuous assignment procedure, the problem disappeared and they were able to benefit from the time savings produced by CBT.

IMPROVED JOB PERFORMANCE

One major reason for using CBT is to improve job performance (or eliminate job performance problems). The capability of CBT to provide interactive individualized instruction means that it inherently has the potential to improve the quality of training. It has been shown that instructional approaches based on passive presentation methods (i.e., classroom lectures, videotape) result in very little actual learning—on the order of a few minutes every hour. Most of the time the student is not attending to the instruction. In interactive individualized instruction, the student spends a very high percentage of the time attending and, hence, learning.[2]

---

[2]This is why students usually find CBT much more demanding and intense than traditional approaches. Students often report being mentally exhausted after two or three hours of CBT, which is likely the equivalent of a full day in regular classes.

The point just made accounts for one of the reasons why CBT efforts do not always result in improved job performance. If the CBT materials are properly designed (i.e., relevant to the job) and take full advantage of the interactive individualized capabilities possible with CBT, then they are almost certain to improve job performance relative to traditional (passive) training approaches. On the other hand, if the other training approaches are also properly designed and involve interactive and/or individualized instruction, the use of a computer is likely to make relatively little difference in terms of improved effectiveness.

CBT can be used to improve job performance directly or indirectly. In direct approaches, it is used to train employees on specific skills needed to do their jobs. One area where CBT is widely applied for this purpose is training individuals to operate or maintain complex equipment. Rebstock and Harkey (1979) describe a typical situation in the context of using a CBT system to train process control operators in the chemical industry:

> The operators comprise a target population of widely varying age, experience and ability. Many possess minimal basic skills, some have virtually no chemical or process control background, and others stubbornly stick to undesirable procedural habits and misconceptions acquired over decades of OJT. Yet their jobs require them to monitor and control a highly technical, complex and volatile chemical process by means of various meters, indicator lights, levels and instruments. Inconsistent performance on their part reduces the unit's efficiency and endangers the safety of fellow workers. Operator errors which cause unit downtime reduce plant productivity and profitability (p. 976).

In this particular example, a process control simulation was developed to improve the operator's understanding of the processes involved (using graphics to show the workings of the unit), teach the correct sequence of actions for specific conditions, and improve the operator's reaction time in performing these actions.

Instead of using CBT to directly improve job performance skills, it may be used to provide instruction that is more general in nature and that broadly affects job performance. For example, Aetna Life and Casualty, as well as other insurance companies, use CBT to provide remedial instruction to employees in basic mathematics as it applies to business and finance. (Lowe 1979). This training opens up job possibilities within the company for employees who lack mathematics skills. Similarly, the U.S. Army has pursued the use of CBT for basic skills education, particularly for remedial reading instruction (e.g., Siegel and Simutis 1979). In the course of a soldier's career, there is a need to read and understand a wide variety of documents ranging from regulations to technical manuals. Clearly, improvements in reading skills achieved through CBT will ultimately result in better job performance for the Army.

CONVENIENCE

In comparison to some of the other reasons previously discussed, convenience may appear to be a relatively weak rationale for the use of CBT; however, as computer systems become more ubiquitous and widespread, it is becoming a very strong and compelling argument for CBT. Insofar as employees already use a computer system for their jobs and have access to a computer terminal, CBT using the same system makes a good deal of sense (as well as cents). Thus, the system can be used to teach employees how to use the system. (This is called "embedded training" or "teaching through the tube.") This approach also has the benefit that the instructional materials can always be available for refresher training or as online job aids. Once of the limitations of this approach is that the kind of CBT possible is limited by the capabilities designed into the system for its actual purpose. Many systems and terminals used for administrative or financial transactions lack graphics capabilities, yet this is generally viewed as an important feature of a CBT system to be used for instruction (see Chapter 4). Another problem encountered is that when the same system is shared for both operational and training uses, system performance often suffers.

Bank teller training is a good example of how CBT can be part of an existing computer system. For example, when Western Bank Corporation decided to install a new financial terminal system in 1978, it was faced with the problem of training approximately 6800 tellers and 1500 bank officers located at many different branches in a very short time period. The obvious solution was to develop this instruction in the form of CBT, which could be delivered using the terminals themselves (Rahmlow 1979).

Airlines and hotel reservation systems provide another example of a computer system that can be used for CBT. For example, United, American, and TWA all use their terminal systems to teach booking reservations, computing fares, and other skills necessary in occupations such as reservations agent, passenger service agent, airport operations personnel, and flight attendants. As new system applications are developed (or old ones modified), the CBT lessons are created or revised as part of the development activity. Holiday Inns, Inc., uses its reservation system for teaching all managers and clerks how to operate the system, as well as providing computer simulations of hotel/motel operations to assist managers in developing business planning and financial forecasting skills.

A more profound kind of embedded CBT is when the instruction is actually designed into the equipment or product. Thus, certain new weapons systems and automated office equipment have been designed to be self-instructional in nature. (The availability of inexpensive microprocessors makes it possible to do this.) What is significant about this development is the fact that training is considered as an integral part of the equipment design process rather than as an afterthought once the equipment is ready for use. To the extent this trend continues, we can expect to see a high demand for CBT expertise on product development teams.

CHANGE AGENT

One important role that CBT has played is as an educational change agent. CBT may be used to force change within the boundaries of a particular organization or institution, or more generally. For example, many large companies now allow employees to take computer terminals home to allow them to learn away from work (e.g., Clogston 1980). Control Data Corporation has developed a program called HOMEWORK, which allows long-term disabled employees to learn and work at home using the CDC PLATO system.[3] The HOMEWORK program allows permanently handicapped or disabled employees to again become productive employees without having to leave their homes. Some of the major outcomes of the HOMEWORK program include: a 50 to 75 percent decrease in health care costs to the employees and company; substantial increase in self-concept and confidence levels of the participating employees; improvement in family relations; and greater involvement in home, community, and professional activities by participants. When it is realized that there are more than 2 million Americans who are classified as homebound due to disabilities and who cost U.S. taxpayers over $750 million per month in Social Security disability insurance, it is clear that the HOMEWORK program represents a very significant humanitarian and economic CBT experiment (see Figure 1-4).

Another example of CBT as a change agent is its use by inmates in correctional facilities. A number of projects have been conducted using the CDC PLATO system (e.g., Siegel 1979; Diem and Fairweather 1980). The purpose of these efforts has been to help inmates obtain improved credentials for employment in terms of high school or GED diplomas. In general, this objective involves remedial instruction in reading and mathematics—instruction that CBT is well suited to provide. Results from the studies showed that the use of CBT in this setting was moderately successful in achieving basic skills instruction and offered considerable potential for educational opportunities that would otherwise not take place. However, like any attempt at innovation, there were numerous problems to be overcome. We will discuss these at length in Chapter 7.

The broadest sense in which CBT is serving as a change agent is in the area of computer literacy. As computers have become more and more ubiquitous in

---

[3]PLATO and HOMEWORK are registered trademarks of Control Data Corporation. PLATO is discussed in detail in Chapter 4.

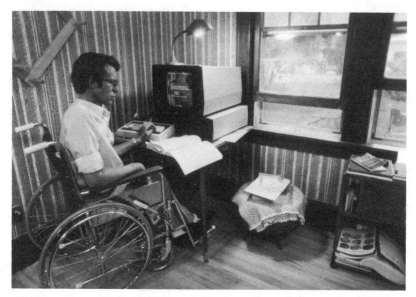

Figure 1-4 PLATO® in Use for the HOMEWORK Program
(Courtesy, Control Data Corporation)

organizations, it has become increasingly important for all employees to have an understanding of how to use computers in their job. This is as true for clerks as it is for senior executives, or for privates as well as generals. In some cases, computers are used to teach about computers. For example, CBT has been used extensively at Honeywell to teach employees how to use terminals, timesharing, job control language, operating system and applications software, and programming languages, as well as to show users of specific business-related application programs how to enter data, generate reports, and apply company policies and procedures (Barry 1982). Kearsley, Hillelsohn, and Hunter (1982) describe a series of workshops using microcomputers intended to teach corporate managers, small business owners, or trainers how to use computers as tools in their work. In many parts of the business world, managers have bought microcomputers on their own initiative to improve their personal productivity (Seaman 1981).

INCREASED LEARNING SATISFACTION

A common outcome of CBT is improved learner satisfaction and enjoyment. Because of the interactive nature of CBT, students typically find it more motivating than other forms of instruction. Because of the feedback provided on responses and the capability to assess progress available on many systems, students are able to develop a sense of achievement while learning which leads to increased satisfaction during training.

The major significance of increased satisfaction due to CBT is that attrition rates (drop-outs) are reduced. Since the selection and enrollment of trainees represent a significant cost, reducing the attrition rate represents a cost savings. Moreover, attrition in training is often associated with job turnover.

Increased motivation and gratification during training is an important factor contributing to achievement in and satisfactory completion of training programs. Poor motivation rather than lack of ability or skill often causes learning problems. Thus, the capability of CBT to improve motivation is an important factor in reducing course failure rates.

REDUCED DEVELOPMENT TIME

One of the significant potential benefits of CBT (which has yet to be realized in more than a few circumstances) is the capability to reduce the time required to develop training programs and materials. For example, most training materials require between 10 to 40 percent revision each year due to changes in equipment or products, organizational policies or procedures, government regulations, and so on. Making such revisions and implementing them is frequently a time-consuming and difficult process. In fact, out-of-date materials are a frequent cause underlying ineffective training. When the majority of training materials are online and delivered via CBT, the revision process is considerably streamlined. For CBT systems in which all courseware is shared from a central database, revisions can be made quickly and take effect immediately.

Consider, for example, a computer system used by the Veterans' Administration to process claims. Terminals are located in VA offices across the nation and claims processing clerks are taught to use the system via CBT courses on the system. When there is a change in government regulations that affect the claims procedures (which is often), the change is implemented in the system software and the online training course at the same time. Once the change has been implemented, existing clerks are apprised of the change the next time they sign on. New clerks to be trained would go through a revised tutorial that incorporates the changes. Because of this capability to make immediate revisions to the training materials, job productivity is maintained at a high level.

One specific area where CBT can reduce development time considerably is testing, particularly competency-based[4] training programs. The develop-

[4]Competency-based training is also called criterion-referenced, performance-oriented, or job-centered instruction. The different terms all mean the same thing—i.e., the desired training outcomes are defined in terms of objectives that are relevant to successful job performance.

ment of tests is very time consuming, especially when multiple test items must be developed for the same instructional objective. With CBT, a large pool of test items can be created and the computer can take care of the formatting and presentation details, including extra benefits such as automatic randomizing and insertion of distractors. Furthermore, CBT allows individualized adaptive testing, which cannot practically be done without a computer. We will discuss computer-based testing in more detail in the next chapter.

Finally, computers offer considerable potential in terms of automating the generation and production of traditional training materials (such as textbooks) as well as the more precise management of the instructional development process. For example, the Training Analysis and Evaluation Group of the U.S. Navy has developed a prototype computer-based publishing system that helps authors generate training workbooks. The system automatically formats text, merges stored graphics, and provides editing "advice" in terms of identifying uncommon or awkward words and sentences, suggesting possible substitutes, and indicating readability levels (Braby and Kincaid 1981). A prototype Author Management System (O'Neal and O'Neal 1979) was developed for the U.S. Navy by Courseware Inc., that helps training managers monitor the status and progress of an instructional development project, as well as "what if" projections for planning purposes. Although both of these examples are prototype projects, they are indicative of the ways in which computers can be used to increase the productivity of training development activities.

You should be aware that while computers have considerable potential to reduce development time, in most current CBT applications they tend to increase it. This is due to a large number of factors. In many cases, authors have little experience with CBT and spend a lot of time learning how to create CBT materials. In other cases, the CBT systems being used do not provide the right authoring tools to make the development of CBT materials quick and easy. Finally, unfair comparisons are often made in comparing the development of CBT materials and other instructional materials. For example, it may take an author ten hours to write a workbook lesson but one hundred hours to develop a CBT version of that same lesson. What is not taken into account is the fact that the CBT lesson is complete and ready for use by the student, whereas the workbook lesson must still be typeset, printed, packaged, and distributed before being ready. Furthermore, because the CBT lesson is interactive, it provides active learning and feedback to the student. It also provides the instructor with student performance data. In the workbook version of the lesson, these features would have to be provided by some form of additional testing or evaluation materials. When differences such as these are taken into account, it is not really clear that comparison of the development times required for CBT with those required for other media are very meaningful. (Issues in the development of CBT materials are discussed in Chapter 5).

SUMMARY

In this chapter, we have examined some of the major reasons that underlie the use of computers in training. The discussion has generally focused on the positive side of these considerations rather than the negative aspects, which will be dealt with in subsequent chapters (particularly Chapters 7 and 8). Figure 1-5 provides a checklist that can be used to assess a particular training situation and determine the potential benefits of CBT. The questions on the checklist are based on the discussions in this chapter. The more "yes" responses checked, the stronger the case for CBT. If this checklist suggests that there are good reasons to explore CBT for a particular training application, the next step is to determine what kind of CBT is appropriate (Chapter 2) and whether it is feasible (Chapter 3).

Each major reason for CBT has been discussed in isolation. While it is possible that a single benefit could be sufficient justification for CBT, normally CBT will address a number of needs simultaneously. For example, consider the use of microcomputers for training field service technicians at Kodak (Duc Quy and Covington 1982). The decision to use CBT was based on: (1) the need to train technicians in thirty-nine U.S. service districts and forty-four other countries on new products and product improvements as quickly as possible, (2) the need to deliver standardized training worldwide, (3) the use of graphics simulations that could effectively teach the complex workings of the equipment, and (4) the need to provide interesting and motivating training that would be used. In other words, CBT was selected to increase control (standardization), reduce resource requirements (decentralized training), increase timeliness (simultaneous training), and improve job performance (better understanding of equipment). The selection of microcomputers was a factor in minimizing the costs.

You may have wondered why reducing costs is not one of the benefits of CBT discussed in this chapter. There are two reasons for its omission. First of all, if costs are reduced due to CBT, it will be in terms of the factors discussed—increased control, reduced resources, increased timeliness or availability, and so on. Any one of these factors could, in principle, reduce the costs of training. The second reason for not mentioning reduced costs is that the use of CBT to improve training may result in increased costs. Even though training costs may go up, the overall savings to the organization in terms of improved job performance may outweigh the cost increase. This type of relationship must be shown by cost/benefits analysis, which is discussed in Chapter 8.

In many instructional situations, the use of computers can make training cheaper and/or better. The main reasons why this is so have been described in this chapter. The rest of the book explains how to determine what type of CBT is appropriate and feasible, select the appropriate system, develop materials, make CBT work, and evaluate its effects. A word of caution: If none of the reasons for CBT discussed in this chapter seem to apply to your training situation, it may be that you have no real justification for using computers in training. No matter how appealing the idea may be, if CBT does not meet a real training need or organizational goal, it is almost certain to flounder somewhere along the way. In other words, if the training application being analyzed results in all "no" answers in Figure 1–5, then you should abandon the idea of CBT and consider a more suitable training medium or approach. This is the wrong book to be reading!

Figure 1–5   CBT Benefits Checklist

		Yes	No
1.	Increased Control		
	Are existing materials poorly used?	[ ]	[ ]
	Are existing training programs taught inconsistently?	[ ]	[ ]
	Is standardization of training important?	[ ]	[ ]
	Is detailed tracking of learning needed?	[ ]	[ ]
2.	Reduced Resource Requirements		
	Is decentralized (field-based) training possible?	[ ]	[ ]
	Is higher student throughput desired?	[ ]	[ ]
	Is a higher student-to-instructor ratio desired?	[ ]	[ ]
	Is expensive equipment needed for training?	[ ]	[ ]
3.	Individualization		
	Is there considerable variation in student backgrounds?	[ ]	[ ]
	Is there considerable variation in student abilities?	[ ]	[ ]
	Is there likely to be considerable student variation in terms of learning progress?	[ ]	[ ]
	Does the instruction have to stand alone (e.g., self-study)?	[ ]	[ ]
4.	Timeliness and Availability		
	Is it necessary to provide training to many students as quickly as possible?	[ ]	[ ]
	Is it desirable to provide training "on demand," i.e., whenever and wherever a student needs it?	[ ]	[ ]
	Is there a problem with students forgetting due to premature training?	[ ]	[ ]
	Is there a problem with a shortage of qualified instructors?	[ ]	[ ]
5.	Reduced Training Time		
	Would time savings in training be worthwhile?	[ ]	[ ]
	Can the training system and organization be changed to capitalize on time savings?	[ ]	[ ]

Figure 1-5   CBT Benefits Checklist (continued.)

	Yes	No
6. Improved Job Performance		
Is the quality of job performance a critical training concern?	[ ]	[ ]
Are there job performance problems that improved training can address?	[ ]	[ ]
7. Convenience		
Do employees already use a computer system for their jobs?	[ ]	[ ]
Could CBT be integrated into existing jobs or equipment?	[ ]	[ ]
8. Change Agent		
Is there a need for new training approaches or methods?	[ ]	[ ]
Could CBT lead to improved personal or organizational productivity?	[ ]	[ ]
9. Increased Learning Satisfaction		
Is the attrition or failure rate high?	[ ]	[ ]
Is there a problem with student motivation?	[ ]	[ ]
10. Reduced Development Time		
Is the large-scale development of training materials and program involved?	[ ]	[ ]
Is immediate revision/update of training materials important?	[ ]	[ ]
Is instruction developed in terms of a competency-based framework?	[ ]	[ ]

2

What Is CBT?

In the first chapter, we considered the major reasons underlying the use of computers in training systems. In this chapter, we will examine the various ways in which they can be used. This includes testing, management, instruction, simulators, and embedded training.[1] It is important to understand the types of CBT possible and the characteristics associated with each since each type typically leads to different selection, development, and implementation considerations. After you have finished this chapter, it should be clear to you that CBT can refer to many different kinds of computer use.

TESTING

One of the simplest CBT applications is the use of the computer to generate, administer, score, or analyze tests, often called Computer Assisted Testing (CAT). Because this is a relatively simple application, you should not make the mistake of thinking that it is unimportant. In most large-scale training systems, testing is the core activity. This is because testing is the means by which training achievement is measured and training accountability is demonstrated. For example, in large Computer-Managed Instruction (CMI) systems such as those used by the U.S. Navy and IBM, the testing component is the key element upon which all other capabilities depend. Testing often plays a major

---

[1]The use of computers to facilitate the design and development of instruction belongs in this list too. This CBT application is discussed in Chapter 6.

role in employee selection, classification, and assignment. In the U.S. Army, computerized testing is used for initial selection and job assignment of recruits and also throughout the career of a soldier to determine qualifications and promotions.

There are many different ways of using computers for testing:

- Scoring and Analysis
- Creation of Tests
- Item Generation
- Interactive Testing
- Adaptive Testing

The use of computers to score test responses and analyze the results (often in terms of certain statistical measures) is the oldest and most common application. Tests can be given in offline form (i.e., "paper and pencil") and the test item responses entered into a computer database for automatic scoring and analysis. If the tests are given using Optical Character Recognition (OCR) or Mark Sense Reader (MSR) answer forms, the data entry can be automated. The analysis of the test data can result in a number of different reports describing individual or group performance scores and test item characteristics.

A second testing application is the creation of tests. In the simplest case, a set of test items (often called an item "bank") are entered into a database by the test developer(s), and the system is then used to assemble the items together into tests. The tests may be printed out for offline testing or displayed on CRT screen for online (interactive) testing. Typically, the computer is used for test construction when the items are to be presented in randomized order or selected on the basis of certain attributes (e.g., as in adaptive testing, discussed later). The various possibilities for computer-assisted test construction are discussed in Lippey (1974).

Item generation is a special kind of computer test construction capability. Instead of storing the items to be assembled in a test, the items are created as they are needed during test presentation. This is usually done by generating numeric values or words to fill certain fields in the questions or problems. For example, the following generative item might be used in a product knowledge test:

If the customer's average monthly copy volume is _____, the best machine is

   a) the 1000 series

   b) the 2000 series

   c) the 3000 series

where the blank is replaced by a randomly generated number in a range that could correspond to either a, b, or c. The computer keeps track of the correct answer for each number generated.

As this example illustrates, the great power of generated items over predefined or stored test items is that a large number of different items can be produced from a single item form. When it is desirable to give each student a unique test, item generation is a good way to do this without having to actually prespecify a large number of items. Roid (1979) discusses the factors involved in item generation.

It should be pointed out that generated test items do not have to be questions involving numbers or words. For example, in a simulator designed to train mail letter-sorters for the U.S. Post Office, item generation techniques were used to create visual images of letters (Gunwaldsen 1975). Since there are a large number of features possible (e.g., size of envelope, location of address, type of stamp, etc.), item generation allowed an essentially infinite number of letters to be generated without the necessity of creating and storing them in a database. Instead of letters, the images could just as well have been bills, invoices, equipment specifications, battlefield configurations, and so on.

Item generation makes the most sense in the context of interactive testing, where the testing takes place online at a computer terminal. Unlike offline testing where the student may have no actual contact with the computer, with online testing the student has direct contact during the test-taking session. Interactive testing allows each student to take a completely unique test. This could be simply a matter of randomization, i.e., a fixed set of test items are presented in a different order for each student (making cheating very difficult), or it could be true individualization in which each student gets a different set of items based on his or her measured skill level or prior learning. Interactive testing is commonly used in the context of criterion-referenced or competency-based instruction where the test items are tied to specific instructional objectives. A pretest is often given to determine which objectives the student does not need to learn or be tested on. A posttest is given following the instruction, which contains only items for the objectives that a particular student studied. The items used on the posttest must be similar to, but not the same as, the items used for the pretest. This means that an item bank must be created that contains sufficient items to allow pre- and posttesting. For example, in a self-study CMI course to teach the programming language BASIC (Heines 1979), sixteen pre- and posttests were needed to correspond to the sixteen instructional modules. The maximum length of each test was 30 items. An item bank of 754 items was created which was sufficient to generate a large number of essentially different tests.

This example also represents an illustration of the most sophisticated kind of interactive testing; namely, adaptive testing. In an adaptive test, the number of test items presented depends on the student's performance on the test. For example, if the student gets a certain number of items in a row correct that correspond to a certain objective or module, it is not necessary for the student to do any more items for that objective or module (see Figure 2-1). Alternatively, items to be used in an adaptive test can be arranged in terms of difficulty level and the items a student receives can vary in difficulty depending upon performance.

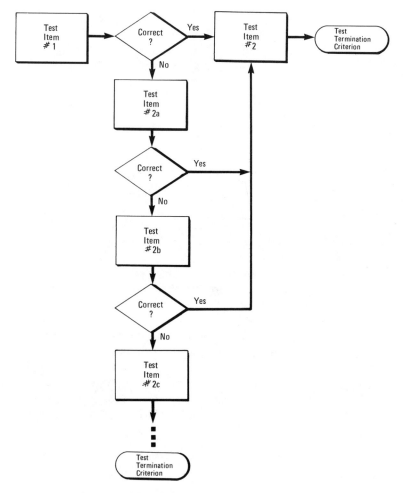

Figure 2-1   Basic Model of Adaptive Testing

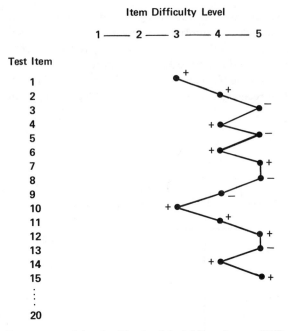

Item Difficulty Level

1 —— 2 —— 3 —— 4 —— 5

Test Item

1
2
3
4
5
6
7
8
9
10
11
12
13
14
15
⋮
20

Figure 2–2   Adaptive Testing Model Based upon Difficulty

Figure 2–2 illustrates the path of a student through such an adaptive test with five levels of difficulty. The test is stopped when the student has gotten ten items correct or twenty incorrect. In this example, the student scores ten correct in fifteen questions, with an average difficulty level of 4.3. Another student could have achieved the same score (10/15) but at a different difficulty level, thereby demonstrating a different level of mastery for the instruction.

The practical significance of adaptive testing is that fewer test items are typically required to test an individual; hence, testing time can be reduced. Weiss (1979) concludes that when a large item pool is available, adaptive testing can provide achievement measures of higher precision with 30 to 50 percent fewer items than a conventional fixed item test. For any training system that involves a lot of testing, adaptive testing has clear-cut benefits in terms of time savings. Furthermore, students tend to find adaptive tests less frustrating since they are being tested at their own level of understanding.

MANAGEMENT

The use of computers for instructional management represents a common form of CBT. In Computer-Managed Instruction, the computer is used to manage student progress and instructional resources (e.g., media, classrooms, instructors, simulators, etc.). CMI is usually used to improve the level of control and efficiency within a training system.

The major components of a typical CMI system are depicted in Figure 2–3. The system consists of four major programs (registration, testing, prescription, and scheduling) plus a "supervisor" program which controls the integration of these four. The four major programs interact with three databases: student records, test, and learning activities. These three databases are used to generate five major kinds of reports: class and student profiles (individual and group progress reports), class lists, test statistics, student schedules, and resource utilization.

Figure 2–4 illustrates how students, instructors or course managers, and these system components interact. When a student is registered in the CMI system, the results of tests and information on the employee's educational or job history are stored in the student record database. The personal goals, needs, and interests of the student along with the recommendations or requirements

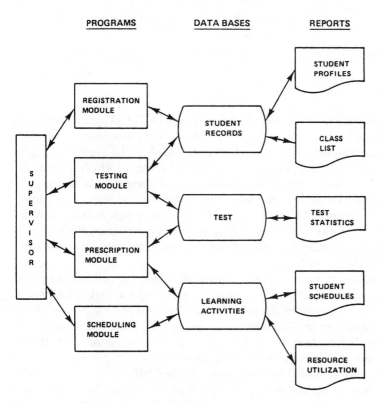

Figure 2–3   Components of a CMI System

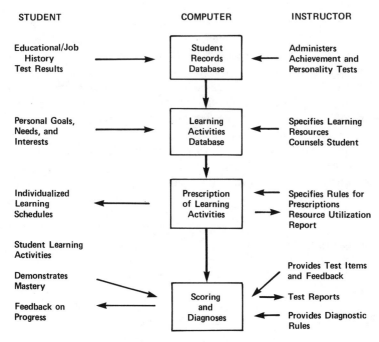

Figure 2–4   Interaction of Student, Instructor, and Computer in a CMI System

of the instructor are used to select an individualized syllabus for the student in terms of specific instructional objectives. The CMI system then generates a schedule of learning activities for each student based on the prescriptive rules provided by the instructor. These prescriptive rules specify which learning activities are needed to achieve various instructional objectives. The learning activities could include multimedia self-study, traditional classes, small group workshops, simulator practice. or even some form of computer-based instruction. As a consequence of the scheduling of learning activities, the system is able to produce a resource utilization report that indicates which resources are being used and how much.

After the student has completed a prescribed learning activity, he or she takes a test corresponding to the objectives for which that activity was assigned. As we discussed in the previous section, this test may be online or offline. The instructor provides the test items, scoring rules and feedback for the tests. The CMI system scores the tests, provides the instructor with test reports, and provides the student with feedback on learning progress. Based on diagnostic rules provided by the instructor, the CMI system may prescribe remedial or review activities depending on test performance. Once the student has demonstrated mastery, a new learning activity is prescribed.

As mentioned in the first chapter, the U.S. Navy operates one of the largest CMI systems in existence. It manages the instruction of about 10,000 students daily in nine schools located in Memphis, Tennessee; Great Lakes, Illinois; Orlando, Florida; and San Diego, California. The system uses offline tests that are entered via MSR. The learning activities involve self-study audiovisual modules and "hands-on" equipment tasks. Printers attached to the MSR units provide students with test results and prescriptive "learning guides." In addition to specific study assignments, the learning guides also indicate a projected course completion date computed on the basis of the student's aptitude and background. The system will also assign additional night school assignments if the student's progress falls behind the projected rate. The following benefits have been derived from the Navy CMI system (Davis 1978):

- Greater flexibility in tailoring course content and training activities to the needs of students and the Navy

- The data required to optimally schedule scarce instructional resources

- Rapid identification of students who are having difficulty so that effective remedial measures can be implemented

- Systematic improvement of instructional materials due to the analysis of performance data

- The capability to handle unexpected increases in student loads without major increases in resources

- The use of instructional strategies such as adaptive testing and individualized learning assignments which reduce course lengths

- The freeing of the learning supervisor from routine record keeping and clerical tasks for the more critical tasks of student tutoring and counseling

Further details of the Navy system are provided in Van Matre (1978; 1980). A demonstration project involving satellite transmissions for shipboard use of the Navy CMI system is described by Polcyn (1976). A comprehensive discussion of CMI systems is provided by Baker (1978a; 1981).

While almost all major CBT systems (see Chapter 4) have CMI capabilities, the CDC PLATO Learning Management (PLM) system is one of the most comprehensive and well designed. Figure 2–5 lists some of the major PLM functions available to an instructor for each group (class) of students being managed. These features allow the instructor to see or change a student's record, modify the class roster, inspect performance statistics, specify curriculum design parameters, and perform other miscellaneous operations. There is another set of PLM options available to the author who creates a PLM curriculum. These include the capability to add, delete, or rename courses or modules, sequence courses/modules, set course or module prerequisites, determine if a course or module is to be required or optional, determine which messages

See or Change Someone's Record
  Change password
  Change spelling of name
  Curriculum status
    Student progress in the curriculum, course, module, and objective.
  Leave a message
  See or change data collection options
  Special options
    See student variables, see router variables, change current lesson, change current unit.

Roster Operations
  See or change someone's record
  See the roster of people
  Add someone to the roster
  Delete someone from the roster
  Leave a message for someone
  See who is now running

Statistics on Records
  Statistics on sign-on and lesson usage
  PLM summary statistics
    Name lists
      Course record data, course progress summary, module progress summary, last module mastery dates.
    Average progress data
      Tables and graphs for summary statistics for each course in the curriculum.
    Scheduling reports
      Deviations from schedule, projected student progress, projected course completion dates, print student schedules.

Special Options
  Set up a template record
    Select a user record to serve as a template for all new records or for existing records.
  Change group-wide data collection options
  Copy a record from another group
  Delete all records
  Print group records data
    Print the total amount of time signed on for each record in the group.

Curriculum Design
  Edit or inspect curriculum
  PLM group controls
    Scheduling
      Determines whether scheduling will be based on course or module durations; or on instructor-specified course completion dates.
    Student gradebook access
    Response recording
      Activates the data collection features of the PLM system.
    Test access controls
      Controls student access to tests.
    Test lockout controls
      Specifies the conditions under which students are allowed to take module tests.
    Test interruption controls
      Determines which options are offered to students when they press SHIFT-STOP during a test.
    Testing and printing controls
      Specifies if students can select testing mode, students must take on-line tests, or students must take off-line tests; allow test question feedback on printed test; allow student to print study assignments; printer type.

Space Usage Information
  Total parts used in the group, total 64-word records, and total names available.

Group Description
  Group information
    Group director information, group information.
  Associated files
    Student notes, data collection, TERM-ask group, routers, curriculum file.
  Security codewords

People Currently Running

Figure 2-5 PLM Instructor Options

will be displayed automatically, specify management strategies, and many other options. PLM also incorporates an authoring system that allows the creation of curriculum without any need for programming.

Reports are a critical aspect of a CMI system from the point of view of the instructor or training manager. The single most important report is that which provides the details of a student's performance and progress. Figure 1–1 in the previous chapter illustrated such a report used in the Navy CMI system. Figure 2–6 illustrates a similar but much less detailed report provided by PLM. In addition to student progress reports, CMI systems typically provide reports on tests (i.e., item analyses), resource or curriculum utilization statistics, and system usage summaries. In most systems, these reports are printed offline but in a few systems (such as PLATO) they are available for online inspection.

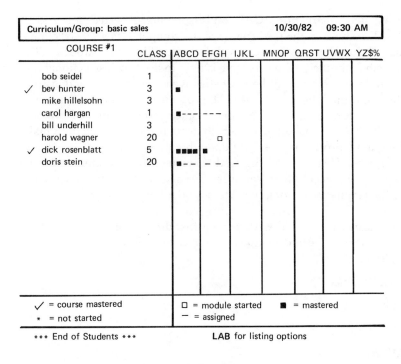

Figure 2-6   PLM Report

CMI is an extremely important kind of CBT. Although the use of the computer for instruction seems a more glamorous CBT application, CMI is often the approach that results in the most favorable cost/benefits case and produces the greatest increase in training efficiency. This is because CMI generally results in significant improvement in the management of a training program or system, which leads to increased efficiency. Furthermore, CMI makes use of existing instructional resources and requires less CBT equipment than instructional applications. In short, CMI is almost always a worthwhile investment in a large training system.

INSTRUCTION

The use of the computer for actual instruction covers a wide range of different instructional strategies and approaches. For example, you will encounter two divergent philosophies about how computers should be used for instruction:

Computer-Assisted Instruction (CAI) and Computer-Assisted (or Aided) Learning (CAL). Those in the CAI camp see the computer as an instructional medium similar to other media such as slide/tape, video, or textbooks. The central problem from the CAI perspective is how to arrange instructional materials delivered via computer in the most effective manner (i.e., good instructional design). On the other hand, the CAL proponents see the computer as a powerful student tool akin to calculators or microscopes. The key problem from the CAL viewpoint is how to teach students to use computers to make their learning most productive. As you undoubtedly realize, there is value in both philosophies. Historically, the CAI view tended to dominate in the United States, but in recent years (catalyzed by easy availability of microcomputers and the emphasis on computer literacy) the CAL outlook has become predominant.[2]

The significance of the CAI-CAL views is that different instructional strategies and systems have been developed around each philosophy. Three major CAI strategies are:

■   Drill and Practice

■   Tutorial

■   Socratic

Major CAL strategies are:

■   Simulations/Games

■   Database/Inquiry

■   Programming

Let's examine each of these strategies in the context of CBT.

Drill and Practice

Drill and practice is the simplest way of using a computer for instruction. As Figure 2–7 shows, it consists of presenting a question or problem, accepting a student response, judging the response and feedback, and branching to another question or problem based on the correctness of the answer or the mastery criterion for the instruction. Generally, drill and practice involves no new instruction—just practice on instruction that has already taken place. Thus, drill and practice is really a kind of testing.

The prototypical examples of drill and practice are arithmetic or spelling problems. Studies with public school children have shown that regular drill

---

[2]It should be noted that the terms *CAI* and *CAL* are often used interchangeably by many without regard to the different philosophies represented.

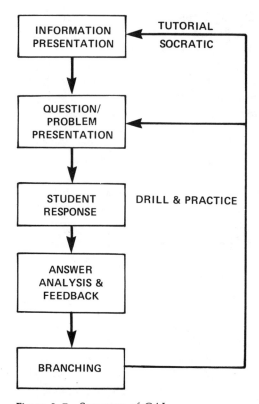

Figure 2-7 Structure of CAI

and practice sessions result in improved learning achievement (e.g., Suppes and Morningstar 1972; Vinsonhaler and Bass 1972). In the training domain, drill and practice has a large number of potential applications such as product knowledge, principles of equipment operation or maintenance, administrative policies or procedures, safety regulations, and fundamental concepts of sales or management. In general, the drill and practice strategy is appropriate for any kind of learning that involves basic facts or terminology. Based on the findings with CAI in public education, it seems reasonable to predict that regular drill and practice in a CBT application would yield improved training results.

Tutorial

In contrast to drill and practice, both the tutorial and Socratic strategies involve the presentation of information. The tutorial strategy typically consists of the discussion of a concept or procedure with interspersed questions or a quiz at the end of the discussion. Tutorial instruction is normally presented in terms of "frames" that correspond to a series of screen displays. Depending on the capabilities of the hardware, the frames may include text only, color graphics, or voice/sound output.

This kind of CAI is often dubbed "electronic page-turning" since the frames (screens) essentially correspond to the pages of a book. The legacy of tutorial CAI comes from Programmed Instruction (Bunderson and Faust 1976), and many PI techniques have influenced the design of tutorial programs. For example, the techniques of shaping and cueing are often used in the construction of feedback sequences to get the student to select the correct answer.

Tutorial CAI is widely used for CBT, particularly for administrative or clerical types of training. Thus, the kind of CBT used by financial service organizations (e.g., banks, insurance companies) or government agencies is primarily tutorial in nature. This is largely because such training involves the understanding of concepts or procedures for which the tutorial strategy is well suited.

Socratic

Socratic CAI is quite different from tutorial CAI in that it involves a conversation or dialogue between the student and the computer in natural language. Since either the student or the computer can ask a question at any point, it is also called "mixed-initiative" CAI (Carbonell 1970). Figure 2–8 illustrates a portion of a dialogue from the SOPHIE system (Brown, Burton, and deKleer 1982) developed for electronics troubleshooting. The student's responses are in capital letters; the computer's are in lower case. In the first part of the sequence, the student is asking questions, but in the latter part the computer questions the student to help the student understand why a particular action ("Replace Q6") is not correct.

Socratic CAI derives from research in artificial intelligence rather than education or the field of CAI itself.[3] Socratic CAI is fundamentally different from drill and practice or tutorial types of CAI in a number of ways. Information is represented quite differently in Socratic programs in order to allow natural language interaction and to allow the program to "understand" what the student is asking about. Rather than measure the student's learning assessment in terms of test scores, progress is determined by the degree of comprehension or problem-solving skill demonstrated.

Socratic CAI has not yet been used in operational training settings. One obstacle is that this type of CAI requires considerable computational power.

[3]Further discussion of "intelligent" CAI can be found in Bregar and Farley (1980), Kearsley (1978), and Sleeman and Brown (1982).

WHAT IS THE OUTPUT?
The Output Voltage is 11.7 Volts.

WHAT IS IT IN A WORKING INSTRUMENT?
In a Working Circuit the Output Voltage is 19.9 Volts.

WHAT IS THE VOLTAGE BETWEEN R8 AND Q1?
The Voltage at N1 is 47.6 Volts.

WHAT IS THE BSE EMITTER VOLTAGE OF THE
VOLTAGE LIMITING TRANSITOR?
= Base
= Transistor
The Base Emitter Voltage of Q5 is −.037 Millivolts.

WHAT ABOUT FOR THE CURRENT LIMITING TRANSISTOR?
The Base Emitter Voltage of Q6 is .349 Volts.

WHAT SHOULD IT BE?
In a Working Circuit the Base Emitter Voltage of Q6 is .593 Volts.

REPLACE Q6
I am Going to Ask You Some Questions About How Q6 is Faulted.

Are Any Junctions Shorted?
   I DON'T KNOW
Are Any Terminals Open?
   YES
Which Terminal(s) Are Open?
   THE BASE
Q6 is not faulted in that manner. Q6 not replaced.

IS IT POSSIBLE THAT Q6 HAS AN OPEN BASE?

Figure 2-8   SOPHIE Dialog

Only recently have sufficiently powerful microcomputers become available to allow Socratic CAI to be done at affordable costs. A second problem is that the author languages commonly used for CAI are unsuitable for Socratic CAI; relatively few people can program in the list-processing languages (e.g., LISP), which are used for constructing these programs. Despite these current limitations, it seems very likely that Socratic CAI will come to be widely used in CBT during the 1980s.

Simulation/Games

Turning now to CAL, let's begin with the simulation/games strategy. Simulations are based on a model of some process, mechanism, or activity. The model allows a student to relate input or change parameters to output or outcomes. Thus, if we have a simulation of a steam plant, it is possible to see the effects that changes in water temperature or pressure have on the generation of steam. If the simulation is of a retail business, we can study the effects of changes in pricing, advertising, inventory, location, and so forth. If we are simulating the flying of an airplane, we are interested in the effects of air speed, altitude, and heading through control of the throttle, flaps, and rudder. Unlike tutorial CAI, there are no inherent instructional objectives built into a simulation. The learner reaches certain conclusions about the system being modeled by exploring the effects of changes on outcomes.

Simulation is best suited to training involving problem-solving or decision-making skills. Thus, it has commonly been used in sales and management training where these skills are paramount. For example, Commercial Credit Corporation, a subsidiary of Control Data Corporation, used PLATO to develop a sales call simulation to train its own salespersons (Warner 1979). A series of sales calls were developed based on "real world" experiences of the sales force. Students had a choice of simulations, including several directly related to their product specialty. During a simulation, the student's choices were scored in terms of sales skills demonstrated.

Simulation is also commonly used for training technicians how to repair equipment. For example, at the Customer Equipment Service Division of Eastman Kodak, microcomputers are being used to provide service representatives with practice in troubleshooting and repairing the electronics components of copiers (Kearsley, Hillelsohn, and Seidel 1981). Schematics of equipment are displayed on the screen and a light pen is used to measure voltages. When a malfunction is located, the light pen is used as a soldering iron to replace and repair the faulty circuit. This example neatly illustrates how simulation can provide a large amount of "hands-on" practice while avoiding costs and availability problems associated with actual equipment.

Simulations and games are basically the same with one key difference — games involve an explicit competitive element. In general, any simulation can be turned into a game by introducing a timer (beat the clock), a point system (beat the high score), or interpersonal competition (beat your opponent). In addition, most games usually involve an element of fantasy, which is not a feature of simulations. Games are typically used for training purposes when student motivation is a concern. Some of the critical parameters of designing instructional games are discussed by Thiagarajan and Stolovitch (1978) and Malone (1982).

Simulation and games are the direct analogs of "hands-on" labs and small group discussions. They provide opportunities for students to gain first-hand experience with complex relationships. For example, Marti and Vogel (1981) describe a management game for production engineers called KOMET, used at the Swiss Federal Institute of Technology. KOMET is used by teams of engineering students who compete against each other in the context of a business with production, marketing, and finance components. KOMET provides a number of computer-based tools to be used in the game including:

- A market database containing information on product demand, sales figures, prices, and expenditures

- A production optimization model to be used for planning personnel, facilities, and equipment

- Price and profit optimization models based on advertising and marketing expenditures

- Inventory and shipping plans for warehouses

All of these capabilities exist for the students to use in their decision making during the course of the game.

Database/Inquiry

Like CAI drill and practice, simulations and games do not provide information presentation—this must be provided in other ways. From the CAL perspective, a good way of doing this is with a database or inquiry (i.e., information retrieval) strategy. The critical attribute of this approach is that information is organized in a database that can be searched or presented under the control of the student for different purposes. For example, suppose you are a salesperson interested in learning about competitive products (or a soldier interested in enemy weapons). By selecting a set of critical product features, it is possible to display all of the products that have these features along with other characteristics. You can then draw your own conclusions about competition (or perhaps they are included in the database). At some later point in your training you may need to work out a sales plan for a potential customer and need pricing and delivery information on certain products. Again you would display this information from the database.

As this example indicates, database CAL involves teaching an individual how to use a computer database to look up information, solve problems, or make decisions. Since many jobs today involve the use of databases (e.g., financial, reservations, inventory, personnel, medical records, etc.) this approach makes sense. In fact, in many cases the same database used on the job can also be used for training purposes.

Even though information retrieval from databases is widely practiced throughout the business, government, and military domains, database CAL has not been a commonly used strategy. There are many reasons for this. Generally, trainers have been averse to teaching students how to use such systems when available due to time limitations or lack of sufficient terminals to provide access; however with the proliferation of information utilities (see Chapter 9) and the easy availability of microcomputers, the major obstacles have been removed. Thus, it seems likely that database CAL will become a much more common form of CBT in this decade.

Programming

Finally, a frequent CAL strategy in the past has been to teach individuals how to actively program a computer in order to use it as a personal learning tool. Once students have learned to program, they are able to use the computer to develop their own simulation models or database systems. While this approach may have made sense at a time when most software had to be written by users themselves, it seems inappropriate today when programs for almost any application and computer can be bought "off the shelf." Instead, it seems reasonable to teach students how to use a set of general software tools (e.g., a plotting program, a database management system, an "electronic spread sheet," etc.) and expect them to use these tools in their learning activities (Kearsley, Hillelsohn, and Hunter 1982).

SIMULATORS

Simulators (also called *trainers*) are physical devices used to train an individual how to operate or maintain a particular piece of equipment (e.g., an airplane, tank, oil drilling rig, radar scope, missile launcher, microwave relay transmitter, cigarette-making machine, etc.). For the past few decades, almost all simulators have been computer-controlled. The computer is used to generate displays, sense that the correct operation has been performed (e.g., a switch setting or button pushed), and provide a trace of the student's actions for the instructor to review.

Simulators can range from very elaborate or expensive, such as the flight simulators used by the military and airlines, to relatively simple and inexpensive, such as "Resusci-Annie" used to teach cardio-pulmonary resuscitation.

One of the ongoing debates in the simulator area is exactly how much fidelity (i.e., realism) the simulator must have relative to the actual equipment. Historically, simulators have resembled the actual equipment as closely as possible; however, there has been a clear-cut trend toward using simplified 3D panel and computer graphics representations over the years. This trend is supported by research showing that realistic equipment is not necessary for effective training (e.g., Adams 1979; Crawford and Crawford 1978; Cream, Eggemeier, and Klein 1978). Essentially, this means that simulation may eventually replace simulators to a substantial degree.

Simulators have been used most heavily in the aviation and aerospace domain—both for air crew training and ground personnel. Shelley and Groom (1970) describe the ASCAT system developed to train Apollo II flight controllers. ASCAT was a team-training simulator used to rehearse various aspects of the Apollo II mission prior to its occurrence. For example, the lunar descent was practiced thirty-three times, the launch twenty-three times, and reentry eight times. Federal aviation agencies and the military use similar simulators for the team training of air traffic controllers (e.g., Blake 1979; Paine 1979).

The military makes extensive use of simulators for weapons system training. Almost every major weapons system involves at least one simulator to train operators or maintainers. Farrow (1982) describes ten types of simulators used in military aircrew training. These range from simple familiarization trainers to sophisticated full mission simulators. Farrow describes how different trainers meet different kinds of training needs, particularly in terms of reducing military aviation hazards. Large strategic air defense systems such as SAGE and successors have involved extensive use of simulators for training (Parsons 1970). In recent years, computer-controlled videodisc systems have been used to provide low-cost simulators for military training. For example, Ketner (1981) describes a videodisc-based simulator used to teach ground satellite station maintenance. Similar videodisc-based systems have been demonstrated for other maintenance training tasks (see Kearsley 1981a).[4]

Simulators are also used in technical training conducted by the government and industry. The Mail Letter Sorter (MLS) system described earlier in the discussion of item generation is an example of a simulator developed for the U.S. Postal Service by HumRRO (Wagner et al. 1978). The MLS simulator was designed to provide postal employees with individualized instruction prior to using actual MLS machines. The simulator featured the same special keyboard and physical dimensions of the actual MLS console, but the screen was a color graphics display used to simulate letters to be sorted and a random access slide/tape unit was used for instruction (see Figure 2-9). Letter images were randomly generated at the rate of sixty per minute—the letter-sorting rate actually used on the job with the MLS equipment.

---

[4]Videodisc is discussed further in Chapter 9.

Figure 2-9   MLS Simulator Used by U.S. Post Office

EMBEDDED TRAINING

Embedded training refers to the concept that a system or piece of equipment be self-training. For example, if you buy a computer or word-processing system featuring embedded training, you should be able to learn how to use it on the basis of instruction provided on the system. Similarly, a weapons system with embedded training should be capable of training its operator without any additional (offline) instruction. Embedded training is possible because so many systems and products are computer-based. Training is accomplished by means of online tutorials and helps. Any of the CAI or CAL strategies that have been described could be used for embedded training.

Embedded training has been quite popular in the banking, insurance, and travel industries. Bank tellers are taught how to operate their terminals and process transactions via online tutorials and practice exercises. Similarly, insurance agents and clerks learn how to use their computer systems through online training. Airline and rental car staff learn how to use reservation and ticketing systems by means of embedded CBT.

Embedded training is also becoming very common for training employees how to use administrative or financial computer systems. In fact, it is reasonable to predict that as more and more aspects of organizations (and everyday life) become "computerized," embedded training will come to be the most prevalent type of CBT application. At this point, CBT may cease to be a specialized type of activity and be considered a standard aspect of hardware and software development.

One aspect of embedded training that has not been mentioned so far is the use of online job aids. A job aid is a set of procedures or guidelines (often in the form of a checklist or decision table) that explain how to do a task or activity. Job aids are often used to supplement or replace training. Some job tasks are so complex that it is not possible to completely train individuals to do them. Instead, it is more reasonable to train people how to do the task relying on job aids. In the context of embedded training, it is possible to provide minimal instruction by ample use of job aids. Alternatively, job aids can be used to provide an individual with prompts outlining recommended actions for given circumstances.

A good example of how job aids can be used is provided by current efforts to design computer-controlled nuclear plant systems. While the operators who work in such environments are well trained, the operation of a nuclear plant is extremely complex and places heavy demands on the operators in terms of mental workload and decision making. It is possible to design the computer system so that it provides the operator with the options possible for a given state of the system. The use of job aids reduces the likelihood that the operator will make a mistake that could have serious consequences.

SUMMARY

In this chapter we have discussed a number of different ways to use computers in training. Figure 2–10 summarizes the major strengths and applications of each. Computer-Assisted Testing (CAT) reduces clerical tasks and allows individualized testing. It applies to any continuous ongoing testing program. Computer-Managed Instruction (CMI) allows existing instructional resources to be used more efficiently and generally reduces training durations. CMI applies to any self-study or multimedia training program. CAI (drill and practice, tutorial, Socratic) provides a high degree of interaction during instruction and provides flexibility in handling fluctuations in student loads. CAI applies to any stable, widely used curriculum. CAL (simulation/games, database inquiry, programming) provides hands-on practice that might not be feasible otherwise and provides the student with control over the learning process. CAL is particularly appropriate to training situations that involve the learning of processes or procedures, or practice in problem-solving or decision-making skills. Simulators typically minimize requirements for actual equipment and increase safety during training. Simulators apply to any situation involving the operation or maintenance of equipment. Embedded training ensures

	STRENGTHS	APPLICATIONS
CAT	• reduces clerical tasks • individualized testing	• any continuous testing program
CMI	• uses existing resources more efficiently • reduces training durations	• any self study or multi-media training program
CAI	• provides high degree of interaction • more flexibility in handling student load fluctuations	• any stable, widely used curriculum
CAL	• provides practice otherwise not feasible • student controls learning	• processes, procedures, problem-solving, decision-making
SIMULATORS	• minimize equipment requirements • increase safety	• operator/maintenance of equipment
EMBEDDED	• avaliabilty and timeliness of training	• computer-based systems or products

Figure 2-10 Summary of Types of CBT

the availability and timeliness of instruction. It applies to any computer-based system or product.

Throughout this chapter, we have considered each kind of CBT separately; however, there are important interrelationships between them. For instance, CAI may be one of the instructional activities managed in a CMI system or used in a simulator. Computer-assisted testing could be a part of any other type of CBT. Embedded training could also involve any type of CBT. Under some circumstances, there may be little difference between a CAL simulation and a simulator. Finally, in any large training program or system, a number of different types of CBT are likely to apply. For example, CAT may be used to determine what training activities are needed for an individual; CMI may be used to manage these activities. The activities could involve a full range of CAI, CAL, or simulator usage.

Figure 2-11 provides a checklist for use in analyzing what kinds of CBT might be appropriate for a particular training application. You may need to review the discussions of each type in this chapter before using the checklist.

Now that you have completed Chapters 1 and 2, you know the why and the what of CBT. The next chapter explains how to conduct a CBT feasibility study.

	Yes	No
1. Testing (CAT)		
Scoring and Analysis	[ ]	[ ]
Creating Tests	[ ]	[ ]
Item Generation	[ ]	[ ]
Interactive Testing	[ ]	[ ]
Adaptive Testing	[ ]	[ ]
2. Management (CMI)		
Registration	[ ]	[ ]
Testing	[ ]	[ ]
Prescriptions	[ ]	[ ]
Scheduling	[ ]	[ ]
System Utilization	[ ]	[ ]
3. Instruction (CAI/CAL)		
Drill and Practice	[ ]	[ ]
Tutorial	[ ]	[ ]
Socratic	[ ]	[ ]
Simulations/Games	[ ]	[ ]
Database/Inquiry	[ ]	[ ]
Programming	[ ]	[ ]
4. Simulators		
Operator Training	[ ]	[ ]
Maintenance Training	[ ]	[ ]
Team Training	[ ]	[ ]
5. Embedded Training		
User Training	[ ]	[ ]
Job Aids	[ ]	[ ]

Figure 2-11   CBT Applications Checklist

3

Getting Started:
The Feasibility Study

The first step in getting started with CBT is to conduct a feasibility study. The purpose of the study is to determine if a particular training application is suitable for CBT. The feasibility study involves an assessment of the degree of risk associated with the use of CBT. It also involves an analysis of the expected costs and benefits that will result from the use of computer-based training. The outcome of a feasibility study is the decision to go ahead with CBT or abandon the idea.

Figure 3-1 illustrates the three preliminary steps that lead up to a feasibility study. A training problem or opportunity is identified that seems appropriate for CBT. The checklist provided in Chapter 1 (Figure 1-5) can be used for this purpose. The second step is to identify the specific training application to be examined. This means a particular training program or course in which CBT might be used. On the basis of this step, the appropriate type of CBT can be identified. The checklist in Chapter 2 (Figure 2-11) should be helpful.

Once the training application and type of CBT have been identified, the feasibility study can be conducted. Four major kinds of feasibility need to be examined: instructional, organizational, technical, and economic. Instructional feasibility deals with the suitability of CBT for achieving the instructional objectives of the training. Organizational feasibility focuses on social, policy, or political issues that may affect the use of CBT. Technical feasibility refers to the availability of the CBT features or capabilities needed. Economic feasibility concerns the affordability of the CBT costs involved. Note that a CBT application may be feasible in some aspects but not others. Thus, CBT may be feasible instructionally and technically, but not organizationally or

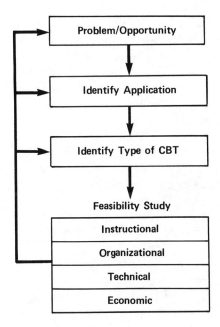

Figure 3-1   Steps Leading to a Feasibility Study

economically. In general, to be successful, a potential CBT application should be feasible in all four aspects.

As Figure 3-1 shows, the conduct of the feasibility study may result in reconsideration of the previous steps, i.e., the type of CBT selected, the application selected, or the understanding of the original training problem/opportunity. Thus, it may be realized that another type of CBT or training application would be more feasible for the problem selected, or that another problem is more suitable for CBT. Determining that the wrong thing is being studied is a relatively common outcome of feasibility studies!

Feasibility studies can vary in their scope and formality depending upon the size of the CBT application being considered. If the study involves introducing CBT for many courses in a large training system, the study is likely to be lengthy and formal. For example, the FAA conducted a feasibility study to determine the potential of CBT for use at the FAA Academy—a large training center involving many courses and students. This study was lengthy (taking years) and employed formal techniques such as PERT charts and requirements specifications (Buck, Bular, and Fagan 1979). On the other hand, some CBT feasibility studies are relatively informal and brief. A feasibility study concerned with only one course or training program might only take a few weeks to conduct and involve nothing more than some interviews or meetings.

Figure 3-2 outlines ten major steps in conducting a CBT feasibility study (assuming that the three steps in Figure 3-1 have been completed). The first step in the study is to develop a plan that specifies what activities will be involved, when they will take place, who will do what, and, finally, what results (decisions) are anticipated. The second step is to organize a study team and hold a planning meeting with this team. The composition of the study team is crucial to the success of the study. It should include key representatives from all parts of the organization that may be involved or affected by CBT and who will need to contribute data to the study. At a minimum, representatives from the training, computing, personnel, and finance departments should be involved since these are the major components of the feasibility study.

The next step is to examine the existing training system, program, or course(s) that has been selected for the CBT application. This should involve interviews with instructors, students, and training managers; observation of the actual training; analysis of the materials used; and analysis of any evaluation data available. Step 4 should involve the collection of data on the capabilities and utilization of any existing computer resources (equipment, software, personnel) available in the organization. The fifth step should be to interview any other members of the organization who are likely to be involved in or affected by the CBT system who have not yet been interviewed.

1. Develop a plan for the study (specifying activities, schedules, responsibilities, and results).

2. Organize and conduct a study team planning meeting.

3. Examine the existing training system, approach, program(s), or course(s).

4. Collect data on existing computer system(s) in use.

5. Interview all other members of the organization who are likely to be involved in or affected by CBT.

6. Collect cost data.

7. Examine CBT systems that appear relevant to the application being studied.

8. Summarize and document all data collected.

9. Prepare preliminary report and briefing.

10. Organize and conduct decision-making meeting with the study team.

11. Prepare the final report, summarizing conclusions and recommendations. (Collect more data if needed.)

12. Present the final report to the decision-makers (if necessary).

Figure 3-2   Major Steps in Conducting a CBT Feasibility Study

Next, cost data should be collected, including information on purchasing/procurement procedures relevant to CBT. Step 7 involves examining CBT systems that appear relevant to the application being studied. These may be systems within the organization or outside. The next step is to summarize and document all of the data collected in the study and then prepare a preliminary report and briefing (Step 9). In Step 10, a meeting of the study team is held to discuss the data and findings and reach decisions about the conclusions and recommendations of the study.

As a consequence of this meeting, it should be possible to prepare a final report indicating the conclusions and recommendations. In many cases, it will be necessary to collect more data before this can be done. Collecting more data may mean repeating any of Steps 3–9 again. In fact, in some studies the outcome of this step will be a recommendation to conduct another entire feasibility study on a different kind of CBT or training application. The last step involves the presentation of a final report to decision-makers regarding the feasibility of the CBT application studied. If the actual decision-makers were part of the study team (a good idea if possible), this meeting will not be necessary.

A few words should be said about the motives underlying the conduct of a feasibility study. Individuals who conduct the studies have either a bias in favor of CBT, a bias against CBT, or are neutral toward CBT. Individuals with a positive bias are liable (deliberately or inadvertently) to highlight the favorable aspects and overlook the unfavorable factors. While this may result in a positive recommendation for CBT, the actual implementation may fail because of the "whitewashed" factors. In contrast, individuals with a negative bias are likely to focus on the unfavorable aspects, paying little attention to favorable factors. As a consequence, a worthwhile CBT application may be passed up. Obviously, a neutral perspective is desired. This is most easily achieved by having the feasibility study conducted by individuals who are knowledgeable about CBT and independent of the organizations affected by the CBT application being studied. In many cases, it is necessary to have an outside consultant conduct the feasibility study in order to meet these requirements.

Normally, the CBT application selected for the feasibility study will be one that offers high potential (otherwise why bother?). Thus, most studies examine an application that is thought to be well suited to CBT. The rationale for doing this is perfectly sound: if it is not possible to make a good case for a high potential CBT application, then clearly a lower payoff or less likely application would be found unfeasible. On the other hand, sometimes the most likely application may run into instructional, technical, organizational, or cost obstacles, whereas a less likely application may be workable. Many times a CBT application with fairly obvious impact on training effectiveness or efficiency has been found unfeasible for technical, organizational, or economic reasons.

In the rest of this chapter, the four types of feasibility are discussed in detail.[1] Following this discussion, a case study is presented, which illustrates a CBT feasibility study.

INSTRUCTIONAL FEASIBILITY

It is appropriate to begin with instructional feasibility since it represents the central core of the study. To a great extent, all other data collected will be determined by the information collected on instructional factors. A major activity in this part of the feasibility study should be a thorough examination of the existing training system, program, or course the CBT application will affect. This will involve interviews with instructors, students, and training managers to determine how CBT will change their roles and their attitudes toward CBT. It will also involve detailed examination of the curriculum or syllabus to determine what changes CBT may lead to. Observation of actual training in progress is usually very valuable since it often identifies important, and often subtle, considerations. For example, it may be noticed that in a large-scale testing program, students frequently change their answers. This observation suggests that if the testing is to be done online via interactive CAT, a method for changing answers will need to be provided (or expect a lot of complaints from students).

Figure 3–3 presents a number of important questions pertaining to instructional feasibility that should be addressed in the study. Some of these questions will apply to any type of CBT, whereas others are more relevant to certain types (i.e., CMI, CAI, embedded, etc.). Questions 1 and 2 focus on the stability of the application and the number of students. Because of the relatively high start-up costs associated with CBT (compared to traditional approaches), it is generally not practical for training courses or curricula that change frequently (e.g., monthly). On the other hand, if material must be changed very frequently (e.g., daily or weekly), CBT may be a good idea since changes in a centralized database system can be available as soon as they are made.

Again because of cost considerations, CBT applications are typically only feasible for applications involving a large number of students. This does not necessarily mean all at once; a training program with moderate enrollment over many years (e.g., equipment training) is often a good candidate. However, there are exceptions to this rule also. A training program may have a very small enrollment but be absolutely essential. Due to a lack of resources (e.g., instructors to teach it), or the impracticality of offering the course when or where needed, it may be a good candidate for CBT even though the total number of students is quite small.

[1]Portions of this chapter are based on Hillelsohn and Kearsley (1981).

	Yes	No
1. Is the training course or curriculum likely to be used long enough to be a good candidate for CBT?	[ ]	[ ]
2. Does the total student volume or throughput (rate) justify CBT?	[ ]	[ ]
3. Is the job performance so critical that a high degree of control over training effectiveness is needed?	[ ]	[ ]
4. Are there pedagogical requirements for interactive instruction (e.g., dynamic graphics, immediate feedback)?	[ ]	[ ]
5. Are there large differences in student entry levels that necessitate individualized instruction?	[ ]	[ ]
6. Is the training environment an extension of the job environment (e.g., do both use computers)?	[ ]	[ ]
7. Is there a strong need for standardized training (particularly at distributed training locations)?	[ ]	[ ]
8. Is there a strong need for on-demand training (i.e., training available whenever and wherever needed)?	[ ]	[ ]
9. Does the training involve expensive equipment or scarce experts?	[ ]	[ ]
10. Is the training relatively independent of human interaction?	[ ]	[ ]
11. Are the present training program and materials competency-based?	[ ]	[ ]
12. Are there aspects of the current training program that can be done well via CBT?	[ ]	[ ]

Figure 3-3   Instructional Feasibility Checklist

Questions 3, 4, and 5 focus on the value of interactiveness and individualization in the application being studied. If proper job performance is very critical, then a high level of control over training effectiveness can be achieved via CBT. The kind of detailed tracking of student progress possible with CAT, CMI, or CAI allows such control.

The training situation may involve pedagogical requirements for interactive instruction. This could include the need for immediate feedback (as in drill and practice) or the need for dynamic graphics (as in a simulation of a procedure or process). In many cases, it may be difficult to identify such needs for interactive instruction since it is not likely to be a characteristic of existing training approaches and hence not obvious. For example, issues with both pro and con sides are often presented via lectures when they really should be done interactively using small group discussions or some kind of CBT.

Large differences in student entry levels due to abilities or prior job/educational background are favorable to the use of individualized instruction and hence CBT. This is particularly common in basic training programs for new employees (e.g., sales, banking, management, insurance, etc.). CBT can be used to bring all trainees up to a standard minimum level of skills and competencies.

Questions 6, 7, and 8 deal with the capabilities of CBT to extend, standardize, or distribute training. If the job environment is an extension of the training environment by virtue of a shared or similar computer-based system, then there exists an opportunity for embedded CBT. Thus, when the job involves the use of a computer system to perform some kind of administrative or clerical function, it may be possible to use the same system for training those functions. This has the further benefit that the employee can be taught to use job aids or via online tutorials, which are then available for use on the job. Another possibility is that employees can be taught to use the computer as a tool (i.e., CAL) during training and then use it subsequently on the job.

CBT can be used to ensure standardization or availability of training at distributed training sites. Since these sites may be unsupervised and lack instructional assistance, this capability could be important in a decentralized training system. A common problem in such decentralized systems is that the nature and quality of instruction delivered via instructors varies from location to location. CBT can significantly reduce this variation. Another problem is that training is not available when needed or is given when not needed. CBT can also eliminate problems due to training unavailability or timeliness.

Question 9 is straightforward and asks whether the training situation involves scarce resources (either equipment or instructors) that could be replaced or supplemented via CBT. In the case of equipment, simulation (CAL) or simulators could be used; for experts, CAI or CAL is a possibility. There are many types of training (e.g., engineering, medical, data processing) where properly qualified instructors are sufficiently expensive and in such short supply that even very expensive CBT still results in cost savings.

The next three questions (10, 11, 12) all provide reasons why CBT may not be a good idea. If the training application is highly dependent on human interaction, then CBT may not be feasible. For example, many types of sales and management training depend on the modeling of interpersonal skills or the learning of group dynamics. If the training program is not competency-based (i.e., uses instructional objectives), then it is quite likely that CBT will make little difference. Often one of the major reasons for improvements brought about by CBT is that the training is converted to competency-based instruction as part of the use of CBT. Finally, it is important to determine if there are aspects of the current training application that cannot be done well by the kind of CBT being considered. For example, CAI or CAL may be used to teach the conceptual aspects of a task but may not be suitable for the psychomotor or affective aspects. A simulator may be needed for psychomotor skills, and the use of CMI with videotapes may be needed for the affective skills. While there are very few training areas that cannot be handled by some form of CBT, there will often be situations where a particular kind of CBT is inappropriate or not very effective for the training application being considered.

In the course of examining the existing training system, answers to these twelve questions should be obtained. There are no absolute answers to the questions, only relative ones. Thus, the members of the study team must make judgments based on their experience with CBT and the training application being studied. To the extent that answers to most of the questions favor CBT, then CBT can be considered instructionally feasible. It is to be expected that not every question will favor CBT; however, even though CBT satisfies most criteria, it may be deemed unfeasible because it fails to meet one critical consideration in the list.

ORGANIZATIONAL FEASIBILITY

Organization factors frequently represent the underlying reasons for the failure of CBT applications. Computer systems of any kind typically change the power structure and roles within an organization (Kling 1980). This is just as true of CBT as it is of a management information or word-processing system. It is necessary to evaluate potential organizational problems that might jeopardize or prevent the success of CBT. (Such problems are discussed more fully in Chapter 7.)

Figure 3-4 lists a dozen questions to be answered for the purpose of assessing the organizational feasibility of CBT. Usually the data needed to answer these questions are not collected directly but inferred from the data-collection activities. One of the reasons for attempting to interact with all individuals who might be affected by, or involved in, a CBT system is to be able to assess any organizational problems.

The first four questions have to do with the availability of suitable personnel to support CBT activities. This includes the computer systems personnel needed to design, develop, implement, operate, and maintain the CBT system; the instructional designers/developers needed to create and maintain CBT materials; the instructional programmers needed to implement, test, and debug CBT programs; and the administrative personnel required to plan, supervise, and manage CBT activities. Whether all four of these types of personnel are needed (and how many) depends on the magnitude of the CBT application and the type of CBT system involved. As we shall discuss in the following two chapters, some systems require large numbers of specialized personnel; others require very few.

	Yes	No
1. Are the systems personnel needed to design, develop, implement, operate, and maintain a CBT system available?	[ ]	[ ]
2. Are the instructional designers/developers needed to create and maintain CBT materials available?	[ ]	[ ]
3. Is the necessary instructional programming expertise available to implement, test, and debug CBT programs?	[ ]	[ ]
4. Are necessary administrative personnel available to plan, supervise, and manage CBT activities and do they have appropriate expertise?	[ ]	[ ]
5. Are the reactions of the training staff and students likely to be positive toward CBT?	[ ]	[ ]
6. Are the attitudes of the key decision-makers positive toward CBT?	[ ]	[ ]
7. Is the application free of any organizational conflicts likely to jeopardize the success of CBT?	[ ]	[ ]
8. Is interest in and support for the use of CBT widespread rather than limited to a few individuals?	[ ]	[ ]
9. Are the expectations of the training staff or decision-makers regarding the benefits of CBT reasonable?	[ ]	[ ]
10. Is the training system and organization flexible enough to accommodate disruption caused by the implementation and testing of CBT?	[ ]	[ ]
11. Does a formal mechanism exist in the organization for the modification of procedures or policies needed to accommodate changes required for CBT?	[ ]	[ ]
12. Is it clear which organizational entity (or entities) will have responsibility and authority for implementing and operating the CBT system?	[ ]	[ ]

Figure 3-4   Organizational Feasibility Checklist

The next two questions (5 and 6) have to do with attitudes toward CBT. It is necessary to know whether the attitudes of training staff and students are positive or negative toward CBT. If the attitudes are negative, then CBT is unlikely to be accepted and used even if it is implemented. It is also necessary to know the attitudes of key decision-makers toward CBT. Even though CBT may be feasible on all grounds, the lack of support from a key decision-maker could mean scuttling the idea.

Question 7 asks if there are organizational conflicts that may jeopardize the success of CBT. Such organization conflicts may stem from many sources: personal rivalries, power struggles, competition for limited resources, differing organizational philosophies, or resistance to change. CBT may become a victim of such a conflict for no reasons having to do with CBT itself.

The next question (8) asks whether interest and support for CBT is limited to a few individuals or widespread. It is normal for an individual to become enamored with CBT and to champion its use in the training system. There is nothing wrong with this situation, provided that CBT interest eventually spreads to all those who will be involved in the operation and use of the system. If the evidence suggests that support for CBT will not become widespread but always localized with the original individual, CBT may be a poor idea. If this individual leaves or loses interest, or antagonizes others in the organization, the CBT application is likely to fail.

Question 9 deals with the reasonableness of the expectations of the training staff or decision-makers regarding the outcomes of CBT. In their zeal to "sell" CBT, it is common for CBT advocates to make promises that cannot actually be fulfilled. Alternatively, individuals may develop unrealistic expectations based on genuine misunderstandings of the capabilities of CBT. For example, a trainer or decision-maker may see a demonstration of a finely tuned tutorial program that accepts open responses to questions and assume that natural language interaction is a general capability. Years may have been spent refining the keyword analysis of the particular sequence observed. Because there are so many "hidden" aspects of CBT software, it is relatively easy to form such mistaken impressions.

If it appears that training staff or decision-makers have unrealistic expectations for CBT that are unlikely to be changed prior to implementation, then this may be a factor contributing to organizational infeasibility.

The implementation and testing of a CBT system usually causes significant disruption to a training system. In general, CBT (involving interactive and individualized instruction) is not something that can be quietly "slipped into place." It normally requires major changes in the way training activities are conducted. Furthermore, implementation times for CBT often stretch over months (occasionally years); hence, the period of disruption may be an extended one. If it appears that the organization cannot cope with such a disruption, CBT may be infeasible.

Along with accommodating the disruption caused by CBT, it will likely be necessary to modify organizational policies or procedures to accommodate the changes (Question 11). It is important to determine if a formal mechanism exists for doing this; if it does not, changes necessary to make the CBT work may not be possible. Many changes are created by CBT that require modifications to organizational policy or procedures. A classic example is whether to allow students to study and use CBT equipment in the evenings and on weekends. This necessitates changes to facility procedures (i.e., access to equipment) and hours of work policies. Another example is the capability to finish training ahead of schedule and return to work. To take advantage of this extra employee time, work scheduling policies must be made flexible. If formal mechanisms do not exist to address such issues, a state of chaos may occur during implementation of CBT.

Finally, and perhaps most significantly, it is important to determine if the organizational entity that will have responsibility and authority for CBT can be identified. If no such entities can be clearly identified, this suggests that CBT may be poorly supported or may induce organizational conflict. In a proverb, "Ships without rudders often run aground."

As with the instructional factors previously discussed, no CBT system is likely to meet all organizational criteria for success. On the other hand, any single factor, if severe enough, could preclude the success of CBT and hence make it infeasible on organizational grounds. The importance of these factors will depend on the extent of the CBT system—the larger it is and the more of the organization it affects, the more important it becomes. A small system for a single training program in one department may be practically immune from all organizational concerns discussed. A large system that will affect the entire training system and all departments will undoubtedly have to deal with all of the preceding issues. Rating of the significance of these factors will have to take into account a good understanding of the organization and the probable effects of the CBT system proposed.

TECHNICAL FEASIBILITY

Technical feasibility is concerned with the availability and affordability of the hardware and software features needed for the CBT application being considered. The purpose of assessing technical feasibility is to determine what kind of system features are needed and how expensive they are. The purpose is *not* to select a particular system but to ensure that the functional capabilities required for the CBT application under study are realistic. The data collected to assess technical feasibility will likely be used later in system selection, if CBT is found feasible.

Figure 3–5 presents ten questions relating to technical feasibility. The first four questions have to do with hardware capabilities. Question 1 asks whether the kind of display, input, or output capabilities needed are available. Display capabilities include screen resolution, color, graphics, special characters, and size. Input capabilities include special keyboards, touch, speech, or digitization. Output capabilities include printers, multimedia devices (such as videotape or microfiche), and 3D display panels (used with simulators). There is a tremendous range of capabilities possible with existing CBT systems, however each system typically has only a certain set of features. For instance, some systems support only monochrome alphanumeric displays; if graphics or color are needed, this system would be inappropriate.

	Yes	No
1. Do available systems/terminals provide the kind of display, input, and output capabilities required?	[ ]	[ ]
2. Is the necessary processing capability available?	[ ]	[ ]
3. Is the necessary offline storage capacity (for lesson material and student records) available?	[ ]	[ ]
4. Are the kinds of communications capabilities needed available?	[ ]	[ ]
5. Is suitable software or courseware available?	[ ]	[ ]
6. Can a system support the number of simultaneous users expected at peak loads?	[ ]	[ ]
7. Will average system response time be acceptable?	[ ]	[ ]
8. Has acceptable system reliability and service been demonstrated?	[ ]	[ ]
9. If the system is to be used concurrently for other applications, is CBT free of adverse effects on other applications or vice versa?	[ ]	[ ]
10. Have other technological alternatives that would have a lesser impact on resources needed been considered?	[ ]	[ ]

Figure 3-5   Technical Feasibility Checklist

Questions 2, 3, and 4 ask about processing capability, storage capacity, and communications capabilities, respectively. Different types of CBT will require different degrees of processing power. Thus, CAT or CMI typically do not require a lot of computation; however, CAI or CAL involving a lot of graphics, complex answer analysis, or simulation are likely to result in significant computational demands. The usual consequences of insufficient processing power are slow display and response times, which may be unacceptable to the student. In some cases, the lack of processing power prevents certain kinds of applications from being attempted.

Similarly, different types of CBT will require different amounts of offline storage capacity, i.e., simulators are likely to require far less than CAT or CMI. Since the storage is used for lessons and student data, the amount needed will normally be a function of the size of the CBT system. The more students and different lessons available, the more storage capacity needed.[2]

Communications capabilities (Question 4) are a critical component of any modern CBT system. In most CBT applications, there will be a need to trans-

---

[2]The total capacity required can be estimated by multiplying the maximum number of students and lessons by average record sizes in bytes. Thus, if average student record size is 75,000 bytes and average lesson size is 500,000 bytes, a CBT system for thirty students and five lessons will require a minimum of: $(30 \times 75,000) + (5 \times 500,000) = 4.75$ million bytes offline storage.

mit lesson materials or student data between student terminals and central databases or between two or more terminals. These transmissions could take place between two rooms in the same building or between two locations on different continents. As we shall see in the next chapter, there are many different types of communication methods, many of which are incompatible. Thus, determining that the CBT system has the specific kind of communications capability needed for the application under consideration is an important aspect of the feasibility study. While it is unlikely that the communications capability needed will be unavailable, it is possible that it will be prohibitively expensive.

Question 5 asks about the availability of suitable software or courseware.[3] The real issue here is whether it can be bought "off the shelf" and used without major modifications or whether it will have to be written especially for the application being considered. If it is available, then the question is what kind of system is needed to run it. If it is unavailable, then the problem becomes the availability of systems and programming personnel with the ability to develop what is needed. In general, most types of software needed for CBT applications are "off the shelf" although the right type of hardware must be available. In contrast, most courseware cannot be obtained "off the shelf" and must be developed to meet the unique needs of the organization.

The next three questions (6, 7, and 8) deal with performance of the CBT system. The system must be able to support the total number of users under peak load conditions. It may be that the number of terminals required is larger than can be reasonably expected for the system under consideration. As well as supporting the total number of users, the system must also be able to provide acceptable response times. A system with consistently slow or highly variable response times will lead to user dissatisfaction. Finally, the system must be capable of meeting certain reliability and service criteria. Normally, a CBT system must have an "uptime" of at least 95 percent or better to be acceptable for CBT. Furthermore, service must be good enough so that any component of the system can be repaired within a day (i.e., maximum "downtime" of less than twenty-four hours).[4] If it appears that the kind of performance conditions needed cannot be achieved, then CBT may not be technically feasible.

Question 9 deals with the issue of shared resources. If the CBT system is to be used for other purposes (e.g., administrative or financial computing) or if the CBT programs are to be run on a system primarily used for other purposes (as in the case of embedded training), then a potential problem situation exists in terms of priorities. There may come times when the performance of the CBT system is adversely affected by the other uses, or when heavy usage of CBT af-

---

[3]The details of CBT software and courseware are discussed in the next chapter.

[4]It should be noted that achieving acceptable reliability and service is not only a function of the hardware/software but also the user (e.g., adequate preventative maintenance, redundant equipment, spare parts, etc.).

fects the other functions. This can happen with the full range of resources —terminals, systems/programmer personnel, offline storage, and so on. The sharing of CBT with other applications may be a good idea economically, but it may be technically infeasible.

The last technical feasibility question has to do with the existence of alternative technological solutions than the CBT approach being considered. There are almost always other solutions possible that require less resources. For example, the U.S. Air Force uses a large scale CBT system called AIS in its pilot and aircrew training.[5] They wanted to enlarge the system to do a lot of adaptive testing, but the cost of the number of terminals needed was unacceptable. Instead, they developed a low-cost keyboard terminal specifically for adaptive testing (McKnight, Waters, and Lamos 1978). A similar problem existed in the development of a CAI system to teach land navigation and map reading to soldiers. The costs of high resolution displays and the programming of maps was too high. The use of computer-controlled (i.e., random access) microfiche meant that existing maps could be used. Thus, other types of technology, instead of, or in addition to, the CBT system being considered may make a particular application feasible.

An assessment of technical feasibility depends heavily on an expert understanding of the capabilities of existing CBT systems and the likely requirements of the application being considered. In the absence of this expertise, the evaluations should be based on the characteristics of similar CBT systems examined and the capabilities of existing computer systems within the organization (i.e., Steps 4 and 7 of Figure 3-2).

ECONOMIC FEASIBILITY

Of the four types of feasibility, economic is probably the most important since it generally sets the boundaries on what is or is not possible. Given an unlimited amount of money, most instructional, technical, and organizational obstacles can be overcome. Of course, this is not realistic in a world of fixed budgets and limited expenditures. What can be afforded is therefore a major consideration in a feasibility study.

Figure 3-6 lists a set of questions pertaining to economic feasibility. Question 1 asks if the existing training costs are known. This is important since these are the costs that the CBT application will be compared with (either explicitly or implicitly). It is very common for such costs to be unknown or drastically underestimated, thereby making comparison with CBT difficult or unfair. Thus, the first step in determining the economic feasibility of a CBT application is to identify all of the costs of current training programs or systems. Without these figures, it may not be possible to properly evaluate the feasibility of CBT.

[5]AIS is described in detail in the next chapter.

	Yes	No
1. Are the total costs (including instructors, administration, facilities, equipment, materials, student travel, etc.) for the existing training program known?	[ ]	[ ]
2. Are the total development costs for the proposed CBT materials (including design, development, programming, evaluation) known?	[ ]	[ ]
3. Are the total delivery costs for the proposed CBT system (including hardware acquisition, system operating and maintenance costs, instructors, administration, facilities, offline materials, etc.) known?	[ ]	[ ]
4. Will the use of CBT result in annual or life cycle cost savings over the existing training?	[ ]	[ ]
5. Will the use of CBT result in value-added benefits over the existing training that can be quantified?	[ ]	[ ]
6. Are assumptions underlying the cost analyses about the throughput or total utilization of CBT reasonable?	[ ]	[ ]
7. Are the immediate or total costs of CBT *tolerable* costs for the organization?	[ ]	[ ]
8. Will the organization fund the start-up costs at a level that is sufficient and necessary to assure a reasonable chance of success?	[ ]	[ ]
9. Will the procurement process allow the CBT system or associated resources to be acquired in the timeframe needed?	[ ]	[ ]

Figure 3-6   Economic Feasibility Checklist

The next two questions (2 and 3) deal with the total development and delivery costs for the CBT application. The development of CBT materials (particularly CAI or CAL) is typically quite expensive. A commonly used rule of thumb for CAI is 100 to 200 hours of development time for every hour of instruction developed. The amount of time required (and hence costs) will vary considerably with the type of CBT involved, the capabilities of the system, and the experience of the personnel. The total delivery costs encompass all of the hardware and software acquisition and operational costs, as well as expenses associated with personnel and facilities. If the CBT development and delivery system costs are not completely known (or cannot be estimated), then it may be difficult to determine the feasibility of the application.

Questions 4, 5, and 6 have to do with cost/benefits analysis of the CBT application.[6] In order to demonstrate economic feasibility it may be necessary to show that the CBT application will result in annual or life cycle savings over the existing training approach. Alternatively, CBT may cost the same as or more than existing training but be cost justified on the basis of value-added benefits—i.e., improved training effectiveness or better job performance. Such value-added benefits are numerous and can usually be quantified. For example, simulators may reduce the accident rate in training to near zero; the value of the medical expenses (or lives) saved is the CBT benefit. Similarly, after a particularly effective sales training course via CAI, new salespersons may actually sell more products than with previous training; the value of these extra sales is a benefit of CBT. Note that if these added-value benefits cannot be quantified, they will not contribute to the economic feasibility of CBT.

Question 6 asks about the assumptions underlying the cost analyses, specifically the student throughput or total utilization assumptions. These two assumptions represent the major ways in which the costs (either development or delivery) of CBT systems are computed. If the number of students using the system is overestimated, the per student cost may be too low; if it is underestimated, the cost may be too high. To get an accurate assessment of economic feasibility, it is important to have reasonable assumptions for these two factors.

Tolerable costs (Question 7) are simply the level of funding an organization is used to or feels comfortable with (Seidel 1980). Even if a CBT system promises to save a million dollars, if the system requires an initial investment of $100,000 when the annual training budget is only $50,000, the costs of the system are not likely to be tolerable costs. If the annual costs of the CBT systems are greater than the existing budgets of all the groups who can share the funding, the system is likely to be seen as economically infeasible.

One of the common reasons for the failure of CBT systems (indeed all technological innovations) is the failure to fund the start-up of the project at a level that is sufficient to ensure its success. Because an idea is new and unproven, the temptation is to provide the minimum support possible in case it fails. Alternatively, insufficient time may be allowed for the project to overcome start-up problems and produce benefits. Thus, if the level of financial commitment at the beginning of a CBT project is not enough to ensure that it will be successfully implemented, the system may be infeasible.

Finally, it is important to examine the procurement process in the organization to determine if it will hinder the timeliness with which the CBT system can be acquired. Often the procurement policies in the military and government are so cumbersome that a CBT system cannot realistically be acquired in a timeframe that will allow it to be useful for the applications in-

[6]Cost/benefits analysis for CBT is discussed in detail in Chapter 7.

tended. A common stumbling block in the procurement of CBT systems is the problem of deciding whether CBT should adhere to the procedures developed for data-processing systems or training equipment. While it is clearly the latter, it usually looks like the former on paper. Another common problem is the acquisition of the necessary expertise to implement and operate a CBT system (e.g., designers, programmers, managers). It is often the case that job positions for such personnel do not exist and must be created—a procedure that causes problems in many organizations. Thus, determining the economic feasibility of CBT should include an analysis of the time delays associated with procurement of the system.

CASE STUDY: SOUTHWESTERN UTILITIES LIMITED

To help illustrate how the preceding discussion would apply to a real training setting, a case study will be presented. The case study deals with a fictitious company called Southwestern Utilities Limited (SUL), which provides natural gas service to about 200,000 customers in southwestern United States. The company consists of about 500 employees, approximately half of which are located in a head office and the rest in field offices throughout the service area.

In order to improve efficiency, SUL has recently implemented a computer-based Customer Information System (CIS). CIS provides a complete database on all customer-related transactions, including meter installations, meter readings, service calls, billings and payments, credits and collections, and customer inquiries. CIS is used regularly by about 60 percent of SUL employees. Almost all employees must understand CIS and how it relates to company operations.

CIS runs off a large mainframe computer located at the SUL head office. There are fifty-two terminals located in the head office and forty-eight terminals located in field offices. CIS is operated and maintained by the Information Systems Department (ISD), which is responsible to the VP, Operations.

While CIS has undoubtedly improved the efficiency of SUL operations and the quality of customer service, it has created tremendous training problems. CIS is a complex information system that requires considerable expertise and understanding to use properly. Failure to learn how to use CIS properly can result in incorrect or inappropriate billing, unnecessary service calls, and poor handling of customer inquiries. These failures could lead to dissatisfied customers and service complaints. Clearly, good CIS training is vital to maintaining a high standard of customer satisfaction.

When CIS was first implemented, the training was handled by ISD staff who knew the system and company operations expertly. They gave small group training sessions, which included hands-on practice, to everyone who initially used CIS. This took many months, but this was acceptable since operations were basically still being done manually.

Although everything went smoothly with initial implementation of CIS, there have been problems training new users on the system. They are trained on the job by their supervisors or co-workers who already know how to use the system. Unfortunately, this training is unsystematic and often of poor quality; hence, it is often a long time before the new users learn to use CIS properly.

ISD is now ready to implement a major new capability on CIS (order entry), which will require additional training for all users. However, ISD is not able to conduct this training since it is totally occupied with implementing new features and maintaining the existing system. ISD asks the Training Services Department (TSD) to do the training. TSD has not been involved in CIS up to this point. Partly out of ignorance and fear, and partly due to lack of resources and expertise, TSD refuses, insisting that support of CIS is an ISD responsibility. Like ISD, TSD also answers to the VP, Operations.

The matter goes to the VP for resolution. She realizes that since CIS training is critical to the smooth operations of SUL (and will become increasingly so), a cost-effective training program for CIS must be developed. While she feels that the responsibility for doing this rests properly with TSD, she recognizes that ISD contains all of the expertise on the system and will therefore need to play a major role in CIS training. She has an insight—perhaps the use of CBT for CIS would be a way of involving both groups and making good use of their respective expertise. She also suspects that it might be a very cost-effective way of doing CIS training.

The VP immediately establishes a CBT Task Force consisting of the managers of TSD and ISD, other major department managers (including customer service and personnel), and four first-line supervisors (two from field locations) known for their candor. The task force is coordinated by an outside consultant with CBT expertise and no particular organizational loyalties. The task force is given two months to collect data and determine the feasibility of CBT for CIS training.

After two months, the task force is convened in a meeting to discuss the findings and reach conclusions. In terms of instructional feasibility, CBT seems like a good idea. One of the findings of the study is that employees seldom get enough practice with the system prior to using it on their jobs. The availability of on-line practice exercises using a "dummy" database as part of training is seen as highly desirable. The number of employees to be trained on CIS is large and ongoing. Good performance on CIS is critical to company operations. CIS experts are scarce, particularly in the field offices. There are large differences in the backgrounds of employees to be trained because the system is used by so many different kinds of people (from salespersons to accountants). The training environment is literally an extension of the job environment. There is a strong need for standardized and on-demand training at all locations. Since training is most effective if feedback to student actions is as quick as it would be with CIS, there is a pedagogical requirement for interactive instruction. The training is not highly dependent on human interaction (quite the opposite) and there are no real aspects of CIS training that cannot be done via CBT. In fact, there is only one aspect that raises a problem of instructional feasibility. The CIS training program is not competency-based. At present there is no way of determining if the training is relevant to job needs. Thus, prior to or as part of implementing CBT, a task analysis would need to be done for all CIS users to identify the objectives and criteria for CIS training.

The findings also indicate that CBT is technically feasible using the same computer system used for CIS. It is clear that the same display, input, and output capabilities used for CIS are quite suitable for tutorial CAI. Due to the foresight of the ISD manager, the system bought for CIS has considerable expansion capability in terms of processing capability and offline storage capacity; these can be expanded as needed at relatively little cost. The current terminals have average utilization rates of about 70 percent allowing sufficient time for them to be used for training; however, they are located in busy work locations that are not considered conducive to learning. Thus, it is determined that an additional twenty-eight terminals would be needed, to be used exclusively for training purposes and located in quiet places.

Because of continual system expansion, the ISD manager has managed to avoid any kind of system performance problems. There is no reason to believe this will be different with CBT. Investigation of CBT systems similar in nature to the one envisioned for CIS indicate that they can run concurrently with the main system function and no performance problems are created. System reliability and service for CIS results in about 99 percent uptime—very acceptable for CBT.

While a good authoring language (explained in subsequent chapters) is available for the system being used, no one in ISD has had experience with it. The ISD department has a strong preference to do any courseware development work in the same programming language that CIS is written in (COBOL), which they have expertise in and can support.

A number of other alternatives to CBT are considered (e.g., videotape, small group classes, self-study workbooks), but none of them meets the instructional requirements as well as CBT.

The evaluation of economic feasibility strongly supports the selection of CBT. The initial CIS training cost SUL $107,000. More importantly, though, computation of employee and supervisor overtime directly attributable to learning how to use CIS amounted to another $100,000 over a one-year period. Thus, if CBT for CIS can be done for less than $100,000, this will result in a cost savings. The total development costs for the development of CIS training online are estimated to be about $40,000 (for a sixteen-hour course and all materials), with annual revision costs of about $15,000. This includes instructional design/development and evaluation time, as well as system design, programming and testing time. The cost of the additional terminals and system capacity is approximately $32,000 per year. In addition, about half the time of a manager is felt to be necessary to supervise and coordinate CBT (a value of about $16,000 annually).

The major costs of CBT are therefore less than $100,000, particularly if the development effort is amortized over a number of years of use. In addition, there are many value added benefits that could be quantified if necessary. These include savings in travel costs to provide training in the field, the immediate availability of training (allowing employees to become productive sooner after being hired or promoted), and the potential for the training always to be up to date (thus avoiding mistakes due to the use of old procedures and hence wasted time). The costs of CBT are tolerable to SUL since they are less than was spent either initially or during the year on CIS training. Because of the importance of CIS training, it will receive the initial and ongoing level of funding that has been shown to be needed. Finally, because TSD and ISD answer to the same VP who has authority to commit this level of funds, there are not likely to be any procurement obstacles to CBT.

This brings us to organizational feasibility. Organizational considerations present potential problems for CBT. First, the systems and programming personnel needed to develop, implement, and maintain CBT are not available in ISD. (Remember, this caused the initial conflict over CIS training between ISD and TSD.) Instructional designers/developers with suitable CBT expertise are not available in TSD. Furthermore, the necessary administrative personnel (e.g., the half-time manager proposed) are not available in either ISD or TSD. There is conflict between ISD and TSD over who should have responsibility for CBT. This has become worse since the study began since both groups are now very excited about the prospect of doing CBT.

Other organizational factors appear favorable to CBT. Employees are generally positive toward CIS (once they learn how to use it) and will approach online training positively. Support for CBT has spread from the task force members into their respective departments. All the key decision-makers (including, of course, the VP) are on the task force and support CBT. Expectations on the part of TSD, ISD, or employees about CBT are not out of line with what can be accomplished. Since the implementation of CIS, the organization has become used to changes in old procedures and policies necessary to make the system work. It is not felt that changes necessary to use CBT effectively will cause problems, especially since no formal mechanisms currently exist for CIS training.

Thus, CBT seems feasible on instructional, technical, and economic grounds, but possibly not organizationally. At the decision-making meeting, no resolution can be achieved between ISD and TSD over responsibility or personnel for CBT. The meeting is adjourned and the consultant and VP retire to discuss the matter. The consultant feels that responsibility for CBT should be joint since both ISD and TSD need to be involved; the VP does not think this will work and feels that TSD should be responsible for CBT.

The consultant suggests the following matrix management plan. TSD should hire a new designer/developer with CBT experience and an instructional programmer experienced on the authoring language available for the system. While both new employees would answer to TSD, they both would be located in ISD. By using the authoring language rather than COBOL, and answering to TSD, control over CBT would stay in the hands of the training group; however, by being located in ISD, they would essentially become a part of the computer group. While this plan will cost more (two new employees are needed as well as the cost of the authoring language), it seems to be a good compromise.

A meeting is held between the consultant, VP, and managers of TSD and ISD. While neither manager is totally happy with the plan, they both agree that it is acceptable. At least both will be involved in the project. At the consultant's recommendation, the VP also establishes a CBT steering committee consisting of the same members who served on the task force (less one person—the consultant).

SUMMARY

As the case study demonstrates, the questions listed in Figures 3–3, 3–4, 3–5, and 3–6 can be used as a set of checklists to guide what information needs to be collected in the feasibility study. Each question can be answered with a positive or negative answer based on the data collected and expert judgment. In order to ensure feasibility, it is necessary to satisfy the majority of questions within any of the four categories. Furthermore, any single factor, if severe enough, could prevent the success of CBT.

Of the four types of feasibility discussed, instructional and technical feasibility are least likely to provide significant obstacles to CBT. Generally, applications can be selected to be instructionally suitable for some type of CBT. Furthermore, current CBT systems can provide almost any kind of instructional capability required, although sometimes such capabilities may be expensive in terms of development or delivery. Economic considerations often make CBT infeasible since start-up costs for large-scale CBT systems are often quite high; however, it is typically organizational problems (as illustrated in the case study) that present the real obstacles to CBT. Organizational problems are often very difficult to resolve—short of significant changes to the organization.

Feasibility studies do not usually lead to full-scale implementation of CBT. Instead, they result in decisions to try a pilot or prototype CBT project.

Because many factors associated with CBT cannot be evaluated well in advance, it is often necessary to try CBT on a small scale to find out the answers. It is reasonable to think of feasibility studies as consisting of two stages. The first stage leads to a decision to forget CBT or to proceed with a pilot demonstration project for the training application with the highest expected payoffs. If the demonstration is successful, the second stage of the study is conducted to determine the feasibility of a full-scale implementation.

Assuming that a decision is made to go ahead with CBT (either as a pilot project or full-scale implementation), the next step is to select the appropriate CBT system. The next chapter discusses alternative CBT systems.

4

CBT Systems

In this chapter, we look at the different types of CBT systems available. Most of these systems can be used for any of the kinds of CBT discussed in Chapter 2. In the next chapter we will look at how to select a particular system in terms of training requirements.

CBT SYSTEM CONCEPTS

Before we discuss specific systems, it is necessary to clarify some basic concepts. First of all, we will discuss four major components of a CBT system: *hardware, software, courseware,* and *humanware.* Hardware refers to all of the physical equipment associated with a CBT system including terminals, disk drives, printers, multimedia devices, etc. Software covers the programs that allow the system to operate and perform instructional functions. Software is usually classified into system software (e.g., the operating system and utility programs), applications software (e.g., word processing, statistics, database management), and courseware. Courseware refers to programs that provide instructional presentations. Courseware is distinguished from other types of software in CBT systems because of its special role of representing a curriculum.[1]

---

[1]Courseware is also called *lessonware* or *teachware.* It is analogous to the information stored in an information retrieval or MIS database. While normally referring to online materials, the term has come to be used for offline materials as well. See Bunderson (1981) for a comprehensive discussion of courseware.

Humanware refers to all of the people with specialized expertise who are required to develop, operate, maintain, or evaluate a CBT system. This can include instructional designers, system analysts, programmers, computer operators, system managers, proctors, and electronics technicians. The number of people required for a CBT system can range from a few to hundreds, depending on the size and type of system involved.

All four of these components are equally important in selecting and implementing a successful CBT system. Without the correct choice of hardware, the instructional capabilities needed for the training application may not be possible. Thus, a training situation may have strong requirements for touch input or dynamic graphics; however, if these features are not present on the hardware, they cannot be provided by the CBT system. Hardware is a necessary but not sufficient component of a CBT system. Without the hardware, the other components have no role; however, the hardware without the other three components cannot provide CBT.

If the appropriate software is not available, then desired features of the hardware or courseware cannot be used. For example, full-scale CBT systems usually provide comprehensive software programs for collecting and analyzing student performance data; this software will normally have to be written when general purpose computing systems or languages are used for CBT.

Without the appropriate courseware, even the most sophisticated hardware and software is of no value. A cardinal rule of CBT is that computers do not magically make poor training materials into good training materials. Adding CAT or CMI to an existing training program may improve its efficiency, but if the training materials or activities are poor, there will be no change in the effectiveness of the training. The design of good courseware and the steps associated with it are discussed in Chapter 5.

Humanware is usually the most critical yet overlooked element of a CBT system. Without the right kind of people (in terms of skills and background), it is easy for a CBT system to fail. During the feasibility and selection process, it is very important to have a high level of CBT expertise available, as well as individuals who are very familiar with the organization. Development of CBT courseware involves people with training in instructional design and technology along with subject matter experts. Implementation of a CBT system requires a high degree of management ability and experience with innovation. Operation and maintenance of hardware, software, and courseware require a stable and highly knowledgeable CBT staff. It is hard to overstate the significance of the humanware component in CBT.

CBT SYSTEM CONFIGURATIONS

One of the major design aspects of a CBT system is the system configuration, i.e., the way the various hardware components interact with each other. Historically, CBT systems were based on *time-sharing* configurations involving large central mainframes with terminals that shared the processing, offline storage (i.e., disk drives), and input/output peripherals (e.g., printers) associated with the mainframe. This sharing takes place via a communications network that may involve remote transmissions over long distances (via telephone or satellite connections) or local transmissions (i.e., a few yards or blocks) using coaxial or fiber optic cables.

With the advent of relatively inexpensive mini- and microcomputers, it has become possible to provide all of the processing and storage capabilities needed in the terminal itself. Thus, *standalone* configurations are being used for many CBT applications without the need for a mainframe computer or a communications network. Simulators have almost always been designed as standalone configurations.

At the present time we are seeing the emergence of *distributed* configurations, which represent the marriage of timesharing and standalone capabilities. In a distributed system, terminals can function in a standalone mode as well as being able to share the processing or storage capabilities of other terminals or computers in the network. Distributed systems may involve either remote or local communications networks.[2]

Figure 4–1 depicts the three types of system configurations just described. In the timesharing configuration, the storage (S) and peripherals (P) are shared by all terminals. In the standalone configuration, each terminal is independent and has its own storage and peripherals. In the distributed configuration, there are both local and shared storage and peripherals, and communication links directly between terminals as well as through a mainframe host.

Figure 4–2 outlines some of the advantages and disadvantages of each system configuration. Timesharing configurations allow the sharing of central processing resources and storage capability. Thus, the power of a large mainframe can be utilized by all the terminals on the network. Similarly, a large amount of storage capacity for courseware or student data can be shared. The sharing of central resources means that the terminals can be relatively simple and inexpensive. Because of this, a timeshared network can be expanded for a relatively low per terminal cost. On the other hand, one of the major limitations of a timesharing configuration is saturation of resources—when too many terminals are simultaneously using the system, performance is degraded resulting in unacceptable response times. Another problem is unreliability—when the central processor fails, all terminals are affected.

Standalone systems provide essentially the exact opposite set of advantages and disadvantages. They offer a great deal of flexibility since each terminal can be equipped with the specific features needed for each particular application. Some terminals might need a lot of processing capability and graphics for CAL (e.g., simulations), others may only need alphanumeric capabilities for CAT/CMI, while some need color, audio, and video interfaces

[2]For comprehensive discussions of computer networks see J. Martin (1977) or Tanenbaum (1981).

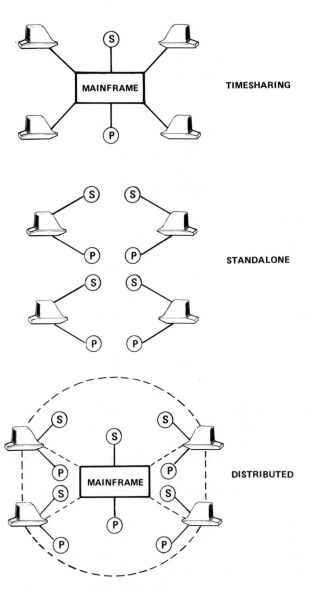

Figure 4-1   System Configurations

	ADVANTAGES	DISADVANTAGES
TIMESHARING	• SHARING OF CENTRAL PROCESSING AND STORAGE CAPABILITIES • LOW TERMINAL ADD-ON COSTS	• SATURATION AND RELIABILITY PROBLEMS
STANDALONE	• FLEXIBILITY • PORTABILITY	• LACK OF SHARING OF CENTRAL PROCESSING, STORAGE AND PERIPHERALS
DISTRIBUTED	• SHARING OF PROCESSING, STORAGE AND PERIPHERALS • FLEXIBILITY • INCREASED NETWORK RELIABILITY	• TELECOMMUNICATIONS CONSIDERATIONS

Figure 4-2   Advantages and Disadvantages of Different Configurations

for CAI tutorials. Moreover, standalone terminals tend to be relatively portable and can be located where they are most convenient for the student (e.g., the workplace, learning center, home).

Standalone terminals are not able to take advantage of shared processing or storage capabilities. Thus, the speed of processing is determined by the particular limits of each terminal. Similarly, the amount of courseware or student data storage possible is determined by the capacity of the disk drives attached to the terminal. Any input/output peripherals needed (such as printers, plotters, digitizers, or multimedia devices) must be provided for each terminal. Clearly, it quickly becomes expensive to configure a CBT system with a lot of standalone terminals.

Distributed systems represent the advantages of timesharing and standalone systems without the disadvantages. They allow the sharing of the processing or storage capabilities of other terminals or computers in the network. This might involve the collection of student records from other terminals in a local network or accessing courseware available on a large mainframe via remote telecommunications. Unlike timesharing configurations, the failure of one terminal or mainframe will not inhibit the other members of the network. Because the terminals are standalone, they can be equipped with different kinds of capabilities and are portable.

Distributed configurations are highly dependent upon communications, whether local or remote. Generally they are designed to take advantage of shared resources. When these are unavailable, use of the system may be degraded. The dependence on communications introduces a number of issues relating to compatibility and costs. Furthermore, because of increased complexity, it is often harder to make distributed systems "user friendly" (i.e., easy to use and learn) than simpler timeshared or standalone configurations.

Because of the inherent advantages of distributed configurations, it is likely that all CBT systems will eventually evolve into such a design. While there will be applications where timesharing or standalone configurations may be suitable, a distributed system can be used for either and offers future flexibility when training needs change. One of the major limitations of past CBT systems has been their lack of such flexibility.

One further concept needs to be introduced before discussing examples of CBT systems. This is the difference between dedicated and piggyback systems. A dedicated CBT system is one in which the hardware, software, courseware, and humanware are all specifically designed for CBT. Thus, the hardware is specifically designed for CAT, CMI, CAI, CAL, or simulation. Likewise, the software is designed for CBT functions. The courseware consists of instructional presentations or practice. The humanware includes people with the particular expertise needed for CBT. In contrast, a piggyback CBT system is one in which the hardware, software, or humanware have a primary role that is not CBT. Thus, in the embedded training found in administrative or management information systems, CBT is simply an additional function or capability provided. In its most simple form, CBT is a set of introductory lessons that teach employees how to use an existing computer-based system. For example, a tutorial program may be written that teaches people to use an information retrieval, electronic mail, word processing, or inventory control system. Whether a CBT system is dedicated or piggyback will significantly affect the scope and nature of the resources required and the capabilities possible.

EXAMPLES OF CBT SYSTEMS

In this section, we will survey some of the different CBT systems commercially available today. The particular systems discussed have been selected because they illustrate the concepts discussed in the first part of this chapter.[3] No endorsement of any of these systems is intended. Baker (1978a) discusses the history of commercially available CBT systems.

Dedicated Systems

This section discusses three examples of dedicated CBT systems: PLATO, TICCIT, and AIS. These three systems represent large-scale CBT systems that have been implemented in many organizations. They also represent systems with mature and sophisticated hardware and software.

[3]Information about computer systems becomes dated relatively quickly because of the fast pace of development in the computer world. You should check with the vendors of the equipment for the latest details when actually doing a selection study rather than relying on the information presented in this chapter (see Appendix).

PLATO

Because of its longevity and size, the PLATO system deserves first mention. PLATO was initially developed at the University of Illinois about 1960 and has gone through many changes and enhancements in the past two decades (e.g., Rahmlow, Fratini, and Ghesquiere 1980). PLATO is marketed by Control Data Corporation and is installed at a number of sites across the world (see Figure 4-3). A complete PLATO system can be purchased, terminals can be leased, or CDC Learning Centers can be used. Hundreds of courses have been developed for the system and can be used on a lease basis. PLATO is a very mature CBT system and provides a full range of CAT, CMI, CAI, and CAL capabilities. It has been used in virtually every CBT application possible in a wide range of training settings. This includes sales and management training, technical and industrial training, military training, medical education, remedial education in basic skills, and hundreds of college and university courses. The use of PLATO in prisons and for home learning has been mentioned in an earlier chapter.

PLATO is a dedicated CBT system that involves specialized terminals, software, and humanware. The system was originally designed as a large time-

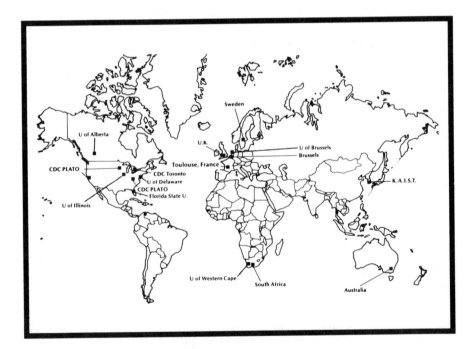

Figure 4-3 Worldwide PLATO® Network

sharing configuration using remote telecommunications. Today, CDC markets a Micro-PLATO terminal capable of standalone operation. At the current time, the standalone terminals must work in the timeshared mode when using the network, but it is inevitable that the terminals will be capable of full distributed network capabilities in the near future. When operating in the standalone mode, the Micro-PLATO terminals access courseware and store data via a floppy disk drive (see Figure 4-4).

Two hardware features have always been distinctive of PLATO: the touch panel and high-quality graphics. The touch panel allows students to indicate responses by touching a screen location with a finger. This is a heavily used feature of the system. It helps make interaction with PLATO "friendlier" (keyboards are not liked by many people) and also allows the simulation of psychomotor skills (e.g., touching buttons on control panels or keys on a piano). The high-quality graphics capability is a function of a screen with a resolution of 512 × 512 addressable locations and the ability to do line/curve generation. These two aspects allow PLATO to display detailed illustrations and do certain kinds of animation.

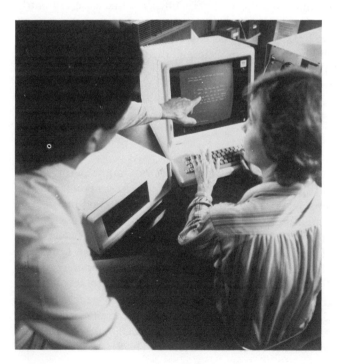

Figure 4-4   Micro-PLATO® Terminal
(Courtesy, Control Data Corporation)

From a software and courseware perspective, PLATO features an extremely powerful author language called TUTOR, which makes it possible to create almost any type of instructional presentation needed. The combination of the good graphics capability and TUTOR has led to PLATO's popularity for simulation. The CMI capability of PLATO (PLM) has already been described in a previous chapter. One very important feature of the PLATO system is its interterminal messaging and mailbox facilities. Through the use of these capabilities, the PLATO community discovered quite early that interpersonal communication between student and instructor, or between student and student could be a very important part of the overall learning process. In fact, PLATO probably represented the first large-scale electronic mail community.

In many ways, PLATO has come the closest of any CBT system to minimizing the humanware considerations. If an off-the-shelf course is used in the context of a CDC Learning Center, there is essentially no special CBT expertise required. The system is operated and maintained by CDC and is transparent to either the students or trainers. If an organization needs its own custom courseware developed, it may simply contract with CDC (or other third-party courseware developers) or create its own development team including at least an instructional programmer familiar with TUTOR. In either case, no hardware or software needs to be acquired; hence, no personnel to operate or maintain such hardware are necessary. Of course, if the PLATO hardware is acquired, a full staff will be needed. For example, the University of Delaware installed its own PLATO system to serve the university in 1975. By 1981, the project had a full-time staff of forty-two (director, managers, secretaries, electronics specialist, user coordinator, systems analysts, programmers) as well as over sixty-seven part-time staff.

TICCIT

Development work on TICCIT began in the early 1970s as a joint effort of the Mitre Corporation and Brigham Young University.[4] The design philosophy of TICCIT differed in many ways from PLATO. Instead of a large timesharing system with remote terminals, TICCIT was designed to be a local timesharing network with up to 128 terminals. In contrast to the special purpose terminals designed for PLATO, TICCIT used off-the-shelf Sony TV monitors. Instead of a large mainframe, TICCIT used a Data General minicomputer. While PLATO has high resolution monochrome (i.e., single color) graphics, TICCIT features seven color graphics. Whereas PLATO used a touch panel, TICCIT used a light pen. TICCIT was also capable of showing video sequences from a central videotape library (see Figure 4–5). Details of TICCIT are described in Merrill, Schneider, and Fletcher (1980) and Reigeluth (1979).

[4]The development of both TICCIT and PLATO were supported extensively by the National Science Foundation. TICCIT is a registered trademark of Hazeltine Corporation.

Figure 4-5   TICCIT® System in Use
(Courtesy, Hazeltine Corporation)

Probably the most dramatic difference between TICCIT and PLATO is the unique instructional framework developed for TICCIT. First of all, it involves developing all instruction in terms of a small set of instructional components (rules, examples, practice, tests, objectives). Second, the learner is given control over these components by means of special keys on the TICCIT keyboard. Thus, the student is able to not only control the rate and sequence of learning but also the nature of the instructional components. In addition, there are "easy" and "hard" keys allowing the learner to alter the difficulty level of the presentation. Instead of being programmed using an author language such as TUTOR, instructional components for TICCIT courseware were "packaged" using a form-driven authoring system. The creation of courseware for TICCIT is therefore fundamentally different from PLATO or other CBT systems (Bunderson 1974).

Like PLATO, TICCIT has undergone significant changes since its initial development. Since 1976, TICCIT has been marketed by Hazeltine Corporation. It is used at a number of community colleges, military installations, and commercial organizations. TICCIT hardware is still based on a local timesharing configuration, although it is presently being upgraded to a full distributed architecture with both remote and local networking. In addition to its original packaging system (called APT), an author language (called TAL) is now offered. Interactive videodisc capability local to each terminal has replaced the central videotape storage system.

AIS

The Advanced Instructional System (AIS) is a large time-shared CBT system developed by McDonnell Douglas Corporation in conjunction with the Air Force Human Resources Laboratory. AIS was originally implemented as a multimedia CMI system and featured offline testing (via mark sense scoring sheets) and specially designed audiovisual equipment. A plasma type terminal (similar to the ones used in the PLATO system) was used for CAI and online student interaction (Rockway and Yasatuke 1974).

In recent years, the system has undergone considerable redesign. While orignally implemented on a CDC Cyber mainframe, it can now run on a DEC VAX minicomputer. The CAI capabilities of the system are now emphasized. Most importantly, AIS-II now supports a variety of terminal types featuring different screen sizes, alphanumeric or color graphics, and various peripherals (printer/plotters, videotape units). This multiterminal capability makes AIS stand out from PLATO and TICCIT, which allow only one type of terminal. It is an important capability likely to show up in future CBT systems.

AIS has been used within McDonnell Douglas Corporation for internal training, by the Air Force for aircrew training, and by the Department of Energy for nuclear safety training. AIS has a powerful instructional language called CAMIL, which is unique in that it is well designed for both CAI and CMI applications (Pflasterer and Montgomery 1979).

Piggyback Systems

Unlike PLATO and TICCIT, which are dedicated CBT systems, a number of CBT systems are piggyback software packages, which run on already existing computer systems.

IIS

One of the most popular of the piggyback systems is the IBM Interactive Instructional System (IIS), a set of two programs that run on large IBM mainframes and use IBM 3270 type display terminals (see Figure 4-6). The two programs are IIAS (for authoring) and IIPS (for instructional presentation). IIS is based on an author language called COURSEWRITER, which has been in use for almost two decades.[5] In addition, IIS includes the capabilities of the Interactive Training System, an earlier CAT/CMI system used extensively in IBM

---

[5]IBM once marketed the 1500 Instructional System, which was widely used during the 1960s. This system used an earlier version of COURSEWRITER.

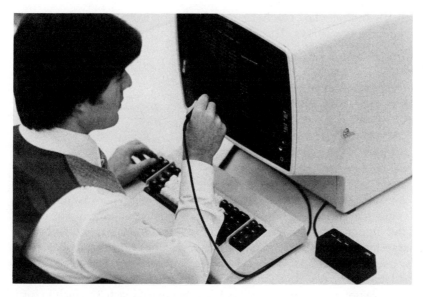

Figure 4-6 Student Using IIS
(Courtesy, International Business Machines Corporation)

for internal training. Besides IIS, IBM markets a set of programs called EPIC for educational administrative applications (i.e., class scheduling, test scoring, and financial management).

While a small selection of courseware is available for IIS from IBM (mostly for DP training on IBM equipment), most users of IIS develop their own courseware using COURSEWRITER or buy it from companies such as Deltak, Advanced Instructional Systems, or Edutronics. IBM provides online courses and offline workshops to train COURSEWRITER authors. IIS has recently been implemented on microcomputers by a number of companies. This means that IIS authoring or instructional delivery can take place using either time-sharing on a large mainframe or in a standalone mode via a microcomputer.

Scholar/Teach 3

Another piggyback CBT system called Scholar/Teach 3 is marketed by Boeing Computer Services. Like IIS, it runs on IBM mainframe computers. Scholar/Teach 3 is used by Boeing for internal training and by major airlines, such as TWA, for training their reservations and ground service crews. Scholar/Teach 3 provides a relatively simple and easy to use authoring system for use in creating courseware. It also features CMI capabilities for student registration, course cataloging, and reporting of student/system statistics.

Both IIS and Scholar/Teach 3 are similar in that they currently support only alphanumeric displays. This distinguishes them from dedicated CBT systems such as PLATO and TICCIT which have extensive graphic capabilities. However, IIS and Scholar/Teach 3 are typically used for administrative or data-processing training applications in which graphics is not a critical instructional requirement. Furthermore, because these systems are able to make use of existing hardware and software (i.e., provide embedded training), they represent a relatively low investment as far as system acquisition and operational costs are concerned.

Other Computer Manufacturers

In addition to IIS and Scholar/Teach 3, most major computer manufacturers provide piggyback CBT systems of some sort for their equipment. For example, Digital Equipment Corporation (DEC) provides Dimension, an authoring language system for its GIGI terminal; Honeywell supports the CAN-8 instructional system and NATAL author language; and Sperry Univac provides ASET (Advanced System for Education and Training). In general, these CBT capabilities are not as comprehensive as IIS or Scholar/Teach 3, which in turn are far less complete than dedicated CBT systems such as PLATO, TICCIT, or AIS.

Besides these software systems provided by major computer companies, a number of companies market "plug-compatible" CBT systems that are compatible with major CBT systems but have enhanced features. For example, Phoenix (marketed by Goal Systems International) is based on IIS but has many additional authoring and student management capabilities. It only runs on IBM systems but it can support a broad range of non-IBM display terminals. Regency Systems Inc. markets a standalone system with a display type essentially identical to PLATO (and a similar language called USE based upon TUTOR), which allows it to run PLATO courseware with minimal translation. However, the Regency system uses the CP/M operating system (discussed later) allowing it to use a wide variety of software. SIMPLER (marketed by Global Information Systems Technology Inc.) is another PLATO-like system that runs on MODCOMP minicomputers and offers a wide range of multipurpose capabilities (i.e., other programming languages, word processing, database management programs, etc.).

Standalone (Microcomputer) Systems

An alternative to the two categories of systems already discussed (dedicated and piggyback) is the use of standalone microcomputers for CBT. Most major brands of microcomputers have been used for CBT applications (e.g., Kearsley, Hillelsohn, and Seidel 1981) and no particular brand has any inherent advantage as far as CBT is concerned. Microcomputer CBT systems are usually not specifically designed for CBT. A general purpose programming language or authoring language/system is used to write instructional programs. Stand-alone systems differ from piggyback systems in that the terminals may feature the kinds of capabilities (e.g., graphics, color, touch input, multimedia, etc.) typically found in dedicated CBT systems. On the other hand, standalone systems, which lack any shared central processing or database capability, often lack many important software features found in systems such as PLATO, TIC-CIT, or AIS. Since most standalone systems have similar hardware capabilities, it is the software they run that distinguishes them.

BASIC

BASIC is a general purpose programming language universally available on microcomputers. It was originally developed at Dartmouth for the purpose of making it easy for college students to learn programming. Because of its relative simplicity and small memory requirement, it became widely implemented on mini- and microcomputers. BASIC was not designed specifically as an instructional language and is cumbersome to use for developing courseware. It has none of the functions provided in author languages for answer analysis, screen layout, or graphics (see Chapter 6); however, because of its widespread availability it is often used for CBT with microcomputers (particularly CAL).

PILOT

PILOT (Starkweather 1969) is a popular author language that is available on most major microcomputers. One of the virtues of PILOT is that it has a small number of commands (about fourteen), which makes it very easy to learn. PILOT provides a good range of instructional capabilities; however, it has no built-in provisions for collecting student data, developing tests, or doing CMI. These functions must be developed by the author. Many testing and CMI programs are available for microcomputers but they are separate programs from PILOT and considerable programming will be needed to be able to share data. Unlike a dedicated CBT system, standalone microcomputers do not provide an *integrated* set of CBT capabilities.

PASS

The Professional Authoring Software System (PASS) is an authoring system marketed by Bell & Howell for their modified Apple microcomputers. PASS includes many CBT capabilities found in full-scale systems such as PLATO, TICCIT, or AIS. It allows easy interfacing of the microcomputer with multimedia devices such as slide tape, videotape, or videodisc units. PASS also provides student management capabilities such as registration, test scoring and grading, and item analysis.

WISE

The Wicat Interactive System for Education (WISE) is an authoring system marketed by WICAT Systems for their microcomputer systems. WISE provides a menu-driven and prompting approach to the creation of courseware including graphics, videodisc, and synthesized speech. The use of function keys allows special instructional capabilities to be defined by the author.

Other Languages and Software

There is a vast variety of languages and software available for microcomputers—a factor that makes them attractive for use in CBT. For example, the general purpose programming language PASCAL has been widely used with microcomputers and for some CBT applications (mostly simulations). An operating system called CP/M is available for many machines and allows the use of thousands of programs that work on this operating system. Some special programming languages have been developed for educational purposes such as LOGO (Feurzeig and Lucas, 1972) and SMALLTALK (Tesler, 1981). Furthermore, there are literally thousands of educational programs available for microcomputers; however, these programs generally have very little relevance to the needs of the training world (about half of them are math drills). In fact, there is very little in the way of "off-the-shelf" programs suitable for CBT. This situation will undoubtedly change over time, but it is likely that training courseware will normally have to be uniquely developed by each organization. Since training needs are usually somewhat different from application to application and organization to organization, "off-the-shelf" courseware will rarely be feasible.

Customized Standalone Systems

A number of standalone systems have been developed for special training applications. For example, a keyboard trainer has been developed by KEE Systems that teaches employees how to use a particular keyboard. Figure 4–7 shows a KEE trainer being used to teach American Express card entry operators how to use the IBM Series 1 computers they use on their job.

Figure 4–8 shows another standalone system, the Primarius Interactive Video System (IVS). The Primarius system uses cassette tapes for program storage and overlays on a touch-sensitive panel for input. It provides inexpensive and easy to use interactive instruction. The IVS has been used extensively for patient education.

One possibility that such standalone systems open up is the idea of developing customized systems for each major training setting. In fact, this has long been the approach of the military (i.e., most simulators). Since microcomputer-based systems can now be built quite inexpensively and configured

Figure 4-7   KEE Trainer
(Courtesy, American Express Company)

exactly as needed in terms of input/output features, this is a feasible approach
to CBT systems that may become common in the future. (Note that such customized systems are not too different from embedded training.)

Microcomputers used as CBT systems offer some tremendous benefits in
terms of low cost, flexibility, and simplicity of operation. On the other hand,
they pose significant limitations in terms of capabilities needed for CBT. Most
of these limitations have to do with insufficient offline storage (for lessons or
student data), lack of appropriate CBT software, and lack of online/offline
support (e.g., documentation, training). The storage limitation is disappearing
as relatively large capacity disk drives (called Winchesters) become affordable
and as local and remote networks (permitting sharing of databases) become
common. The software limitation is likely to go away more slowly since hundreds of person-years are required to create, test, and debug the kind of software needed for serious CBT. Finally, a large array of documentation, training, and procedures are needed to support CBT activities. They are almost
totally absent in standalone systems, but an integral part of established (dedicated or piggyback) CBT systems.

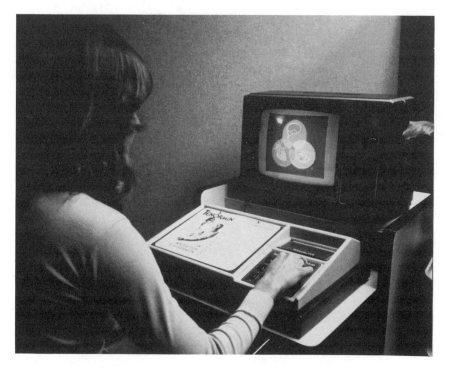

Figure 4-8 Primarius Interactive Video System
(Courtesy, Primarius Inc.)

Distributed Network CBT Systems

Figure 4-9 summarizes the preceding discussion. Dedicated CBT systems provide a full range of CBT capabilities and represent a high level of vendor and user support. However, dedicated systems are relatively expensive and involve equipment and resources specialized for CBT. Piggyback systems are low cost and provide added value for existing computer equipment. Because piggyback systems must work with existing terminals and software, they are typically limited in their instructional capabilities. Also, resource conflicts (over equipment, people, or facilities) are likely to occur as use of the system for training competes with operational uses. Stand-alone CBT systems are also low cost and provide multipurpose functions, unless they are customized. They also have limited capabilities, primarily due to lack of shared databases, and usually have limited support in terms of service, documentation, training, etc.

	ADVANTAGES	DISADVANTAGES
DEDICATED CBT SYSTEMS (e.g., PLATO, TICCIT)	• FULL RANGE OF CAPABILITIES	• RELATIVELY EXPENSIVE
	• HIGH LEVEL OF SUPPORT	• REQUIRES SPECIALIZED EQUIPMENT/RESOURCES
PIGGYBACK CBT SYSTEMS (e.g., IIS, ST/3)	• LOW COST	• LIMITED CAPABILITIES
	• ADDED VALUE FOR EXISTING EQUIPMENT	• RESOURCE CONFLICTS
STANDALONE CBT SYSTEMS (e.g., PILOT, PASS)	• LOW COST	• LIMITED CAPABILITIES
	• MULTIPURPOSE	• MINIMAL SUPPORT

Figure 4-9 Summary of CBT System Types

At the present time, a convergence of the three types of CBT systems is underway toward a distributed network configuration.[6] Established CBT systems such as PLATO, TICCIT, AIS, IIS or Scholar/Teach 3 (all originally based on timesharing architecture) are being modified to utilize standalone terminals with remote and local network sharing of databases and processors. At the same time, standalone microcomputers are being linked together in remote and local networks to provide the kind of database sharing capability that has always been available on timesharing systems (e.g., Saal 1981). As far as hardware is concerned, there will eventually be little significant difference in the configurations of the various CBT systems; however, there will be significant differences in training capabilities as a consequence of the different software available.

Three general principles for selecting a CBT system should be clear from this chapter. *First, CBT systems must be selected on the basis of functional capabilities dictated by training demands, not on the basis of external hardware features.* Instead of making a decision based on the type of system (i.e., dedicated, piggyback, standalone), a set of training requirements should define the functional capabilities needed (e.g., color, graphics, calculation, electronic mail, etc.) and these should be matched up with system types. *Second, pay more attention to the software than to the hardware.* This includes the software for authoring, student interaction, and instructional management. It is

[6]There are some other important trends too, such as interactive video, information utilities, and hand-held computers. These will be discussed more fully in Chapter 9.

much easier to obtain an additional hardware feature for a CBT system than to obtain software enhancements. *Third, be sure you understand the humanware demands associated with each system being considered.* This includes the amount of time required by students, instructors, or managers to learn how to use it as well as the authoring skills needed to develop and revise courseware. In the final analysis, the user and staffing requirements of a CBT system will strongly affect its success or failure.

In the next chapter, we will examine a detailed set of functional capabilities to be used in the selection of a CBT system.

5

Selecting a CBT System

The previous chapter surveyed major types of CBT systems. This chapter provides guidelines for selecting a particular system in terms of specific training needs. It is assumed that the kind of CBT desired has been identified and is thought to be feasible. As mentioned at the end of Chapter 3, the initial system to be selected is more likely to be for a pilot test of CBT rather than a full-scale implementation. The selection process should be conducted as if the full-scale system is being chosen—even if only one or two terminals will be used in the pilot study. This will help to ensure that the results obtained in the pilot evaluation are genuinely representative of the eventual operational outcomes.

Figure 5-1 depicts six major steps in the selection of a CBT system. Step 1 involves the specification of training requirements for the application(s) involved. This consists of detailed descriptions of the instructional tasks and objectives, the desired student throughput, the anticipated entry levels of the students, and so on, corresponding to the questions discussed for instructional feasibility in Chapter 3. In fact, training requirements should be easily derived from the information collected in the feasibility study.

Similarly, the information needed for Step 2 of the system selection process, namely, needed system capabilities and characteristics, should also be derived from the feasibility study. The information collected to assess technical feasibility will define the functional characteristics of the system. A set of detailed selection factors is discussed in the rest of this chapter. Normally, system capabilities will be classified in terms of essential (mandatory), desirable, and not important.

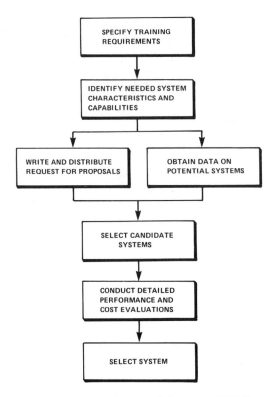

Figure 5-1   Major Steps in Selecting a CBT System

Once the necessary system capabilities have been identified, one of two things can happen. In a military or government agency (and sometimes in commercial organizations), systems are likely to be selected through competitive (i.e., public) procurement. This means that a system specification must be written and a Request for Proposal (RFP) developed. The RFP will also specify the criteria to be used for selection of the successful bidder. This RFP is distributed to qualified bidders (or simply published and bids invited) and the responsibility rests with the bidders to demonstrate in their proposals that the proposed system meets the system specifications.

The other alternative is that once the requirements have been identified, the individuals responsible for system selection collect data on potential systems. This will likely involve vendor demonstrations, visits to conferences, and discussions with current users of the systems. This approach is usually much faster than the RFP method but not usually as systematic or objective.

Step 4 involves selecting the candidate systems. Normally all systems that fail to meet the essential (and possibly desirable) requirements will be eliminated at this point. With an RFP or when a formal checklist is being used, the top ranking systems will be selected. Usually this will mean three or four systems.

At this point, detailed performance and cost evaluation of the "finalists" is in order. The candidate systems are likely to have been selected on the basis of individual features and capabilities. In the detailed evaluation, the performance and costs of the entire system configuration matching the requirements should be evaluated. This often means running "benchmark" comparisons between systems in terms of various performance factors (see the next section). It also means looking at specific examples of performance rather than general averages. For example, CBT vendors will provide performance and cost data based on experiences with their past customers or industry averages. A detailed evaluation will often involve the development of small amounts of courseware for the particular training application(s) being considered. This will be used to benchmark system performance and courseware development costs.

Once the detailed evaluations have been completed (a stage that could take months), a final selection will be made. It is important to accept the fact that the final selection may be made on political grounds or for reasons that are not wholly rational. The way people select new cars is not a bad model for understanding the selection of a CBT system. People try to select a car that meets their needs in terms of size, fuel economy, price range, and self-image (e.g., sensual, practical, authoritative, etc.). The advice of friends and the reputation of the dealer for "good deals" and service are likely to be weighed. However, the final selection, consciously or otherwise, may be a function of the fact that the car dealer lives on the same block, attends the same church, or is a brother of your boss. Alternatively, the selection may be based upon a particularly compelling advertisement or the sincerity of an attractive salesperson.

While the selection of CBT systems is normally a little more rigorous and comprehensive than the selection of new cars, it is subject to some of the same influences. Once a set of candidate systems have been selected that meet the critical requirements, the final selection is a matter of getting the best possible match. In many cases, the exact system selected will not be the primary determinant of whether or not CBT is successful. The quality of the courseware developed (Chapter 6), how well the system is implemented and managed (Chapter 7), and the nature of the evaluation activities (Chapter 8) are much more likely to seriously affect the success of CBT than the relatively small details that discriminate between acceptable systems. This is not an argument against conducting a good selection study, but a plea for a corresponding level of attention to the aspects discussed in subsequent chapters.

CBT SELECTION FACTORS

In order to select a CBT system, it is necessary to match the training requirements with specific system characteristics or capabilities. This section discusses the six major categories of system characteristics listed in Figure 5-2.

I. Hardware Characteristics

Display characteristics include the capability to display text and graphics. The range of character sets possible (variable character size, special symbols) affects the text display capabilities. Graphics capabilities can cover simple graphics (e.g., charts, graphs, boxes), complex graphics (e.g., illustrations, equipment panels), dynamic graphics (i.e., animation), and 3D (perspective) graphics. The type of CBT involved will strongly influence the kind of graphics needed. For example, administrative training often requires only simple alphanumeric (i.e., textual) displays, whereas simulation and simulators typically create a requirement for complex, dynamic, and 3D graphics. Display capabilities are affected by screen resolution, refresh rate, and screen size. Color is also an important display characteristic for some training applications where it is used for motivation, cueing, or realism.

Input characteristics include keyboard/keypad, pointing or cursor control, MSR/OCR, and voice (speech). While the standard keyboard (QWERTY) will suffice for most applications, some training situations require special keys or a special-purpose keypad. Many training requirements favor some type of pointing (i.e., touch panel, light pen, graphics tablet) or cursor control (i.e., arrow keys, joystick, trackball, mouse) for input rather than a keyboard. For example, training an electronics technician to pinpoint circuits or a pilot to identify control switches requires pointing or cursor control input. In many CAT and CMI applications, Mark Sense Readers (MSR) or Optical Character Recognition (OCR) input can reduce the number of terminals needed. Some applications provide strong justifications for voice input, e.g., foreign language learning or air traffic controller training.

Output capabilities encompass printing or plotting, control of multimedia devices, and speech. Printing capability can include raster type printers capable of providing students with copies of screen displays, line printers used for reports and listings, and plotters for printing graphics (e.g., blueprints, illustrations, etc.). Multimedia devices can include slide/tape units, microfiche, videotape, videodisc, and actual equipment. Speech output can be prerecorded or synthesized. Multimedia output is often used to reduce the development costs of CBT (in the case of offline graphics) or to provide capabilities not feasible online (e.g., the realism of photographs/video). Speech output is used when reading skills are low or when voice is an important attribute of the content (e.g., language learning or interpersonal skills).

	Inadequate	Satisfactory	Excellent
I. HARDWARE			
1. Display	[ ]	[ ]	[ ]
2. Input	[ ]	[ ]	[ ]
3. Output	[ ]	[ ]	[ ]
4. Portability	[ ]	[ ]	[ ]
5. Ruggedness	[ ]	[ ]	[ ]
6. Ergonomics	[ ]	[ ]	[ ]
7. Security	[ ]	[ ]	[ ]
II. SOFTWARE			
1. Student	[ ]	[ ]	[ ]
2. Authoring	[ ]	[ ]	[ ]
3. Management	[ ]	[ ]	[ ]
4. Programming Languages	[ ]	[ ]	[ ]
5. Application	[ ]	[ ]	[ ]
6. System	[ ]	[ ]	[ ]
7. Interterminal Communications	[ ]	[ ]	[ ]
8. Ergonomics	[ ]	[ ]	[ ]
9. Security	[ ]	[ ]	[ ]
III. COURSEWARE			
1. Availability	[ ]	[ ]	[ ]
2. Transportability	[ ]	[ ]	[ ]
3. Development Sources	[ ]	[ ]	[ ]
4. Demonstrated Effectiveness	[ ]	[ ]	[ ]
IV. SYSTEM PERFORMANCE			
1. Display Quality	[ ]	[ ]	[ ]
2. Response Time	[ ]	[ ]	[ ]
3. Maximum Storage Capacity	[ ]	[ ]	[ ]
4. Maximum Processing Capability	[ ]	[ ]	[ ]
5. Processor/Database Sharing	[ ]	[ ]	[ ]
6. Maximum Number Terminals	[ ]	[ ]	[ ]
7. Reliability/Dependability	[ ]	[ ]	[ ]
V. SYSTEM SUPPORT			
1. Service	[ ]	[ ]	[ ]
2. Updates	[ ]	[ ]	[ ]
3. Documentation	[ ]	[ ]	[ ]
4. Training	[ ]	[ ]	[ ]
5. User Groups	[ ]	[ ]	[ ]
6. Extent of Usage	[ ]	[ ]	[ ]
VI. COSTS			
1. Base System	[ ]	[ ]	[ ]
2. Per Terminal	[ ]	[ ]	[ ]
3. Operation/Maintenance	[ ]	[ ]	[ ]
4. Courseware Development	[ ]	[ ]	[ ]

Figure 5-2   CBT Selection Checklist

Portability refers to the capability to easily move terminals or systems from place to place. For example, many kinds of technical training are done in field locations and it is desirable to have a terminal that can be moved. Portability characteristics include size, power requirements, and communications capabilities. Microcomputer-based CBT systems obviously provide a considerable degree of portability. Hand-held computers, discussed in Chapter 9, represent the ultimate degree of portability for CBT systems.

Ruggedness determines the dependability and lifetime of CBT terminals and systems. Certain types of keyboards, displays, input/output devices, central processors, and peripherals are more rugged than others. The degree of ruggedness needed is a function of the degree of usage and abuse anticipated. For example, portable CBT systems used regularly for field training must be much more rugged than a system in an office environment that is used occasionally for new employees or refresher training.

Ergonomics covers all the factors that make CBT hardware easy or difficult to use or maintain. For example, terminals can be designed to minimize user discomfort by means of adjustable displays and detachable keyboards. Similarly, system units and peripherals can be designed to make maintenance easy and, hence, less expensive. Ergonomic considerations become particularly important if the users or operators of the system have nontechnical backgrounds and/or must spend relatively long periods of time (days or weeks) using CBT.

Security of CBT hardware covers the capability to prevent unwanted or unauthorized access to a CBT facility, courseware, or databases. Hardware security includes keys to turn on terminals or system units, as well as shielding of communications networks. Certain types of CBT systems (e.g., local timesharing) are easier to secure than others (e.g., remote timesharing of microcomputer systems). In certain military and industrial training environments, security of CBT materials is very critical.

II. Software Characteristics

Student (or user) software features span sign-on/sign-off, learner control, tutorials/help, calculation, and performance evaluation capabilities. *Sign-on/sign-off* refers to the simplicity or difficulty of initiating or terminating activity on the system. This includes signing on from a remote terminal via telecommunications, logging on, and accessing lessons or programs. It also includes the ease of restarting a lesson from a previous session. Having to start a long lesson from the beginning when it was half completed the day before is often unacceptable to students.

Learner control refers to the capabilities available to the student to control the rate, sequence, difficulty level, or style of interaction with the system. This can range from the simple provision of menus allowing the student to select their next learning activity to the elaborate control options provided in the

TICCIT system (e.g., Bunderson 1974). Learner control is primarily an issue in CAI since the student basically controls the learning activities in CMI, CAL, or simulators. Learner control can be an issue in CAT when students do not have options to correct or change answers and review or skip questions. Learner control is a longstanding issue in CAI (e.g., Bunderson 1974; Merrill 1975; Seidel et al. 1978; Steinberg 1977).

Help/tutorial capabilities allow students to get immediate online assistance by pressing a "help" key or branching to a special help program. Help features may refer to explanation of the content being studied or of the meaning of a certain command or action. For example, in the middle of a CAI lesson on the function of BASIC commands, the use of a help feature might provide a more detailed explanation of the current command being studied. Similarly, while using a BASIC programming laboratory, the use of "help" would explain the options possible at a particular stage of programming (e.g., Barr, Beard, and Atkinson 1975). In the TICCIT system, an "advice" key provides students with recommendations on what to do next. It is common to develop tutorials for introductions to the use of the terminal or system (e.g., Al-Awar, Chapanis, and Ford 1981).

Calculation refers to the capability to use the terminal as a calculator. This is particularly useful in courses that are quantitative in nature (e.g., accounting, engineering, budgeting, etc.). In some systems, the bottom line of the screen can be used without interrupting the rest of the display. In other systems, it is possible to suspend the current instruction activity, write and execute a program, and then return to the original instruction exactly where it was interrupted.

Performance evaluation capability involves the ability of students to examine their progress in the course. Thus, a student can display a progress report that indicates lessons completed, test scores, or learning rates. For certain kinds of students (e.g., highly motivated) or instructional situations (e.g., learner control), this may be an important feature.

Authoring software characteristics include response analysis, data collection, editing capabilities, availability of built-in strategies, and extensibility. Response analysis (or answer judging) capabilities refer to the ability of the system to evaluate input responses and provide feedback. The lowest level of response analysis is the ability to make exact matches of alphanumeric strings (as is possible with any general purpose programming language). Most author languages provide a full range of matching features including missing letters, misspelled words, shifting to upper or lower case, Boolean logic (AND/OR combinations), and the use of word stems. In addition, most author languages provide automatic logic for handling correct, incorrect, and unexpected responses.[1] The degree of sophistication of the response analysis needed is a

[1]The capability to understand natural language responses is a sophisticated level of response analysis demonstrated in a few prototype "intelligent CAI" systems. This is discussed in Chapter 9.

function of the instructional requirements. If multiple choice input is sufficient, then only simple response analysis capabilities are needed; if open-ended responses are desired, then complex response analysis capabilities are required.

Data collection capabilities refer to the ability to specify what student response data will be automatically collected. This could include number of questions correct/incorrect, response latency, number of attempts, or the actual response typed in. Some systems provide very rudimentary capabilities for data collection (i.e., counters or buffers), while others provide complete selections including specification of data summaries, analysis, and reports. The importance of this capability will depend on the nature of evaluation planned (see Chapter 8).

Editing capabilities cover the ability to create and revise text, graphics, programs, and lessons. Almost all interactive systems today feature some kind of text editor that facilitates the creation and modification of text (i.e., replacing, inserting, copying). In CBT systems that involve graphics, a graphics editor is important. This allows the creation of character sets and the rotation and modification of graphics. Many CBT systems provide capabilities to edit programs or lessons in terms of deleting, replacing, inserting, or copying entire blocks or units. Because so much time is spent creating and revising CBT materials, the editing capabilities of a system are often very significant. (See the discussion of authoring in the next chapter.)

Another authoring capability that may be quite valuable is the availability of built-in instructional strategies. For example, in the construction of multiple choice tests, it is possible to have the system automatically format the question and alternatives, randomize the order of the alternatives, and provide appropriate feedback. The author simply provides the content and indicates the correct answer. Similarly, authoring systems can provide built-in formats for drills, tutorials, simulations, or games, which minimize the amount of time an author must spend in creating lessons.

One of the problems with the use of such built-in strategies (or author languages in general) is that they do not always provide the capabilities needed for a particular instructional sequence. Hence, it becomes important that the authoring software is extensible, allowing for the creation of new functions or strategies beyond what is built-in. For example, many organizations have a particular instructional model they use in the development of their training materials. In these circumstances, it is desirable that the authoring software allow templates to be created, permitting courseware or instructional sequences to be created according to this model.

Management software refers to capabilities needed to manage students and instructional resources. Generally, these are the capabilities found in CMI systems, although they may be needed for any kind of CBT application, depending on size. This includes various kinds of student and class performance reports, test item analysis, student registration and scheduling programs, and programs for generating learning prescriptions or allocating instructional resources (classrooms, equipment, materials, etc.).

Programming languages refers to the capability to use various general-purpose programming languages (e.g., BASIC, PASCAL, COBOL, FORTRAN) or specialized author languages (such as IIS, PILOT, PLANIT) on the system.

Application software includes the capability to run word processing, database management, information retrieval, statistics, readability analysis, and other noninstructional programs on the system.

System software refers to the type of operating system, telecommunication control, and utility (i.e., backup, diagnostics) programs available on the system.

Interterminal communications software allows online interaction between terminals. This includes real-time messages from one terminal to another (either student to student or instructor to student), electronic mailboxes, broadcast messages and bulletin boards, and the capability for an instructor to monitor a student terminal to diagnose a problem.

Ergonomic characteristics of software focus on how easy it is to learn, use, and maintain (i.e., revise) programs. This could be from the point of view of the student, instructor, training manager, or system analyst/programmer. For example, a complex sign-on procedure may not bother a system analyst but it might frustrate a student, instructor, or manager. There is a reciprocal relationship between the extent of human factors engineering of the software and the amount of user training required.

Security characteristics of software refer to built-in capability to prevent accidental or unauthorized access to courseware, student databases, files, or programs. This usually consists of passwords for sign-on, use of lessons, use of student data analysis programs, and so on.

III. Courseware Characteristics

Availability of courseware refers to the existence of CAI, CAL, or simulator materials that are suitable for actual use or serve as models for curriculum development. Unlike courseware used in educational settings, most courseware needed for training must be custom developed. With the exception of a few subject areas (e.g., data processing, sales/management skills, safety training), most organizations have different ways of doing things (even for the same jobs within an industry, agency, or service) and therefore require uniquely developed courseware. On the other hand, existing courseware can often be adapted, thereby saving time and money. Consequently, the existence of relevant courseware may be an important consideration.

Transportability of courseware is an important factor in organizations where material is to be shared over different locations or sites. Transportability can be of three kinds: physical, electronic, and software. Physical transportability refers to the ability to load lessons on a storage medium (e.g., disc, tape) and physically ship it to another system at a different location. This will work for identical systems. Electronic transportability refers to the ability to share lesson materials via communications. This will work for systems that have common communication protocols. Software transportability refers to the ability to use the same author/programming language (e.g., PILOT, BASIC, PASCAL) even though it may be a different version of the language. The courseware is usable to the extent that differences between versions of the language can be identified and changed.

Development sources refers to the suitability of the sources for developing courseware. With some systems (e.g., PLATO, IIS) the hardware vendor or independent contractors provide courseware development services. For other systems (particularly standalones) such services do not exist and all courseware development must be done in-house. This will affect the organizational resources and timeframes associated with the development of CBT materials.

The demonstrated effectiveness of courseware refers to the existence of studies that measure the comparative validity, student performance outcomes, or student attitudes associated with the use of a particular CBT system. While these results will not normally apply to the specific courseware you expect to use, they do provide some assurance that the use of that CBT system has been demonstrated to be effective.

IV. System Performance Characteristics

There are a large number of system performance characteristics that should be taken into account in the selection of a system. In fact, in any major CBT system selection study, a set of benchmark tests should be run with candidate systems to determine whether they can meet desired performance criteria. Major performance factors are display quality, response time, maximum storage capacity, maximum processing capability, processor/database sharing, maximum number of terminals, and reliability/dependability. System performance data is usually provided by the system vendor, by tests run as part of the selection study, or by interaction with existing system users.

Display quality includes screen refresh rate, degree of flicker, brightness variation, and sharpness. It is a function of many of the hardware characteristics already discussed (e.g., resolution, color, speed of processor, and storage).

Response times refer to the average and maximum latencies and the overall consistency of system response. It is important to measure response times under anticipated student loads and also during authoring and management activities.

Maximum storage capacity refers to the total amount of peripheral storage available for courseware, software, and student data. It is important to determine that the capacity can be expanded easily and that it is sufficient to allow all of the instructional activities planned. It should take into account the space needed for lessons and data once the system is fully operational (which may not be for many months or years).

Maximum processing capability refers to the size and nature of the processing unit. This is usually measured in terms of total bytes of Random Access Memory (RAM) ranging from 16,000 (16K) for small microcomputers to millions of bytes for large mainframes. The significance of the processing capability is that it will determine the kinds of CBT possible (e.g., tutorials, simulations, testing, management) and other system performance factors (e.g., display quality, response times).

Processor/database sharing capability refers to the ability to share lessons, data, or programs via remote or local telecommunications. This capability is essentially defined by the configuration of the system (i.e., timesharing, distributed, standalone). It has highly significant implications in terms of the kind of CBT usage expected (i.e., CAT, CMI, CAI) and courseware sharing.

Maximum number of terminals refers to the total number of terminals that can be part of the system and the total number of simultaneous terminals that can be used. Both of these affect the number of students who can be accommodated by the system, either over time or at once. As with maximum storage capacity, it is important to project to a fully operational stage of the system.

Reliability/dependability is usually measured in terms of "uptime" and "downtime." Uptime is defined by average Mean Time Between Failures (MTBF), i.e., how long the system operates without failing. Downtime is defined as average Mean Time To Repair (MTTR), i.e., how long it takes to get the system operating again after it has failed. Different instructional settings will require different degrees of reliability and dependability depending on the urgency and scheduling of training. However, almost all CBT systems must meet standards of at least 95 percent uptime and downtime of less than one hour per week to be useful.

V. System Support Characteristics

System support characteristics have to do with the level of support available (either from the system vendor or the user community) for a particular CBT system. This includes service, updates, documentation, training, user groups, and extent of usage.

Service includes the amount of time required for initial system installation and the maintenance of the hardware/software after it is operational. Warranties and service contracts may be provided. An important factor in service is the time delay in responding to a trouble call. A more general factor affecting service is the commitment of the vendor to CBT and your installation.

Updates refer to the way in which hardware and software upgrades or modifications are made. It is important to determine whether they will be provided automatically by the vendor and the extent to which they will be tested before being released to customers. It is also important to determine the policy regarding system modifications either requested or made by customers.

Documentation is a critical feature of system support that affects many aspects of system operation. Different kinds of documentation will be needed by students (users), instructors, managers, and systems personnel. Furthermore, both reference and tutorial documentation will be needed (see Chapter 7).

Training is closely related to documentation and the ergonomics of the system hardware/software. As with documentation, different training will be needed for students, instructors, managers, and systems staff. Ideally, as much training and documentation as possible will be online.

User groups are an important aspect of system support since they provide a formal mechanism for sharing experiences and obtaining information. They exist for most major CBT systems and microcomputers. (See the Appendix for further details.)

Extent of usage is an important characteristic since it generally determines the degree of support associated with a system. For example, CBT systems such as PLATO or IIS, which are in widespread use, have well-developed support. In addition, they have undergone extensive changes to meet user demands and are therefore likely to have the features needed for most training applications.

VI. Cost Characteristics

Four major cost characteristics to be examined in system selection are base system, per terminal, operation and maintenance, and course development costs. Detailed discussion of CBT costs and benefits is provided in Chapter 8.

Base system costs include all the hardware, software, and support services that are to be acquired to have a completely operational CBT system. These costs will vary substantially depending on the type and size of the system involved. The presence or absence of all of the characteristics discussed in this chapter will affect the base system price. Base system prices can range from $5,000 for a microcomputer-based CBT system with limited capabilities, to $5 million for a large mainframe CBT system intended for thousands of users.

Per terminal costs refer to the costs of adding additional terminals to the system. The number of terminals needed will depend on the anticipated number of users (students and instructors) and the type of CBT. For example, a CAT or CMI system involving offline activities will require far fewer terminals than a CAI or CAL system in which every student requires a terminal. The price range of terminals can range from $500 to $5,000 (or more) depending on the display, input, and output characteristics of the terminal.

Operation and maintenance costs include all the ongoing expenses associated with a CBT system (excluding courseware) once it is installed. This includes power and facilities costs, repair, spare parts, software modifications, and training/documentation to the extent that it is not supplied with the system. These costs typically range from 5 to 10 percent of the total base system costs.

Courseware development costs cover all expenses associated with the design, development, testing, and revision of courseware, including tests for CAT or programs for simulators. While many of these costs would be incurred for any type of instruction, CBT involves additional costs associated with programming. Furthermore, because CBT materials are interactive, they typically cost more to develop, test, and revise. The cost range will depend on the type of CBT, the use of author languages or systems, and the quality of the courseware. A rule of thumb often used is that 100 to 200 hours of total development time are required for each student-hour of CAI or CAL developed, although this rate can be higher for complex simulation and simulator programs and lower when authoring systems are used.

These four cost components will vary for the different kinds of systems described in Chapter 4. For example, the base price of a dedicated CBT system ranges from hundreds of thousands (TICCIT) to millions of dollars (PLATO or AIS). This base price includes a mainframe, a large amount of central off-line storage (i.e., disk drives), peripherals such as printers or multimedia devices, system authoring and application software, documentation, training programs, maintenance agreements, as well as a sizable number of terminals (20 to 200). The base price of a piggyback system basically amounts to the rental or lease of the software package plus the personnel time to implement it. This ranges from approximately $500 per month (for IIS) to a one-time license fee of $40,000 (for Scholar/Teach 3). Since existing terminals, offline storage, or peripherals are used, the hardware costs are relatively nominal. The base price for a standalone system ranges from $3,000 to $9,000, depending on how much offline storage capability, how many peripherals, and what software is included. However, this base system price is essentially for a one-terminal system.

Per terminal costs also differ among the three types of systems. Dedicated CBT systems usually involve specially-designed terminals that cost $3,000 to $5,000 each. Piggyback systems can use regular data-processing terminals that range from $500 to $2,000. The per terminal cost for standalone terminals is usually in the same price range as the base system cost ($3,000 to $9,000), although student terminals may share the resources of the system terminal and therefore cost less.

Operation and maintenance costs are a function of total system size. They are not likely to differ much for either dedicated, piggyback, or standalone systems serving the same number of students. The operation and maintenance costs for piggyback CBT systems tend to be lumped together with the costs for the entire system; thus, they may be "hidden" for this type of system. Furthermore, the operation and maintenance costs for dedicated CBT systems tend to be explicit and identified in advance (e.g., service agreements, facilities costs), whereas these typical costs for standalone systems are dealt with on a case-by-case basis as they arise (e.g., service calls, monthly utility payments). This makes the operation and maintenance costs for standalone systems look almost nonexistent compared to dedicated systems; however, standalone terminals use as much power, take up as much space, and break down as often as the terminals of a dedicated system.

Courseware development costs are a function of a number of factors (to be discussed in the next chapter), a critical one being the type of author language or system used to create materials. To the extent that author languages/systems exist for all three types of systems, the courseware development costs should be similar. While the author languages of the dedicated systems are more sophisticated than those available on piggyback or standalone systems, it is not clear that this makes a significant difference for the kind of courseware usually developed on the latter.

To summarize this discussion of cost factors in system selection, it should be evident that the greatest variation in price range between different systems is in base system price. This is a function of what features the system offers. There is a tremendous difference in capabilities between a dedicated CBT system such as PLATO, a piggyback system such as IIS, or a standalone microcomputer with PILOT. Per terminal, operation and maintenance, and courseware development costs tend to be not too different for a given size of system and level of usage. In fact, as the number of terminals and courses offered increases, the cost difference between different systems tend to disappear. For small numbers of students or courses, the differences are much more pronounced.

CASE STUDY: MABEL

In response to the need for a multipurpose, all-terrain combat vehicle, a new weapons system designated MABEL is being planned by the military. MABEL can operate in land, sea, and air (see Figure 5–3). You are part of a training command and your specific task is to select CBT systems that might be suitable for use in MABEL training programs. This includes operator, maintenance, and crew (i.e., tactical) training. CBT is already used for all three types of training in similar weapons systems; hence, feasibility has already been established. In fact, CMI and CAI are routinely used at the schools that teach the baseline skills (i.e., basic principles of navigation, electronics, tactics, etc.) needed for MABEL operator, maintenance, and crew training.

Figure 5-3   MABEL

Operator training for MABEL consists of three positions: commander (pilot), navigation officer (co-pilot), and weapons officer. Because of the versatility of MABEL, a higher level of training is needed for all three positions than in other combat vehicles. Thus, the pilot must be able to maneuver in air, sea, and land; likewise, the navigator must be proficient in air, sea, and land navigation. Both the commander and navigator must also be able to operate a range of sophisticated radar and communication equipment. Because MABEL is equipped with a broad range of air-ground and surface rockets, as well as cannons, training for the weapons officer is extensive. Because of the high level of interdependency of tasks, a large amount of cross-training is planned.

The maintenance training requirements are equally, if not more, demanding. Three maintenance positions are associated with MABEL: mechanic, electronics technician, and systems engineer. The mechanic is responsible for the maintenance of the engines and all moving parts (e.g., tracks, turret, guns, rudders, etc.). The electronics technician has responsibility for the upkeep of all navigation, guidance, ordnance, and communications equipment. The systems engineer is responsible for repair of the computer systems that basically control all aspects of MABEL operations. Unlike the operations crew, which is dedicated solely to MABEL, the maintenance crew is responsible for the repair of other weapons systems.

Crew training goes beyond the basic operator and maintenance training. It involves capability to effectively operate and maintain MABEL in its mission environment. This means practice under combat conditions as part of an attack force. The operations crew must be able to execute the correct tactical maneuvers with MABEL; the maintenance crew must be able to keep MABEL operational in the field.

Training syllabi have been developed from task analyses and objectives hierarchies based on MABEL specifications and similar weapons systems. The syllabi have been used to generate a comprehensive set of training requirements. Projected throughput requirements for MABEL are as follows: 150 operational crews (i.e., commanders, navigators, weapons officers) per year will be trained for the first three years, followed by 30 per year for the rest of the MABEL life cycle (estimated at ten years). A total of 300 maintenance crews (i.e., mechanic, technician, engineer) will be trained each year for the first three years, followed by 50 per year thereafter. The operator training is estimated to require about sixteen weeks; maintenance training, about ten weeks; and crew training (both operators and maintainers), about five weeks. The three types of training would take place at different locations.

Three types of CBT are seen as appropriate for MABEL training: CAL (primarily simulations), simulators, and embedded training. A great deal of the initial operator and maintenance training can be taught via simulation provided that good representations of control panels and equipment operation can be portrayed. Thus, high resolution and dynamic graphics are important display features. It is desired that input be via touch on simulated control panels rather than using keyboards. Photographic and video representations of actual equipment (i.e., computer-controlled multimedia devices) are seen as essential. In addition, for maintenance training it is important that the CBT system be able to interface with and monitor actual equipment (e.g., multimeters, oscilliscopes, etc.). Since these terminals will be used in a school environment, portability and ruggedness is not a major concern; however security is important since most levels of training on MABEL will be classified.

Simulators will be used for the more advanced stages of operator and maintenance training and for crew training. These simulators will be computer-controlled mock-ups of actual MABEL equipment components. There will be separate simulators for the equipment clusters associated with pilot, navigator, and weapons officer, as well as simulators of the major subsystems (e.g., engines, turret, communications, guidance) for mechanic, technician, and engineer training. For crew training, mission simulators will be developed that consist of all major components of MABEL under computer control. Such mission simulators must allow realistic depiction of the effects of operational or maintenance actions by the crew members in realtime situations.

As far as embedded training is concerned, it is desirable that MABEL minimize the training load as much as possible by including electronic job aids in the equipment design. Thus, the panels used for navigation, weapons, communications, and control can be created in such a way as to always make online help available. Similarly, portable electronic test equipment can be designed that provides maintenance personnel with diagnostic and troubleshooting help. Note that such embedded training capabilities must be conceived of as an integral part of the weapons system—it generally cannot be added after the design is completed.

Because of the shortage of appropriate CBT expertise within the military, the vendor of the equipment will be expected to provide the necessary software and courseware as part of the system. However, sufficient documentation and training will need to be provided to allow military personnel to maintain and revise the software and courseware after initial installation. The kind of student, authoring, and management capabilities required are uniquely tailored to the needs of the MABEL training syllabi. Certain kinds of software features will consequently be required (e.g., helps/tutorials, easy editing, individual student progress reports), whereas others will not be important (e.g., student control options, extensibility, test item analysis). Furthermore, capabilities such as the availability of other programming languages or application software and interterminal communications capability are not needed.

As far as courseware characteristics are concerned, the availability of off-the-shelf courseware is not relevant to MABEL training. It is important that the existence of development sources be affirmed since the military does not expect to do the development itself. Physical transportability of courseware is an important consideration since it is to be anticipated that MABEL training will be conducted at multiple sites. Note that electronic transportability (i.e., via communications) is not desirable for security reasons. Demonstrated effectiveness will be a major concern and it is to be expected that a comparative evaluation of the CBT training versus classroom/actual equipment training will be required as part of the benchmark tests for the candidate systems.

System performance characteristics are of utmost importance. Display quality, in terms of adequate resolution and suitable graphics, has already been mentioned. Response time must meet the needs of simulation, simulator, and embedded training (often realtime response). The systems must have adequate storage capacity and processing capability. Because the requirements of MABEL training depend so heavily on complex simulation, adequate processing capability is a vital consideration that will be scrutinized carefully.

Given the student requirements, the maximum number of terminals/simulators can be calculated. For operator training, students can be scheduled in classes of fifty at a time (i.e., three classes of fifty in a year). Since there are three positions, at least 150 student terminals will be needed. For maintenance training, five classes of sixty pupils per year will be needed, or 180 total terminals for the three positions. Assuming that an entire crew can be trained on a mission simulator at the same time, 15 operational and 30 maintenance simulators are required (i.e., ten classes per year). Thus, systems comprising at least 150 and 180 student terminals plus 45 simulators will be needed. While it is possible that all three systems could be supplied by the same vendor, it is much more likely that they would be completely different systems from different companies since they must meet somewhat different training requirements.

System support from the vendors is important since the military expects a "turnkey" operation as far as CBT is concerned. The vendor will be expected to provide complete maintenance of the system, as well as make any hardware/software updates needed. The importance of good documentation and training has already been mentioned. User groups and widespread usage are not particularly important since this application is unlikely to have much in common with other system users (except similar military applications).

Cost, one of the major system characteristics for most systems, is not a major selection factor in this particular case. Because weapon systems such as MABEL are so expensive and because their value cannot be achieved unless they are properly operated and maintained, it is allocated whatever funds are necessary for training. Spending the money on CBT rather than some other approach (i.e., classrooms or actual equipment) depends on demonstrations of improved training effectiveness due to CBT. There is ample evidence in the military sphere that CBT is a good approach (e.g., Orlansky and String 1981a).

These remarks notwithstanding, the per terminal cost is clearly an important consideration in the selection of the CBT system for MABEL training since so many terminals are required. A price difference of $1,000 for the number of terminals required would amount to $100,000 to $200,000.

For the mission simulators for crew training, the price of the base system (each simulator being effectively an entire system) is critical. The operation and maintenance costs are likely to be included in the base system costs (i.e., via service agreements), as are the costs of initial courseware development.

Based on the foregoing discussion of training requirements and considerations, it seems evident that piggyback systems and standalone microcomputers can be eliminated as suitable candidates due to lack of essential characteristics or capabilities. The MABEL training environment clearly requires a dedicated CBT system rather than the type of multifunction capabilities associated with piggyback systems. Furthermore, it is clear that the kinds of CBT needed for MABEL training will require substantial processing and storage capabilities, which are more cost effectively supplied by shared resources rather than standalone terminals. Because of the security considerations, a local network system is to be preferred over remote networks involving telecommunications. Finally, because of the high level of support required, an established CBT vendor is preferred.

As a consequence of this selection process, the basic system capabilities needed and the kind of systems suitable have been identified. At this point an RFP could be created and sent to appropriate vendors. While any vendor could bid on the RFP, it will have been conceptualized in the context of a certain type of system and therefore biased toward companies that market a particular type of CBT system (i.e., dedicated, local networks, shared processor/storage). This bias is necessary in order for the bidders to be able to respond in a specific and meaningful fashion. The point of the RFP is to select the particular vendor who offers the best "deal" on the type of system required.

SUMMARY

In this chapter, a basic selection process and selection factors for CBT have been described. It should be emphasized that this selection process is not infallible. It is axiomatic that a choice made tomorrow will be better than one made today, due to hindsight and the fact that CBT systems continually get cheaper and more powerful over time. However, decisions left to tomorrow never get made. The purpose of the description provided in this chapter is to make the selection of a CBT system as comprehensive and objective as possible. It certainly will not guarantee success, although it should raise the probability.

6

Designing and
Developing Courseware

This chapter assumes that the decision to implement CBT has been made and a particular CBT system has been selected. The next concern is in the design and development of courseware. This could be tests for a CAT system; learning prescriptions, or materials used in a CMI system; actual instructional programs for CAI, CAL, or simulators; or job aids/tutorials for embedded training systems. Courseware typically refers to whatever combination of online and offline materials comprise a training course or program (e.g., Bunderson 1981).

In this chapter the considerations and methods associated with the design and development of courseware for CBT systems are discussed. This includes the use of systematic instructional development procedures, design concepts, different authoring approaches, and available authoring languages/systems.

The development of courseware is probably the most critical aspect of a successful CBT effort. While deficiencies in CBT hardware and software can often be overcome, ineffective courseware (or an inefficient courseware development process) is likely to be the death knell for a CBT project. After all, it is the courseware that ultimately determines whether CBT accomplishes its training goal (i.e., testing, instruction, management, etc.).

The topic of courseware development is even more critical in the training domain than in public education. Schools and colleges are much more likely to buy or share "ready-made" courseware than training organizations. Thus, courseware for elementary math or reading, high school physics or chemistry, or introductory statistics or calculus is likely to be useful at many institutions.[1]

---

[1]In practice, however, this has not happened a great deal despite almost Herculean efforts to make it work. See the discussion of transportability in Chapter 9.

However, a simulator for a specific weapons system, a CAI tutorial on billing procedures, or online job aids for maintaining a company's product line is likely to be useful only to a particular organization. This means that in the training domain, most organizations will have to develop their own courseware rather than buy it from an existing selection. This is likely to be true even with "generic" subject areas such as sales or safety training; each organization tends to have its own idiosyncratic ways of doing things based on different traditions, values, and missions.

SOME MYTHS ABOUT CBT

It seems appropriate to begin the discussion of courseware development with some remarks about three fairly widely-held myths concerning CBT:

Myth #1: If it's on the computer, it must be good.

Myth #2: Only certain subjects are suitable for CBT.

Myth #3: CBT is just another computer application.

It is common to find training or operational personnel who assume that if training is delivered or managed by computer, it must automatically be "good stuff." Nothing could be further from the truth! Taking a bad training course or materials and implementing them on a computer still results in bad training. There is no magic inherent in CBT that will change bad training materials into good. This misunderstanding often comes from a naivete about the authoring process. For example, because it is known that instructions to computers must be made very specific (i.e., in the form of programs), the inference is made that any instruction delivered by a computer must also be well defined. The fact is, however, that much CAI or CAL is developed without any clearly defined objectives or purposes. It is true that CBT possesses some inherent capabilities (e.g., immediate feedback, automatic data collection, dynamic graphics, etc.) that can easily result in very powerful training, but this potential can easily be abused or not taken advantage of. Without careful attention to the considerations discussed in this chapter, CBT is likely to be a waste of time and money.

Myth #2 derives from the history of computers and their instructional use (e.g., Bunderson and Faust 1976; Suppes and Macken 1978). Early computers and software were basically designed for numerical computation. This led to the (originally) correct inference that computers were best applied to quantitative problems and topics. Since most early pioneers in computer-based instruction had mathematical or scientific backgrounds, this was the subject area where CBT started; hence, the notion that CBT applied best to quantitative subjects. In addition, the input/output capabilities of most early CBT systems were fairly primitive (e.g., teletype keyboards and upper case only output). This also tended to limit use to quantitative subjects.

Today, computers are well recognized as all-purpose symbol manipulation devices and are used for just about every application imaginable. Furthermore, the input/output interfaces are quite rich in terms of capabilities (e.g., graphics, color, speech, video, touch, etc.). Today there is really no area of training (including psychomotor and affective skills) that cannot be handled by some form of CBT. It is true that some subject areas are easier or harder to develop courseware for than others, but this has nothing to do with CBT—it is a function of the subjects themselves.

Myth #3 is one that frequently causes major problems in both the development and implementation stages of CBT projects. In a literal sense, the statement is true: CBT is just another computer application like data processing, airline reservation systems, or online banking systems. The trouble is that CBT normally requires specialized hardware, software, and, most of all, expertise (humanware). Trying to approach the development of CBT courseware in the same way as a payroll program or information retrieval database usually results in disaster. The fact that frequently escapes computer (or training) people is that while courseware must ultimately be programmed (like any other computer application), it must also be developed. This requires content and instructional expertise. Furthermore, courseware is not finished after it is debugged and tested—it requires a long and ongoing "tuning" period, often lasting years, to make and keep it effective. CBT is sufficiently different from most computer applications that it should not normally be viewed as an activity or task appropriate for computer departments or staff.[2] Instead, it should be the primary responsibility of training organizations with the necessary CBT expertise. Given the large amount of money and time that will likely be invested in the development of courseware, it is clearly important to put the investment in the right hands.

The three myths just discussed lead us to three general design/development considerations: how do you ensure that the training delivered via CBT is good; how can CBT work for any training area; and what kind of CBT expertise is needed? These considerations plus others are discussed in the rest of this chapter.

ISD AND CBT

Instructional Systems Development (ISD) is a general term that refers to the systematic approach to the design and development of training materials and systems. It rests on the common acceptance and use of certain procedures and components. These include job/task analysis, behavioral objectives, criterion-referenced or competency-based testing, and formative evaluation. While there are many variations on ISD methodology, most frameworks are based

---

[2]These remarks are less applicable to embedded training than other types of CBT, although they still hold for courseware development.

on the five-phase model depicted in Figure 6-1. The analysis phase involves identifying the training need(s) in terms of specific job tasks and performance standards. Design involves the definition of objectives and the structure/sequence of the training. The development phase encompasses the exact specification of the learning activities or events and the creation/production of necessary materials. Implementation includes the actual delivery and management of the training as well as instructor training activities. Evaluation consists of trying out, revising, and validating the training. It usually takes place during the design, development, and implementation phases, as the arrows in the diagram signify. One of the eventual consequences of the evaluation phase is that the training will be found to no longer meet the original needs (i.e., the needs change) and so the analysis phase must be started again. Thus, the ISD phases and procedures are part of a cycle that is continually being repeated.

It is not the intent of this section to explain the basic principles of ISD. For readers who want further background, see Butler (1972); Davis, Alexander, and Yelon (1974); Gagne and Briggs (1981); Kemp (1971); Mager (1975); Merrill (1971); or O'Neil (1979a&b).

Why use ISD procedures? ISD procedures have been developed to ensure that training programs and materials are relevant, complete, lean, and effective. These four attributes describe the most common failings of training programs and materials: (1) they do not train the appropriate skills needed for the job, (2) they are missing important content or instructional components (such as examples or practice), (3) there is too much irrelevant or "nice-to-know" content or activity, and (4) they simply do not teach well. ISD procedures help to minimize these problems.

The first two phases of ISD (analysis and design) are no different for CBT than any other approach. Thus, job/task analysis, objectives, and lesson specifications are needed to develop effective courseware regardless of what type of CBT is involved. As part of the design phase, the appropriate media should be selected. If the type of CBT has already been selected (based on the considerations discussed in Chapter 2), then media analysis amounts to deciding

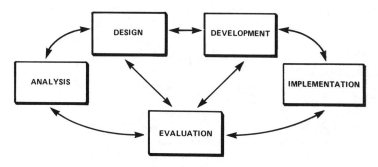

Figure 6-1   Major Phases of ISD

what kind of system characteristics (i.e., display, input, output) are needed based on the objectives. For example, the objectives may dictate the need for color, dynamic graphics, video, touch input, maximum response times, etc. If the type of CBT has not been selected, then the media analysis amounts to determining which kind is most appropriate as well as what characteristics are required. Media selection models may prove helpful (e.g., Anderson 1976; Boucher 1973; Bretz 1971; Tosti and Ball 1969).

The third phase, development, is significantly different for CBT. First of all, the courseware will usually involve interaction. Exactly how much and what kind of interaction will depend on the type of CBT, i.e., testing, drills, tutorials, simulations, dialogues, simulators, job aids, etc. Invariably, such interaction means multiple paths through the materials and course. For example, consider the simple tutorial lesson shown in Figure 6-2. This module has an introduction, two levels of explanation (one for review or remediation), four practice problems, and two parallel tests. These nine components allow for sixteen different sequences the student could go through (e.g., I-E1-P1-T1, I-E1-P2-T1, etc.). Regardless of whether the selection of these sequences is under program or student control, the instructional designer must plan for all sixteen possible sequences. This lesson could just as well be an adaptive test, a CMI lesson, or a simulation. Since any normal training course consists of dozens of lessons, it should be clear how easy it is for the design of CBT courseware to get complex in a hurry.

In most kinds of CBT it is necessary to specify branching rules, i.e., how a student gets from one lesson, component, or display to another. These rules are often defined as part of the Instructional Decision Model (IDM) for the materials. A number of models have been developed and used for CAI. They include mastery, adaptive, learner control, and aptitude/treatment interaction. In the mastery model, pre- and posttests are used to determine if the student has achieved the desired mastery level. If the student does not achieve mastery, remedial instruction and/or additional practice is given until mastery is demonstrated. In the adaptive model, the student is continuously branched to varying levels of difficulty based on immediately preceding performance (e.g., Suppes and Morningstar 1972). In the learner control model, students are given the responsibility for choosing their own sequencing and compo-

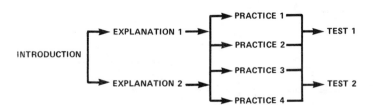

Figure 6-2   Structure of Simple Tutorial Lesson

nents, with the help of an advisor (e.g., Bunderson 1974). In the aptitude/treatment interaction model, branching decisions are based on the personality attributes of the learner (e.g., Pask and Scott 1972).

Once the sequencing (i.e., decision model) has been specified, the actual content must be developed and produced. In the case of CBT this refers to the authoring process, i.e., the creation of instructional programs. There are four basic steps associated with authoring: the representation of the content and logic of the learning activities in some way (e.g., handwritten notes, flowcharts or diagrams, storyboards, forms); the programming of the content and logic; the debugging and testing of the programs; and the development, production, and integration of any offline materials involved such as video, microfiche, workbooks, slide/tapes, etc. If these offline media are to be under computer control (i.e., interactive video or random access microfiche), then further programming, debugging, and testing will be involved. The authoring process can be done in a variety of different ways, which are discussed in the next section. Furthermore, special programming languages and systems have been developed for authoring; these are also discussed subsequently.

Once development is completed, the implementation phase of CBT begins. This involves the installation and startup of the system and daily operation. It involves the initial and ongoing training of all system users (i.e., students, instructors, managers, operators). It also involves the initial "shakedown" and ongoing revisions of the courseware and software. More profoundly, implementation is likely to require some major organizational and procedural changes. Instructor and student roles will change, as will training regimes. For example, with self-paced (individualized) instruction, more importance is placed on the management of time and resources, and student motivation becomes an important consideration. The next chapter discusses the implementation phase of CBT in detail.

Although the evaluation phase is discussed last, evaluation is an activity that goes on during the preceding three phases shown in Figure 6–2. During the design phase, various alternative formulations of objectives and lesson specifications are likely to be reviewed by subject matter experts and instructional designers. During the development phase, prototype lessons are likely to be created to test out ideas. Once pilot versions of lessons or courses are ready, they should be tested via small group tryouts. As well as testing out the effectiveness of the courseware, the usefulness of instructional management capabilities (e.g., student progress reports, test item analyses, scheduling or registration programs) should also be evaluated. During the implementation phase, the effectiveness of the courseware is evaluated in an operational setting with actual students. The evaluation data is used to assess student performance, revise courseware, and monitor system utilization and efficiency.

All of the preceding evaluation activities can be considered *formative* evaluation, i.e., data collected to make decisions about revisions and improvements. At some point in the implementation phase when the system and courseware are considered to be fully operational, a validation study may be conducted that compares the outcomes of CBT courses with on-the-job performance or another training approach. This constitutes a *summative* evaluation, i.e., data collected in order to make decisions about the overall value of CBT. On the basis of a summative evaluation, decisions may be made to continue with, expand, or drop a CBT system in a particular application. Chapter 8 discusses evaluation in the CBT context in further detail.

The extent to which these five phases of ISD are evident in a CBT project are a function of the type of authoring approach involved, the size of the project, and the experience of the organization with ISD. Some authoring approaches (discussed later) are much more conducive to the use of ISD than others. The larger (and hence more costly) the project, the more likely that ISD procedures will be essential.

It is important to understand the critical contribution that ISD makes to successful CBT. Oftentimes the improvement in training attributed to CBT is really due to the use of ISD methodology, i.e., the systematic design of training program or materials. For example, it is common to convert testing programs to a criterion-referenced framework as part of CAT. The increased effectiveness that results is most likely due to the criterion-referenced basis of the tests rather than computer administration (although computer scoring and analysis will undoubtedly improve testing efficiency). Similarly, existing materials may become much more effective with CMI because they are now tied to specific objectives and job tasks. Instruction presented via CAI or CAL may be effective, not because of the inherent interactive capabilities, but because they are relevant to the job needs. For these reasons, taking a training course or program that has already been properly developed via ISD and implementing it on a CBT system may yield little improvement in instructional effectiveness. On the other hand, CBT is likely to increase the efficiency of the training, i.e., yield improved cost/benefits. This is particularly true for CMI, simulators, and embedded training.

To summarize our discussion of ISD and CBT, ISD represents the foundation for designing and developing effective CBT courseware. To the extent that ISD principles and procedures are followed, CBT is likely to be instructionally sound. CBT introduces some new aspects to ISD methodology, primarily in the development, implementation, and evaluation phases. This means that ISD expertise will need to be supplemented by CBT expertise in order to develop good CBT courseware.

CBT DESIGN CONCEPTS

Up to this point in the chapter we have basically discussed *macro* variables, i.e., how to determine what content should go into a CBT program. Once this has been accomplished, it then becomes necessary to consider *micro* variables (not to be confused with microcomputers) that have to do with the actual design of lessons. We will divide such variables into two functional categories: displays and interaction. As you will see, however, the distinction will quickly get blurred.

Displays

The first major category of factors has to do with what the students or users see on their screen. This will be either text or graphics of some kind. There are many dimensions to be taken into account in creating text for a screen display. This includes topography, readability (vocabulary, sentence length), emphasis (highlighting, underlining), and so on. The techniques that apply to good writing in any medium (e.g., amplification, examples, metaphors, conciseness) also apply to creation of text for CBT displays (see Burke 1982; Merrill 1982). Second, graphics (either online or offline) can play many roles in creating effective displays (Bork 1977). This includes presenting concepts that are dynamic or hard to explain in words, the creation of imagery to improve retention, or simply to increase motivation or attention. The use of audio (i.e., music, narrative) is another display characteristic to be considered.

Beyond the details of text or graphics, there are many further display variables to be taken into account. Frame size—how much information is presented in a single display—is important. It is common to try to pack too much into each display. A single frame should present one major idea (concept, example, rule, test question, etc.). After all, blank space on a display screen costs literally nothing, unlike white space on a piece of paper.

Another common problem with display design is the nature of instructions given to students. Authors should never assume that students will carefully read and follow instructions! Consequently, important instructions should be repeated (perhaps in both text and audio) and their understanding checked via a question. In fact, good design involves structuring activities so that the expected behavior/response is self-evident and instructions are basically superfluous. Note, however, that such design requires a great deal of thought and tryouts.

Lack of modularity is another common limitation in the design of CBT courseware. This leads to two major problems. When material is organized in big "chunks," it is difficult to allow students to move around easily in programs since they generally must wait until they finish a section before branching. Second, smaller units make it easier for the author to revise—long lessons typically require more effort to change. Some systems such as TICCIT with its componentized lesson structure help guide the author toward creating smaller rather than larger units.

The most profound problem with the design of displays in CBT courseware, however, is none of the preceding factors. It is the lack of understanding or imagination on the part of authors about how to exploit the unique interactive characteristics of CBT. There is a strong tendency for authors to create interactive tests along the lines of paper and pencil tests or tutorial screens similar to pages of a textbook. This is nothing unique to CBT courseware; think of instructional television programs you have seen that consist simply of a televised lecture, or the overhead transparencies that are copies of full pages from a textbook (and quite illegible). Authors need to grasp how to create interactive displays that make the student an active participant in the instructional process.

Interaction

Interaction can be broken down into two major aspects: control and responses. Control means exactly what it says—providing the user (student, instructor, course manager) the capability to be in control of the program. This means being able to branch to another question or part of a lesson when desired. It means being able to ask for help or further explanation on some concept. It also means being able to sign on and off easily, send messages, browse, and change the courseware to suit personal tastes (i.e., electronic note taking). Control can be something as simple as the ability to skip a test item and come back to it in an online test to the complex learner control features of TICCIT. One of the reasons that CAL (particularly games and simulations) is so popular with students is that it allows a very high degree of student control. This automatically leads to active participation in learning.

Responses refer to any input that a user makes either via keyboard, touch input, cursor movement, speech, etc. One of the unfortunate historical legacies of the computer field is that the keyboard became entrenched as the standard input mode. This is unfortunate because it means that it will take us a long time to fully take advantage of other input modes, particularly touch and cursor control (e.g., joysticks, mouses, paddles), which are now quite reliable. There are a number of good reasons for avoiding typed responses when it is not instructionally necessary, including avoidance of typing errors, slowing down students, difficult answer analysis. On the other hand, the indiscriminate use of multiple choice input (i.e., selections from menu or answer options) rather than open responses is often a problem. While it is evident that there are times when it will not make any difference (e.g., Lockhart et al. 1981), it is also clear that there are many occasions where a constructed response would have been more instructionally valid than a forced choice. Almost all author languages in use today feature keyword analysis routines that allow open responses to be parsed. Presumably, the eventual use of natural language interaction will eliminate this problem.

A basic principle of good software design is that any input from the user should be acknowledged by the system. In the case of CBT, this acknowledgment usually takes the form of reinforcing feedback. The idea is to make it clear to students that their response was correct, incorrect, along the right track, not understood, etc. One of the most important aspects of creating an instructional program is the development of "prompts," which shape the student toward the correct answer and "helps," which allow the student to get further explanation of anything he or she does not understand. In the more sophisticated forms of CAI (i.e., Socratic dialog systems), the courseware includes tutoring rules that allow the program to diagnose the nature of a student's misunderstanding and present information to correct the misconception (e.g., Brown and Burton 1978; Collins 1977).

Even though a number of useful guidelines are available for the development of good CBT courseware (e.g., Burke 1982; Caldwell 1980; Kingman 1981), there are two critical elements that do not come from following these guidelines: creativity and tryouts. Courseware is often instructionally sound but fails because it lacks the touches of the creative mind—spontaneity, humor, variety, and pizzazz. On the other hand, much of what makes courseware successful may not have been there originally but was added after the second, fifth, or twenty-ninth tryout. There is no better way to design good CBT programs than to let them design themselves at the hands of students, instructors, and managers.

THE AUTHORING PROCESS

As previously explained, the authoring process involves the creation, programming, debugging, and testing of courseware. Authoring can involve a single individual who does all these steps; a small group consisting of an instructor, programmer, and instructional designer; or a large interdisciplinary group made up of subject matter experts, instructional specialists (e.g., writers, graphics designers), and computer scientists (e.g., analysts, programmers). In general, the larger the CBT project, the more likely a group or team approach will be used.

When authoring is done by a single person, that individual must be able to program, debug, and test courseware. Using an authoring language or system (described in the next section), an author can create and edit text, graphics, sound/speech, or special character sets. The author must do the analysis and design, as well as provide all the content. The solitary authoring approach has the advantage that it requires only one person to develop courseware. If the author is very talented, the resulting courseware is often outstanding. On the other hand, to create courseware, the author must take the time to master an author language or system, a process which may take months or years. Furthermore, not all subject matter experts or instructors have the necessary interest or ability to develop good CBT courseware.

Standalone microcomputers represent the most likely CBT environment in which solitary authoring is likely to occur. Using an author language such as PILOT or an authoring system such as PASS or WISE, an author can create, program, debug, and test courseware in a fairly straightforward fashion with relatively little training in the authoring process (e.g., a few days or weeks). This does not necessarily mean that an author will produce good courseware, especially if he or she lacks instructional design expertise or if ISD methodology is not used. Burke (1982) provides an excellent guide for the solitary author who is developing courseware on a microcomputer.

Small group approaches to authoring divide up the development steps in a functional way. The instructor or subject matter expert provides the content and recommendations regarding appropriate teaching strategies, the instructional designer helps translate the content into CBT courseware (i.e., interactive sequences, screen displays, helps, etc.), and the programmer takes responsibility for coding, debugging, and testing the programs. The instructional designer is likely to conduct the analysis, design, and evaluation phases in conjunction with the instructor or subject matter expert. The programmer or systems analyst typically looks after CBT hardware and software concerns.

Bork (1981) describes an authoring model based on this small group approach. Bork suggests that authors should work in groups of three with one member being experienced in the creation of computer "dialogs." Bork also suggests that courseware should be developed using flow charts or diagrams to outline the content and logic of the lessons.

In a large team approach, each aspect of the authoring process is the joint result of a number of people with different skills or expertise. The subject matter expert may work with a graphics designer, a writer, or a test specialist to develop the content. CBT designers or instructional technologists may be involved in the analysis and design of the courseware. System analysts or programmers may be required to develop necessary software or courseware. Even electronics technicians or engineers may be needed for hardware development (as with simulators or embedded CBT).

Courseware development for the TICCIT system exemplifies the team approach (e.g., Merrill, Schneider, and Fletcher 1980). The authoring process is broken down into two major parts: content generation by the subject matter expert(s) and packaging in which displays, lesson files, and answer processing (i.e., branching) logic are created. All content is provided in terms of the instructional components used in TICCIT (e.g., objectives, rules, examples, helps, practice). Graphics are normally prepared by an artist or graphics designer who works from the content. "Packagers" have responsibility for editing the content and entering it on the system (designing the displays in the process). An authoring system called APT (Authoring Procedure for TICCIT) is used by the packager to put materials online. Since the instructional logic (learner control) is built into TICCIT, neither the content providers nor packagers have to worry about specifying or programming this.

It should be noted that the single author, small group, and team approaches to authoring are not a function of any particular kind of CBT or specific CBT system, but a consequence of the nature and scope of training organization and application involved. For example, suppose a large company decided to adopt CBT for its training activities. Authoring could take place by having each department contribute subject matter experts or instructors to work as part of a large authoring team; it could take place in small groups by providing an instructor, designer, and programmer to each department; or individuals in each department could be taught the necessary instructional design and programming skills and be allowed to author on their own (with help when needed). There are good rationales for each approach. The large team will probably be able to produce a lot of courseware relatively quickly and with efficient use of resources; the small groups will require significantly less management structure and may be organizationally (i.e., politically) more stable and accepted; and the single author approach increases the likelihood of widespread CBT acceptance and allows for local revision and maintenance of the courseware after initial implementation (which may be good or bad).

Regardless of which approach or CBT system is used, a number of common tools or techniques are likely to be involved. Almost every authoring effort depends on some kind of written directions. At a minimum, they take the form of scrawled notes that an author follows while sitting at a terminal. Normally, some type of form is used that allows the content expert to describe the desired displays and associated learning activities. Figure 6–3 depicts the kind of information such a form would typically contain. The first section contains identification information including a unique frame (display) identifier. The second section contains a screen grid and is used to show exactly what should happen in that particular display (e.g., display certain text or graphics, ask a question, provide a feedback message, etc.). It is also necessary to indicate how much of the previous display should be erased before displaying the new one. Because of the capability of overlaying information, one display may actually be built up from a series of different frames.

The third section of the form provides branching information. This may simply be a matter of showing the next consecutive frame in a text display, or it may involve a series of branches contingent upon specific responses. For example, if this is a multiple-choice question frame, there will be branches to feedback messages specified for each answer alternative. The fourth section of the form is for explanation of what the author intended to happen in this frame. In many cases, it will be necessary to describe a complicated display or answer sequence in order for it to be programmed correctly.

In most systems, the different kinds of information indicated in Figure 6–3 will be separated into two or more forms. For example, in the TICCIT system, different forms are used to specify the display, content files, and answer processing logic (e.g., Merrill, Schneider, and Fletcher 1980). In some CBT systems (e.g., PLATO, TICCIT, AIS), these forms exist in both offline and online versions so that specification can be done with or without a terminal available.

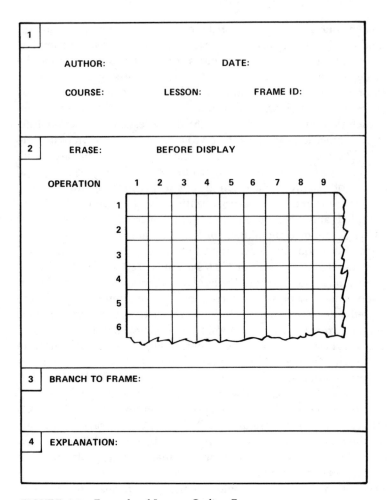

FIGURE 6-3   Example of Lesson Coding Form

The advantage of online forms is that they can be immediately accessed (for review or action) by someone at another terminal in a different location. They also can become part of the online documentation of the courseware. In some cases, the information in an online form is used to automatically generate the program.

No matter which authoring approach is used, courseware development is a highly labor-intensive process, requiring specialized skills. It is the delivery aspect of CBT, where hardware is substituted for humanware, that results in labor savings. This contrasts with traditional training approaches (i.e., classroom lecture, on-the-job apprenticeship), which is usually labor-intensive in delivery but relatively light in terms of development requirements. A significant portion of the development process is attributable to ISD procedures that should apply to any training development effort; however, the bulk of the labor is devoted to the programming, debugging, and testing of the courseware. For this reason, a great deal of attention has been devoted to the development of programming languages and software systems that simplify or streamline the courseware development process. These languages and systems are described next.

AUTHORING LANGUAGES AND SYSTEMS

Over the years a large number of programming languages and systems have been developed for CBT (for reviews, see Brigham 1978; Frye 1968; Zinn 1970). There are three major types of programming languages that can be used: general purpose languages, system-specific author languages, and system independent author languages (see Figure 6–4). General purpose languages such as BASIC, PASCAL, or FORTRAN are designed for any type of programming applications. They are widely available and very flexible, but because they are not specifically designed for instructional applications, it usually takes longer to program than with an author language that is designed for instructional programming. System-specific author languages have been developed for a particular CBT system (e.g., Tutor for PLATO, Coursewriter for IIS, TAL for TICCIT, or CAMIL for AIS). While these author languages take full advantage of the capabilities of the CBT system they are part of, they will not work on any other system. On the other hand, system-independent author languages such as PILOT (Starkweather 1969), PLANIT (Feingold 1968), or

	EXAMPLES	ADVANTAGES	DISADVANTAGES
GENERAL PURPOSE LANGUAGE	BASIC PASCAL FORTRAN	• VERY FLEXIBLE • WIDELY AVAILABLE	• TAKES LONGER TO PROGRAM
SYSTEM SPECIFIC AUTHOR LANGUAGE	TUTOR (PLATO) COURSEWRITER(IIS) CAMIL (AIS)	• OPTIMIZES CAPABILITIES OF SPECIFIC SYSTEM	• WON'T WORK ON ANOTHER SYSTEM
SYSTEM INDEPENDENT AUTHOR LANGUAGE	PILOT PLANIT LOGO	• RUN ON MANY MACHINES	• MAY NOT OPTIMIZE CAPABILITIES OF SPECIFIC SYSTEM

Figure 6–4   CBT Programming Languages

LOGO (Feurzeig and Lukas 1972) are available on a number of different systems. In order to be general enough to run on multiple systems, however, they often do not optimize the capabilities of any specific system.

Author languages possess a number of features that make courseware development easier. This includes capabilities for display formatting, graphics creation, test scoring, answer matching, student data collection, and report generation. All of these capabilities can be achieved using a general purpose language, but in an author language they are built-in. (In fact, author languages are written in general purpose languages, usually an assembly language.)

Figure 6–5 provides a comparison of each of these three different types of CBT programming languages. A small fragment of a lesson frame written in BASIC, PILOT, and TUTOR is shown. The frame involves the presentation of a question, which refers to an offline graphic, and analysis of the response. All programs start with the frame label (Step 1). The BASIC and PILOT programs display the question on the next available lines; TUTOR displays the question starting at line 12, column 3, and places the arrow for the response at line 14, column 1. The answer specification in BASIC requires an exact match—anything else typed in (e.g., PHILIPS, PHILLIP) will be judged as a nonmatch. To indicate other alternative answers in BASIC would require each one to be listed exactly. Both PILOT and TUTOR allow for more sophisticated answer analysis. The *Match (M)* command in PILOT allows for missing or incorrect letters via the "*" symbol, which means accept anything or nothing in this position. Thus, "philip," "Phillips," or even "Fillips" will be correctly matched. The TUTOR *specs* command indicates that all answers should automatically be put in lowercase (bumpshift) and that incorrect spellings or extra letters are acceptable (okspell, okextra). Both PILOT and TUTOR are capable of many other types of answer analysis options such as numerical ranges, logical (and/or) combinations, and pointing (touch) input.

The branching for the correct and incorrect answer messages must be specifically identified with BASIC. In author languages such as PILOT and TUTOR, branching following answer analysis is implicit, i.e., if the answer is judged as correct, the correct feedback message is displayed; otherwise the incorrect message is displayed. The TUTOR program shown in Figure 6–5 uses a *wrong* command to specifically identify a set of wrong answers to be matched to provide more detailed feedback. This allows a number of alternative wrong answers to be checked, each with an appropriate corrective response.

This example illustrates how author languages can make courseware development easier or more sophisticated than by using a general purpose programming language. PILOT shows how an author language can make lesson programming relatively easy; TUTOR demonstrates how a powerful author language can lead to more robust courseware. The example also illustrates that

LABEL	BASIC	PILOT	TUTOR
	STEP 1	*STEP 1	UNIT STEP 1
DISPLAY QUESTION	10 REM STEP 1 20 PRINT " WHAT KIND OF SCREWDRIVER DO YOU NEED TO DISASSEMBLE PANEL 19?" 30 INPUT R	T: WHAT KIND OF SCREWDRIVER DO YOU NEED TO DISASSEMBLE PANEL 19? A:	AT 1203 WRITE WHAT KIND OF SCREWDRIVER DO YOU NEED TO DISASSEMBLE PANEL 19? ARROW 1401
ANSWER SPECIFICATION	40 LET A = " PHILLIPS "	M: **i!*ip*	SPECS BUMPSHIFT, OK SPELL, OKEXTRA ANSWER phillips
CORRECT ANSWER	50 IF R. NE. A THEN 80 60 PRINT " THAT'S CORRECT " 70 GO TO 99	TY: THAT'S CORRECT	WRITE THAT'S CORRECT
INCORRECT ANSWER	80 PRINT " NO, THE CORRECT ANSWER IS PHILLIPS." 99 END	TN: NO, THE CORRECT ANSWER IS PHILLIPS.	WRONG STANDARD, SLOTTED, SQUARE HEAD WRITE NO, THE SCREWS ARE CROSS-HATCHED. WRITE THE CORRECT ANSWER IS PHILLIPS.

Figure 6-5   Comparison of BASIC, PILOT, and TUTOR

no matter what kind of language is used, programming CBT is a detailed and often tedious process. Many factors affect the choice of a particular language, including availability, need for transportability, and the specific needs of the application. For example, some author languages (e.g., Coursewriter) are not well suited to simulation or simulators; a general purpose language would be more suitable for this purpose.

Furthermore, there are many variables that influence the effective use of authoring languages in producing courseware. Avner (1979) presents data from a number of studies on PLATO authors using TUTOR. Avner found that the nature of the courseware being developed and the experience of the author were two major factors affecting production rates. For example, Figure 6–6 shows a comparison of different degrees of authoring experience (less than one year or greater than two) and different pedagogical structures (existing or newly generated). Clearly, inexperienced authors developing new materials take much more time to create (i.e., 165 to 610 hours of authoring time per instructional hour) than experienced authors working with existing instructional formats (i.e., 6 to 34 hours of authoring time per instructional hour).

Because programming is such a tedious and time-consuming aspect of courseware development (even using an author language), many attempts have been made to develop authoring systems (Kearsley 1982a). An authoring system is a set of programs that eliminate or minimize the amount of actual programming required. They allow content experts or instructional designers to author courseware without having to use or know an author (or other programming) language. Alternatively, they provide powerful tools for pro-

PEDAGOGY	AUTHOR EXPERIENCE	
	LOW	HIGH
EXISTING	8-63 Hrs./Hr.	6-39 Hrs./Hr.
NEW	165-610 Hrs./Hr.	27-180 Hrs./Hr.

Figure 6–6   Effects of Experience and Pedagogy on CBT Authoring Times

From R. A. Avner, "Production of Computer-Based Instructional Materials," in *Issues in Instructional Systems Development*, H. F. O'Neil, Jr., ed. (New York: Academic Press, 1979).

grammers or CBT experts to develop courseware faster than by using an author language.

Authoring systems go a number of steps beyond author languages in terms of the capabilities they provide. At a minimum, they provide a high-level interface for the creation and editing of content. Such interfaces usually perform error checking on all input so that relatively little debugging will be needed when the authoring session is complete. Authoring systems allow the selection or specification of particular instructional strategies (i.e., drills, tests, tutorials, etc.). They also make the development and integration of multimedia materials (e.g., video, slide/tape) easier. Capabilities are provided for manipulation and reorganization of entire lessons. Finally, authoring systems usually provide a number of features for storing and reporting student records.

Authoring systems have one of three types of author interface: macros, forms/fields, and prompting. Macros are English-like statements that allow the author to create courseware by substituting critical parameters. These macros are automatically translated into programs by the authoring system. A form- or field-based authoring system provides the author with screens of options and fields that are filled in to create courseware. Programs are generated on the basis of the information provided. Prompting type authoring systems ask questions to elicit the information required. This information is then converted to programs by the authoring system. Figure 6–7 shows an example of a prompting type authoring system called Coursemaker, which generates COURSEWRITER code. The content in the example corresponds to Figure 6–5.

Most major CBT systems and standalone microcomputers feature authoring systems. A number of different form type authoring systems have been developed for PLATO. For example, PLM features an authoring system for the creation of tests and prescription displays. TICCIT was originally designed around a form type authoring system to be used in conjunction with offline forms. Today, TICCIT has both the original authoring system (APT) and a powerful author language (TAL). Coursemaker, the authoring system for IIS, was illustrated in Figure 6–7. AIS also features a form-driven authoring system. Numerous authoring systems have been developed for microcomputers. The most powerful of these at the current time are PASS marketed by Bell & Howell for their modified Apple microcomputers and WISE marketed by WICAT Systems for their microcomputers. PASS uses a prompting type of author interaction and allows specification of instructional strategies, creation of graphics and character sets, student management, and reports. The various components of PASS are shown in Figure 6–8. WISE uses both menu and prompting methods for the creation of courseware.

Authoring systems improve the productivity of authors in developing CBT courseware. However, authoring systems pose some limitations. The run coursemaker

WHAT IS THE NAME OF THIS LESSON?
Step 1
TYPE YOUR TEXT. WHEN FINISHED, PRESS ENTER
Look at the illustration on page 232 of your manual.

TYPE YOUR QUESTION. WHEN FINISHED, PRESS ENTER TWICE.

What kind of a screwdriver do you need to disassemble panel 19?
IS THE QUESTION MULTIPLE CHOICE (1), TRUE/FALSE (2),
COMPLETION (3), OR MATCHING (4)? TYPE 1, 2, 3, OR 4.

3
ENTER A LIST OF POSSIBLE CORRECT ANSWERS.
PRESS ENTER TWICE WHEN DONE.

phillips   phillip

ENTER A LIST OF POSSIBLE INCORRECT ANSWERS. PRESS
ENTER TWICE WHEN DONE.

standard slotted square-head

ENTER RESPONSE TO AN UNANTICIPATED ANSWER. PRESS
ENTER TWICE TO EXIT.

The answer is phillips. Please enter it now.

Figure 6-7   A Prompting Type Authoring System

most significant of these is that the structure imposed by the authoring interface sometimes inhibits the imagination of the author (and hence the quality of
the courseware). Current authoring systems are most usable for CAT, CMI, or
CAI, and not well suited for CAL or simulators. It seems likely that in a large-
scale courseware development effort, authoring systems could be used for
many aspects of development with an author language being used for all
unique components.

   There are many further developments that can be expected in terms of
automating the CBT courseware development process. For example, a comprehensive online authoring curriculum called CREATE[3] exists to prepare au-

[3]CREATE is a trademark of Control Data Corporation.

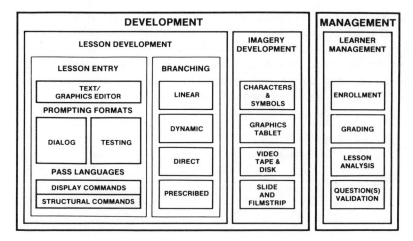

Figure 6–8   Major Components of PASS (Courtesy, Bell & Howell Corp.)

thors to develop courseware for the CDC PLATO system (Taylor 1979). O'Neal and O'Neal (1979) describe an Author Management System (AMS) that provides an online system for monitoring the progress and resource utilization associated with an instructional development project. Brecke and Blaiwes (1981) describe CASDAT (Computer Aided System for Developing Aircrew Training) that allows automated generation of task lists, objectives hierarchies and lesson specifications. Braby and Kincaid (1981) discuss an authoring system for computer generation and editing of text materials. These projects and others suggest that future CBT systems may offer highly comprehensive authoring systems that encompass author training, management of the development process, and computer support for all aspects of the ISD cycle.

SUMMARY

This chapter has surveyed the considerations associated with the design and development of CBT courseware, which included the importance of ISD methodology in developing effective CBT courseware, the nature of the authoring process, and the use of author languages/systems. No single set of CBT authoring procedures or guidelines can be provided because authoring differs significantly across different training applications, organizations, and CBT systems. Thus, authoring tutorials for administrative training will involve somewhat different processes than creating simulations for technical training. Different organizations will use different authoring approaches, e.g., solitary authoring versus groups or teams. Finally, the courseware development process will be affected by the capabilities of the system. A CBT system that involves color graphics or interactive video will present different authoring considerations than one that involves only alphanumeric displays for CAT or CMI. Any detailed discussion of authoring needs to be in the context of a specific application, organization, and system. This chapter has discussed the general aspects of courseware development common to most CBT situations.

7

Implementing and
Managing CBT
Projects

So far in this book we have discussed the assessment of CBT feasibility, the selection of the appropriate system, and the development of courseware. The success or failure of these steps will first appear during the implementation stage of a CBT project. If these activities have been done well, the implementation of the project should go smoothly. On the other hand, a poor job of implementation can ruin a project even though the preceding steps have been successful.

Implementing any kind of new technology (whether it is CBT, commercial products, weapons systems, or whatever) is an extremely difficult undertaking. Innovation means the introduction of new traditions, roles, and relationships. It means changing the way things have been done, perhaps for many years. Few human beings or organizations accept change without some kind of resistance. Thus, to achieve successful implementation of a CBT project, a great deal of planning and coordination is required. Successful CBT projects do not simply happen; they result from careful management.

One of the most unfortunate aspects of CBT projects is that much of the attention and resources are devoted to the acquisition of the hardware/software and the development of the initial courseware. The implementation phase of the project is often given very little thought and minimal funding. As a consequence, the project may fail despite large investments of time and money made up to the implementation stage. For example, initial courseware may be quite effective, but no procedures are defined or funds allocated for revision of the courseware. This means that the courseware soon becomes obsolete and the value of the CBT therefore declines quickly after its initial (successful) implementation. Similarly, the problem could be failure to provide for adequate maintenance or replacement of hardware or software.

This chapter discusses the factors and issues associated with successful (and unsuccessful) implementation of CBT projects.[1] Be forewarned that there are no simple formulas that can be provided for CBT implementation. Just as each training situation presents a unique set of instructional requirements, it also presents a unique set of management considerations. CBT must meet both to be successful.

IMPLEMENTATION CONSIDERATIONS

There are many considerations that must be taken into account in implementing a CBT project. Some major categories are staffing, training, documentation, scheduling (time management), and reliability.

Staffing

The staffing of a CBT project probably represents the most important set of implementation considerations. This includes staff selection and retention, leadership, and morale/motivation. Selection of a staff should focus on the skills needed for CBT. While the skills needed will vary with the kind of CBT involved and the size of the project, it is likely to encompass subject matter expertise, instructional design/development experience, systems analysis/programming experience, administration/management, and CBT background. Francis (1979) stresses the importance of selecting individuals on the basis of specific skills needed rather than filling job positions or roles. This increases the likelihood that the diverse range of capabilities needed for a CBT project will be available.

Selection, or finding authors, is one of the most difficult staffing considerations. Authors may have a teaching or instructional development background, a subject matter or technical content background, or a computer programming background. Each of these three different backgrounds presents its own problems. Both the subject matter expert and computer programmer may pay little attention to pedagogy (for different reasons). The teacher/instructional designer may lack an understanding of the content and CBT. Clearly, it is desirable to use a team approach in which the strengths and weaknesses of each perspective are accounted for. In addition, adequate training and orientation is needed for developers to achieve an understanding of the validity of each perspective (discussed later).

One critical dimension of CBT projects that is often overlooked initially is that different kinds of skills are needed at different stages of a project. For

---

[1]Some of the discussion in this chapter is based on Kearsley and Hillelsohn (1982).

example, in the beginning of a project, usually a great deal of analysis and design expertise is required. Development typically involves different kinds of skills and personalities. Similarly, implementation and evaluation requires yet another set of skills and dispositions. In many cases, it is necessary to acquire new staff at different phases of a project; however, major problems can arise when new staff are added during a project. This includes different perspectives on the purpose of the project, effects on morale, and variations in the nature of the courseware or system.

Turnover or attrition of project personnel is a major problem in a CBT project of large scale or long duration. It can result in lost time, replacement costs, and loss of morale. Often in a team environment, individual members receive little recognition for their work. There are a number of steps that can be taken to remedy this situation in terms of giving proper credits and highlighting individual contributions. Another problem that leads to loss of project members is boredom or lack of challenge. There is always a strong tendency in a project to have an individual continue to do a task because he or she has mastered it. At some point, individuals should be given the opportunity to train their own replacements and take on new tasks within the project.

As in most projects, the leadership provided by the project director or coordinator is a critical factor. Effective leadership of a CBT project requires a good understanding of CBT in general and the purposes of the project in particular. It also requires the capability to take into consideration the perspectives of all those who use the CBT system: instructors, managers, students, and authors.

Planning and communication should be the highest priorities of the project leader—if these two key tasks are not done by the project director, they surely will not be done by any other member of the staff.

Training

One of the major flaws in the implementation stage of many CBT projects is the lack of attention given to CBT training or orientation. The lack of such training/orientation is often a fatal mistake since it represents a major way of overcoming the natural resistance that occurs due to innovation. Sometimes good training is given at the beginning of a project, but no provision is made for providing this training on a recurring basis for new staff or decision-makers. Since regular turnover of staff and decision-makers is unavoidable in many settings (e.g., military), this lack of ongoing CBT orientation often results in misunderstanding or motivation problems. Thus, CBT training must not only be comprehensive in terms of being addressed to all participants in a project, but it also must be designed to be given on a continuing basis. This latter need can be met by always having CBT training as a job responsibility of a project member and/or "packaging" initial training programs so that they are available for use whenever needed (e.g., online instruction, slide/tape lessons, workshop guides, etc.).

It is essential that training and orientation for CBT directly address the changes in roles and new responsibilities introduced by CBT in a training system. There are four major types of training required: (1) training for those involved in the design/development of CBT materials, i.e., authoring; (2) training for those who will monitor CBT activity; (3) training for those who will manage students in a CBT environment; and (4) orientation for students.

Training for CBT authors should involve an overview of the entire development process and the responsibilities of each member of the development team. For example, the subject matter expert should be familiar with the activities of an instructional designer or programmers.

Each member of the team should understand the basic instructional model or procedures that will be used for development and their role in the process. It is critical that all members understand the significance of basic ISD concepts such as task analysis, objectives, criterion-referenced testing, and so on. It is also critical that team members new to CBT be given an understanding of the capabilities and limitations of CBT and their system by studying examples of courseware and, preferably, actually taking CBT courses. Online CBT orientation achieves this purpose very well.

Training for those who will monitor a CBT activity should include operation of all equipment, a knowledge of how to handle hardware, software and courseware problems, and an understanding of the options that are available for help or assistance (e.g., hotlines, mailboxes, messaging). It is essential that this training be "hands-on" in nature and that monitors completely master tasks such as signing on, recovering from problems, sending messages, etc., so that they will be confident in their interactions with students and instructors. Students will look toward these individuals as system experts; therefore they must be very knowledgeable regarding how courses are implemented on the system.

Training for CBT course managers (as well as field managers and supervisors who have training responsibilities) should include a thorough overview of the entire CBT process, i.e., what happens from the time students are enrolled until they complete their training. Second, they should have a good understanding of the nature and appropriate uses of student performance records in terms of tracking student progress and assessing the effectiveness of instruction. In addition, course managers should know how to interpret system utilization data if these are available.

Orientation for students should involve a comparison between learning via CBT and other approaches they are familiar with (e.g., classroom lectures, laboratories, etc.). It is important that students understand the responsibility they have with CBT for managing their own learning activities (i.e., self-pacing, choice of learning strategies). It is also important that students understand how to perform basic operations on the system (such as signing on/off, sending messages, repeating or reviewing materials, control of sequencing, etc.). To ensure this, students should be required to practice and show mastery on these tasks before using the system for actual learning. Since this may be a student's first contact with CBT (or computers), it is critical that such an orientation be well designed, thoroughly debugged/tested, and be as "friendly" (i.e., simple, humorous, nonthreatening) as possible.

The nature and extent of CBT training will obviously depend on the kind of CBT involved and the size of the project. For example, in a small project, the same instructor may fill the three functions described (author, monitor, manager) and will need training that spans all three. Or, a single individual may both monitor and manage CBT activities. If the kind of CBT involved is embedded training, it is likely that the individual responsible for monitoring and managing CBT is the employee's immediate supervisor or manager on the job. On the other hand, in a large CMI system used at a training center, the monitors and managers are separate individuals responsible for certain courses or classes. The way in which the training is given, the frequency, and the performance measures used are all functions of the size and nature of the CBT project as well.

Documentation

Documentation of software, courseware, and procedures is another factor that affects the overall success of a CBT project. Good documentation is one way of minimizing the adverse effects of staff turnover in a project. Documentation of software or courseware is essential to provide smooth operation and maintenance of a CBT project. If programs are poorly documented, they are less likely to be used, will be difficult to fix or revise, and will be difficult to transfer from one system or location to another. Furthermore, good documentation of performance data is essential to the development and revision of courseware.

A variety of different kinds of documentation are required for a CBT system (Kearsley and Hunka 1977). All courseware should have a standard description page that includes the following information:

1. Topic or subject matter of program

2. Brief description of program content or function (including objectives)

3. Amount of time required to complete program (average and range)

4. Support materials required (e.g., handouts, workbooks, manuals, audio/videotapes, etc.)

5. Author(s) of program and address for further information

6. Date of creation or latest revision (plus copyright notice if applicable)

7. Characteristics of intended student group (e.g., preentry skill levels, reading levels)

8. Status and usage of program to date

9. Availability and conditions for use

10. Programming and system involved (i.e., language, type of hardware, terminals, operating system)

11. Available evaluation data

12. Description of other documentation that exists

13. Date of this documentation

This level of information should be used to catalog existing programs and should be coded at the beginning of the program as a comment field. In addition, the first six items should be displayed whenever the program is used as the first screen a user sees. This is especially true if the program is copyrighted or trademarked (e.g., Kearsley and Hunka 1979).

The other kinds of documentation required are intended for particular classes of users and needs. The classes of users include authors/instructors, monitors/managers, operators, programmer/analysts, and students. The three major types of needs are tutorials, reference, and job aids. Tutorial information should serve as an introduction and orientation; reference documentation should be comprehensive and detailed; job aids should be very concise and procedural. For example, documentation on the use of the system should include a tutorial intended for all users (preferably online), a system reference manual for programmers and operators (offline text), and various job aids that might be used by authors, students, operators, and managers for different purposes (online and offline).

Program documentation for authors/instructors should include the following information:

1. Instructional objectives associated with program

2. Preentry skills required for each objective

3. For each distinct instruction unit (e.g., lessons) within the program, a description of content, instructional strategies, media support required, and completion times (average and range)

4. Nature of performance data collected

5. Hardcopy of all screen displays

6. Nature of any instructor intervention required

7. Description of all evaluation data available

8. Assumptions, disclaimers, and restrictions about use or modifications

Documentation for monitors (proctors) or managers of programs should include:

1. Nature of student registration procedures (including passwords)

2. The nature of any proctor intervention required, including a list of all messages and appropriate actions

3. Complete list of all questions or problems presented and corresponding correct/incorrect answers

4. Description of procedures for allowing a student to change the presentation sequence (i.e., for review or skipping of material)

5. Description of all entry points in the course and sequencing of units

6. Nature of all student performance reports available and how to access or generate

7. Procedures for handling special situations such as cheating or system failure during tests

Reference documentation for the system operator(s) should include:

1. Operating details of all hardware (e.g., cpu, disc drives, terminals, printers, other peripherals)

2. Operating procedures for operating system and all software (including details of startup, backup, and emergency situations)

3. Factors that will improve or degrade system performance (e.g., student load, graphics, simulation, background activities)

4. Recovery procedures for system failures

Documentation for programmer/analysts should include:

1. Listing of and location (including file names) of all source code

2. Names and locations of all functions, macros, variables, labels, etc., in the program(s)

3. Particular algorithms or logic used to create certain instructional displays or effects (e.g., animation, decision tables, response analysis)

4. Complete listing of all error messages that might occur, their meaning, and corrective action

Finally, student documentation should cover at a minimum:

1. Organization or structure of course, test, program, etc.

2. Description of how to use terminals, system, programs

3. How to use any special system functions (e.g., calculation mode, function keys, mailbox or messaging, etc.)

4. Description of any scheduling or availability considerations

5. How to get assistance on use of system or content problems

Project directors or system developers may cringe at the idea of spending the time and money required to develop the documentation just described; however, not producing this kind of documentation can be very costly in terms of misuse of a system or misunderstandings about how programs work. The existence of adequate documentation is often the distinguishing factor between an amateur and professional CBT effort—and also a successful implementation and a failure. Remember the DDDD rule: Doing Documentation Discourages Disaster.

Scheduling (Time Management)

Scheduling, or time management, is a major consideration in CBT because it usually involves individualized or self-paced learning rather than group-based instruction (i.e., lectures or classes). This introduces the need to develop plans and strategies for time management on the part of the instructor/author, course/system manager, and student.

A major issue in the design of a CBT course is the optimal duration for lessons, tests, terminal sessions, or entire courses. There are no procedures for determining optimal or maximum durations apart from the content and objectives of the instruction. The number and complexity of tasks to be taught or tested determines the length of courseware. There are certain practical considerations to be taken into account, however. For example, lessons and tests should usually be designed so that they can be completed in one terminal session. Environmental and equipment factors will affect the length of a session. Poor equipment design (e.g., screen glare, chair height) can produce physical fatigue and this will limit session length. The length of a terminal session is also a function of the student's motivation, attention span, and learning habits.

Scheduling of media or equipment is a major time management consideration in CBT. The appropriate scheduling of media should be determined by an objectives hierarchy that indicates the sequence in which media associated with specific objectives should be scheduled. In situations such as CAT or CMI where a variety of learning activities are involved, it is important that the online and offline activities be as integrated as possible. For example, the system should direct the student to read a chapter, watch a videotape, or attend a class and then take an online test following the activity. If the computer is managing all of the instructional resources, then the use of each piece of equipment can be optimized and, in some cases, reduced amounts of equipment will be required. Thus, if time in a simulator is required as part of a course, the system can schedule learning activities so that simulator utilization is spread out and bottlenecks are avoided.

An important CBT scheduling consideration has to do with terminal usage when there are a limited number of terminals available. Often it is necessary to establish priorities in terms of different types of users. For example, a set of priorities for terminal use might be as follows:

1. Students taking scheduled courses

2. Instructors/monitors assisting a student with problems

3. Authors creating or revising courseware

4. Instructors/managers performing student management activities

5. Students taking unscheduled courses (for review or general interest)

6. Programmers working on applications software

7. Demonstrations of courseware or system

Clearly any such priority scheme is likely to be unpopular, leading to the conclusion that having an adequate number of terminals for all types of users is a critical implementation consideration.

Probably the most significant time management consideration in a CBT system has to do with getting students to take advantage of the time savings that are possible with individualized instruction. The problem is that many students lack sufficient motivation to do this. Such motivation can be extrinsic or intrinsic. For example, students may be able to start or return to work as soon as they complete training and therefore be eligible for full salary or a promotion. This usually provides an extrinsic motivation to finish a course as quickly as possible. On the other hand, if a student must leave a plush training center to return to a high-pressure job that is disliked (and is being paid full salary while training), there is little incentive to complete a CBT course in minimum time.

A number of techniques can be used to increase the motivation of students and achieve time savings. For example, providing students with access to their progress records may increase their motivation to complete training faster (Van Matre et al. 1979; Hamovitch and Van Matre 1981). Such access should be on demand rather than automatic (i.e., students can check their progress when they want but not have it forced upon them continually). Another technique that can be used to increase motivation is to introduce an explicit competitive element into training by allowing students to compete against each other to finish training first. Provided that the testing is mastery-based, such competition should not adversely affect the quality or effectiveness of the instruction. Since the amount of time spent at the terminal, rather than ability or achievement level, is the primary factor in "winning," individual success depends on willingness to spend more time studying.

Another technique that can be used to increase student motivation and produce faster or better learning is having students go through lessons in pairs or small groups. Studies have shown that there are no negative effects to multiple students sharing the same terminal (e.g., Reid et al. 1973; Smith and Duggan 1965). In fact, it has been suggested that the opportunity for mutual assistance is quite beneficial, and that students may reinforce each other in learning activities. Since students still take tests individually, it is still possible to assess student performance on an individual basis. Motivation can also be improved via the use of game strategies or humor. Malone (1982) has studied computer games and identified challenge, fantasy, and curiosity as the important factors in successful games.

Reliability

The reliability of a CBT system is an important factor in the success of a CBT project. System response time and downtime affect user acceptance and confidence in CBT. In surveys of user attitudes, the reliability of the system is repeatedly identified as a critical dimension determining overall satisfaction. Much of the time, CBT hardware, software, or courseware is inadequately debugged and tested before being put into operational use. Often this is because of time limitations preventing proper "bullet proofing" of a system. Yet it is an extremely foolish decision to skimp on adequate testing to make a deadline since, in most cases, the lack of satisfactory reliability will lead to user dissatisfaction and ultimate failure of the system.

A number of steps can be taken in the design of hardware, software, and courseware to improve its reliability and make it "fault tolerant." The use/availability of redundant hardware and software components can overcome inevitable hardware failures. No CBT project should go to an operational stage without backup for critical hardware components (e.g., terminals, disc drives, central processor) and software (e.g., operating systems, program libraries, storage files). Clearly, system configurations involving distributed processing and storage offer much greater inherent reliability over timesharing or completely standalone configurations since the shared components can overcome failure of any single unit.

The reliability of courseware can be increased by means of systematic debugging and testing techniques. This involves trying out every possible input response and branch in the program. With real courseware, this is generally impossible to do manually, so special simulation or "exerciser" programs need to be written to generate all responses and learning paths. While such simulations take time and money to develop, they are the only way of ensuring that courseware is robust prior to actual use. The alternative is to conduct extensive field tests and pilot try-outs with students. While this will identify most problems (and is a necessary step anyway for formative evaluation purposes), it will not catch all bugs.

Finally, satisfactory response time is an important dimension of reliability. It has repeatedly been shown that it is not length of delay itself that bothers people as much as extreme variability in response times (e.g., Carbonell, Elkind, and Nickerson 1968). There are many ways in which such variability can be introduced into a system. Any system based on shared resources will eventually "saturate," producing delays in response times once the number of users exceeds some threshold. Certain kinds of CBT (e.g., graphics, simulation) require more computational or storage requirements than other types (e.g., tests, tutorials). As more users on a system engage in such demanding activities, delays in response time may occur.

The system configuration also makes a difference in ensuring satisfactory response times (normally less than two seconds for response). Timesharing configurations are notoriously susceptible to saturation problems. Standalone configurations are good until the limits of the available processing speed and memory are reached. Distributed configurations are obviously more satisfactory because of theoretically infinite expandability, but in practice also show saturation problems. The only guaranteed way to avoid response time problems is to always ensure that the system has excess processing and storage capabilities. Wise system designers and managers know that whatever processing and memory capability is initially obtained, it will not be enough for very long.

Figure 7-1 provides a checklist of the major considerations discussed in this section. Positive responses to the questions in the checklist will increase the likelihood of a successful CBT implementation. Negative answers should be cause for concern and remedial action.

FACTORS UNDERLYING SUCCESSFUL CBT PROJECTS

A number of major factors can be identified that are associated with successful CBT projects. Six such factors are discussed below. Branson (1979) discusses how some of these factors affected the success of three actual ISD projects in the military.

	Yes	No

STAFFING

1. Do the project staff possess the right mix of skills needed for the project? [ ] [ ]

2. Do authors have appropriate backgrounds? [ ] [ ]

3. Can turnover/attrition be minimized? [ ] [ ]

4. Does the project director possess good leadership qualities? [ ] [ ]

5. Are the individual contributions of project members likely to receive due recognition? [ ] [ ]

DOCUMENTATION

1. Do good tutorials exist for authors, instructors, monitors, managers, and students? [ ] [ ]

2. Are necessary job aids available for all classes of users? [ ] [ ]

3. Do all programs have satisfactory descriptions? [ ] [ ]

4. Is reference documentation for authors/instructors, monitors/managers, system operators, and students adequate? [ ] [ ]

SCHEDULING

1. Are the durations of courseware units practical? [ ] [ ]

2. Are online and offline learning activities well integrated? [ ] [ ]

3. Are adequate CBT resources available or priorities defined for use of limited resources (e.g., terminals)? [ ] [ ]

4. Can steps be taken to improve student motivation to complete training? [ ] [ ]

RELIABILITY

1. Is the reliability of hardware, software, and courseware satisfactory? [ ] [ ]

2. Is response time adequate under full system loads? [ ] [ ]

Figure 7-1   CBT Implementation Considerations Checklist

User Involvement

Of all the factors that affect the success of CBT projects, user involvement is probably the most important. This involves the sharing of control, commitment, and coordination with all participants in a CBT project. Each participant must have some degree of "pride of ownership" in the system. For this reason it is particularly important that those responsible for implementing and administering CBT be involved in the design, development, or selection of the system, including hardware, software, and courseware.

Figure 7–2 shows a comparison of different kinds of user involvement in the implementation of an actual CBT system at two different sites (Wagner et al. 1978). On-the-job performance by course graduates was essentially identical at both sites, but site 1 had the system removed as soon as the study was completed, whereas the system at site 2 was kept. Three activities appeared to be especially important. Successful training of on-site people allowed them to be in-house experts when the system was installed. Having the computer prepare reports in the form already in use eliminated the need to change procedures or create duplicate reports. Finally, since the on-site users ran the system themselves, it gave them a sense of ownership that could not be accomplished any other way.

Evaluations of CBT projects (e.g., Alderman, Appel, and Murphy 1978; Misselt et al. 1980; Van Matre, 1980) clearly show that the instructor plays a critical role in the success of a system. If instructors participate actively, they

	SITE 1	SITE 2
PRIMARY CONTACT	Head of Site	Head of Training
PERCEPTION	Experimental System	Operational (Proven) System
PLANNING	Involvement only of high level personnel in planning. Instructional design delivered in system.	Involvement of on-site personnel (Supervisory and Worker) in planning of implementation. Solicited instructional design suggestions from on-site personnel.
PREPARATION	Developer responsible for design, preparation and setup of training center (on-site personnel provided support). On-site personnel were inadequately trained prior to system delivery.	On-site personnel responsible for design preparation, and setup of learning center (developer served advisory/consulting role). On-site personnel (maintenance and instructor) went to developer's site to familiarize themselves with the system prior to shipment.
ADMINISTRATION	Developers retained control of system. Developers provided all maintenance of the system. System management remained the developer's job. Computer-produced student management reports did not meet on-site needs.	On-site personnel ran the system. Site provided first echelon maintenance. System management is part of regular duties. Computer-produced student management reports replaced hand-done reports.

Figure 7–2   Effects of User Involvement

tend to become the best supporters. However, if the instructors are given passive roles or ignored, they will be neutral at best and most likely negative. This holds for training managers and administrators as well.

Level of Commitment

A factor commonly identified in successful CBT projects is a high degree of commitment on the part of top and middle management, instructors, project members, and other administrators who will influence the project. A high level of commitment manifests itself in qualities such as enthusiasm, dedication, persistence, and cooperation. A high level of commitment from top management manifests itself in terms of the quality of people assigned to the project and the closeness with which the project is monitored. Concern with slipped deadlines or delays suggests that completion of the project is of some importance; lack of concern indicates that the project has lack of priority.

The dedication and enthusiasm of the project leader is a critical dimension. Most successful CBT projects can be traced to the tireless efforts and persistence of one or two key individuals. This high level of commitment is needed to keep a project together during the inevitably difficult spots and to continually inspire the staff over a long duration.

Necessary Resources

It is clear that many CBT projects have failed for lack of necessary resources, either human, financial, equipment, or facilities. It is important to have available or access to the kinds of instructional, subject matter, and computer expertise needed. A common problem in CBT projects is that staff (such as subject matter experts or computer personnel) are loaned to the project on a part-time basis. This means that their energies and attention cannot be totally devoted to the project, often leading to less than totally satisfactory results. Another common resource problem is the lack of adequate funds, staff, or equipment for the implementation phase of a project. Often most of the resources are utilized for the initial acquisition of the system and development of courseware. Little money may be left to actually operate and maintain the system, revise courseware, and support the staff.

The solution to adequate resources is proper planning. This includes the knowledge of what levels of resources will be needed at different stages of a project. It is important to know that at least half of the initial budget should be devoted to courseware development and that approximately 25 to 40 percent of this initial budget will be needed for annual courseware revision. Similarly, it is important to allow 10 to 20 percent of the original system cost for annual operation and maintenance. Furthermore, it is important to realize that if a CBT project is successful, the demands on the project staff will increase. More courses will be requested as well as additional system functions.

Readiness of Technology

One problem that often arises in CBT projects is that the hardware, software, or courseware is not ready for operational use. Sometimes this is simply a matter of inadequate debugging and testing, as discussed in the previous section. In other cases, it is a matter of technology not being sufficiently advanced to meet the requirements and constraints of actual training. It is common to find that something that has been demonstrated in a laboratory setting is a long way from practical implementation.

For example, natural language capability for CBT has been demonstrated as feasible (e.g., Burton and Brown 1979); however, the amount of time required to develop suitable programs and the response time involved makes it unsuitable at the present time for actual use in CBT projects. Similarly, speech input (recognition) and output (synthesis) has been demonstrated in many CBT projects during the past decade, but the present level of speech input/output is only practical and affordable for a small number of CBT applications (Halley and Kearsley 1980).

It is important that the technology selected for a CBT system application be clearly operational. This advice does not apply, of course, to research projects in which the purpose of the project is to develop a prototype. Moreover, it is important to distinguish between research and operational CBT projects so that expectations regarding the robustness of technology can be reasonable. (See the discussion in the next section.)

Acknowledgment of Training Need

Another major factor that affects the success of a CBT project is the acknowledgment of a training need that can be met by CBT. If there is not unanimous agreement on the existence of a training need, then it is likely that any results produced by CBT will go unappreciated or unnoticed. More importantly, if the training need is not clearly recognized, it is unlikely that a high level of commitment to CBT, or any other solution, will be present. Branson (1979) points out that without a "documented outcome gap," the necessary support or momentum for innovation and change will not be present. He also points out that innovation is only one possible approach to the problem; the other is a public relations or political solution which tries to alter perceptions of the problem or find a scapegoat.

Demonstrated Results

CBT projects that are able to demonstrate clear-cut success in terms of improved job performance, training efficiency, or worker satisfaction are likely to be successful. This is often difficult to do, as we shall discuss in the next chapter. One of the important considerations is to identify at the begin-

	Yes	No
1. Does a high degree of user involvement exist?	[ ]	[ ]
2. Is there a high level of commitment towards CBT and the project?	[ ]	[ ]
3. Are the necessary resources available to carry out the project?	[ ]	[ ]
4. Is the technology (hardware/software/courseware) ready for operational use?	[ ]	[ ]
5. Is there a clear acknowledgment of a training need which CBT can address?	[ ]	[ ]
6. Can the project demonstrate meaningful results?	[ ]	[ ]

Figure 7-3   CBT Success Factors Checklist

ning of the project what outcomes are achievable and measurable. Baseline data must be collected before CBT is implemented so that changes due to CBT can be measured.

Alternatively, simultaneous comparisons can be made between an existing training approach or media and CBT. Generally, statistical significance is less important than results which are easily discernible to decision-makers (e.g., improved job performance, reduced training time, increased number of graduates with the same level of resources or budget).

Figure 7-3 summarizes the six major success factors just discussed. This checklist can be used to assess the likely success of a CBT project while in the planning or development stage. If the answers are negative to more than two or three questions, the prognosis for success of a project is not good.

MANAGEMENT PRINCIPLES FOR CBT

As was pointed out in the beginning of this chapter, successful CBT projects do not just happen—they are the result of careful planning and good management. In this section we discuss some essential management principles for CBT projects (see Figure 7-4). A large part of this discussion is based upon Seidel and Wagner (1981). These principles follow directly from the preceding discussion of implementation considerations and success factors.

1. *There must be an unambiguous understanding of the purpose and nature of the project.* One of the common problems that arises is conflict between a research and a development (i.e., operational) effort. If top management views the project as an exploratory study, but first-line management sees it as an

	Yes	No
1. Has a clear-cut understanding about the purpose and nature of the project been established?	[ ]	[ ]
2. Are all individuals who will be affected by CBT actively involved?	[ ]	[ ]
3. Has adequate training and orientation been planned and conducted?	[ ]	[ ]
4. Are adequate controls over project resources and progress available and used?	[ ]	[ ]
5. Have explicit criteria been established to assess system and courseware acceptability?	[ ]	[ ]
6. Have project tasks been assigned according to skills needed?	[ ]	[ ]
7. Has an appropriate evaluation model and plan been developed and implemented?	[ ]	[ ]
8. Has a stable system been established before starting courseware development?	[ ]	[ ]
9. Does everyone understand the iterative nature of a CBT project?	[ ]	[ ]

Figure 7-4   CBT Management Principles Checklist

operational project, then it will be very difficult for the project to succeed. Another problem that may arise is over the kind of CBT involved. It is not uncommon for a project to be planned as a CAT or CMI effort but to have to meet demands for CAI or CAL. Because different hardware and software are needed, this is unlikely to work. In short, it is essential that the project manager ensure that the purpose and nature of the project is understood by all levels of management, by the project staff, and by all who will be affected by the project. False or unrealistic expectations have prevented the success of many CBT projects. It is the manager's major responsibility to make sure that everyone has correct expectations about the nature and outcomes of the project.

2. *All participants must be actively involved.* The problems associated with lack of active participation of those who will be affected by a CBT project have already been discussed earlier in this chapter. The project manager must devise strategies in the form of meetings, surveys, memos, or committees to establish communication with everyone who might have some interest (positive or negative) in the project. Second, the manager must structure project tasks and activities such that they involve in some fashion all individuals and groups who could affect the success of CBT. This includes instructors, training managers and administrators, field managers and supervisors, and students. It also includes clerical staff, vendor representatives, consultants (as designers or evaluators), and other influential members of the organization. Involvement of others in the project is one area that cannot be overdone.

3. *Conduct training and orientation for all users involved.* As a corollary of the previous principle, all users of the system will need adequate training and orientation. The different types required have already been described in this chapter. It is the responsibility of the project manager to ensure that this training takes place in a timely and effective manner. All system users must have an understanding of what they are doing and why. The purposes of the project and their role in achieving the purposes is an important aspect of training and orientation.

4. *Establish and maintain adequate controls over project resources and programs.* Techniques developed for managing project resources and progress apply as much to a CBT project as any other. Milestones and checkpoints for system and courseware development are critical; without them it is impossible to determine whether a project is going well or getting into trouble. Continued coordination and communication among project members is necessary and the responsibility of the project director. Regular meetings of project staff with progress/problem reports are critical. Anticipating and preventing potential problems is the essence of good management.

5. *Establish explicit and objective criteria to assess system and courseware acceptability.* It is a mistake to let system developers or authors make their own decision regarding system or courseware readiness. Generally, the tendency to continue "tinkering" will delay the availability of the system or courseware beyond scheduled dates. Conversely, developers may occasionally release the system or courseware before it has been adequately debugged or tested. Either outcome can be avoided by defining explicit performance criteria at the beginning of the project that the system and courseware must meet and then having these criteria judged by competent and credible individuals, different from the original project staff.

6. *Assign project tasks according to skills needed.* It is important not to simply assign tasks on the basis of job functions or past practice. It must be realized that CBT requires a unique mix of talents in instruction, computing, and content areas. Since it is unlikely that any single individual has this mix, it is usual to use a team approach for most developments tasks in CBT. For example, while authoring can be done by single individuals, it is accomplished much better by a team consisting of separate individuals with skills in instructional design, the subject matter involved, and programming. It is the project director's responsibility to acquire and keep the right mix of skills and talents needed for the project. It is important to realize that this mix will likely include individuals of different temperaments, e.g., technologists who are good at following systematic procedures and creative artists who can devise novel solutions when needed (e.g., Kearsley and O'Neal 1979). It is also important to ensure that the contributions of each project member receive due recognition.

7. *An appropriate evaluation model and plan must be developed.* It is the role of the project director to see that an evaluation model and plan is developed at the beginning of a project which will appropriately measure and determine whether the project met its intended goals. As mentioned in the previous section, it is critical that a CBT project be able to demonstrate its success in a way which is meaningful to the sponsors of the project (e.g., top management). This can only happen if a suitable evaluation approach is followed.

8. *Establish a stable system before developing courseware.* It is essential that the system hardware and software be fully developed before courseware development is begun. While this seems almost obvious, there is a strong tendency in CBT projects to work on courseware development concurrently with the evolution of the system. Unless prepared to completely throw away this courseware, it is necessary to wait until the system is stable. In most projects it is necessary to set a "freeze" date after which time all further system development is suspended until a major update is implemented. This provides the kind of stable system needed for courseware development.

9. *Prepare everyone for the iterative nature of the project.* Something that is often poorly understood about instructional and software projects (and CBT especially) is that they are iterative in nature, i.e., they must go through many repeating and recurring cycles. It is the nature of instruction and software to be continually changing as training and job needs change. The basic ISD process itself is a cycle, as described in Chapter 6. As new tasks and objectives are defined and old ones become obsolete, the instruction (i.e., courseware) must be modified and revised. A CBT project manager must plan for continuing revisions and repetition of activities. Factors such as good documentation and provisions for staff advancement/turnover will help; so will continual briefings and presentations on the status and accomplishments of the project.

CASE STUDY: FBN COMPUTER CORPORATION

FBN Computer Corporation is a mid-sized company that manufactures and sells hardware and software for a variety of different application areas. In response to customer needs, FBN has recently developed an authoring system which they intend to market as a software product. The manager of the authoring system project wants to conduct an in-house try-out of the product before releasing it to customers. The request is made to the director of that division (Product Development) who asks the director of the manufacturing division (a golfing buddy) to host the try-out. The manufacturing division director agrees, sends a memo to a loyal manager in the division requiring her cooperation, and forgets about the matter.

The two managers meet and the product development manager outlines the nature of the try-out and what will be involved. Basically what is needed is a course that can be developed in CBT form using the new authoring system. The plan involves bringing in a couple of people who have developed the authoring system and allowing them to use it to write a CBT course which will then be used by manufacturing for training. One of the manufacturing training specialists will assist in the development of the course by providing content expertise.

The manufacturing manager is willing to cooperate, of course, but is not willing to risk a major disruption of the training program or a drain on training staff. Consequently, she suggests that the course selected be a new one on safety procedures and assigns a new and relatively inexperienced member of the training staff to provide content expertise. There are other training programs that are badly needed, but this seems too risky and would involve some of the more valuable members of the training staff.

All courseware development work will take place in the product development department, which is located in another building from manufacturing. The plan involves installing some terminals in the manufacturing training center, which are linked to a host computer in product development, for the try-outs. It is felt that this approach will minimize the resources (i.e., equipment, facilities, people) needed from manufacturing.

This project does not go well. The manufacturing training staff is never briefed properly on the project and assumes that it is some kind of surreptitious plot to replace them with computers. As a consequence, they ostracize the new training staff member who has been assigned to the project. Since this person is new, he is unable to provide the kind of expertise desired by the authoring system group. Furthermore, because of the ostracism, other training staff will not cooperate in providing information or help.

Nevertheless, courseware is developed and two terminals are installed in the training center for the try-out. Because the course developed is new, there is no current time slot for teaching it. The training staff argues that since it is individualized instruction, no specific time slot is needed; students can take the course before or after their other courses. No incentives are provided for the students to take the extra course—it is made an "optional" activity. Predictably few students are interested in spending precious time on such an activity. Worse yet, even when students do try out the program, the software or courseware often fails because of "bugs." The authoring system group sees nothing wrong with this situation—after all the whole point of the project is to test out the system. However, students and training staff are not aware of this and think that the course is supposed to be operational. Eventually, dissatisfaction with the project among the training staff reaches a peak and serious objections are expressed to the manager of manufacturing. Not wanting a mutiny, she calls the product development manager and insists the project be terminated. The product development manager agrees since no useful data is really being collected by the exercise. The fate of the authoring system is now jeopardized since it has not received adequate testing nor any positive response from the training staff in manufacturing. Eventually the product is scrapped.

This case study exemplifies the various implementation considerations and factors discussed in this chapter. Looking at the CBT Success Factors Checklist (Figure 7-3), it is clear that most of the questions can be answered negatively: there was very little user involvement, a low level of commitment, the technology was not ready for operational use, there was no real training need addressed, and the project could not have demonstrated meaningful results (i.e., improvements in course development time) as conducted. Using the CBT Implementation Considerations Checklist (Figure 7-1), it can be seen that there were significant failures in all categories. The project staff lacked the necessary subject matter and training expertise, there was no user (i.e., instructors, students) training or orientation, no documentation was provided, there were scheduling problems, and the system was unreliable. Finally, in terms of the CBT Management Principles Checklist (Figure 7-4), most of the major principles were not practiced in this project. There was misunderstanding about the purpose and nature of the project, the training staff were not actively involved, there was no training or orientation, the evaluation model and plan was unsatisfactory, and a stable system did not exist.

There are many true ironies in this case study. For example, it should not be assumed that a computer company nor its staff will be more receptive to CBT. It also should not be assumed that training groups will necessarily embrace an innovation intended to make their jobs easier or more productive. Finally, it should not be assumed that minimizing the time and resource requirements of participants will make the project work—sometimes this may sabotage it by reducing essential commitment or involvement.

It is not easy to successfully implement and manage a CBT project. In fact, it is incredibly difficult; relatively few projects survive long enough to meet their initial objectives and produce the desired outcomes.[2] Most of the reasons for failure have been described in this chapter. They have little to do with limitations of the hardware, software, or courseware. Rather, they are a function of poor management. Use of the checklists provided in this chapter should alert a project leader to the pitfalls to be avoided.

[2]Some of the successful projects have been described in the first two chapters of this book.

8

Evaluating CBT

As was pointed out in Chapter 5 during the discussion of ISD methodology, evaluation is a process that occurs during all stages of an instructional development project. These various evaluation activities can be grouped into two major types of evaluation: formative and summative. Formative evaluation is conducted by the instructional team while the system (hardware, software, courseware) exists in prototype form; its purpose is to improve the efficiency or effectiveness of the system. Summative evaluation is conducted after the system is operational and usually by evaluators external to the project. The purpose of summative evaluation is to allow decision-makers to assess the value of the system in terms of alternative approaches (comparative), effects on job performance (validation), or cost/benefits.

It is very important to distinguish between these two different types of evaluation since the purposes and methods of each differ significantly. If the kind of evaluation desired is summative (i.e., for decision-making) but a prototype system is involved or the evaluation is conducted by the system developers, it is unlikely that the purpose of the evaluation will be satisfied. Similarly, if information is needed to revise the system but a summative evaluation is conducted, the data collected are not likely to be helpful for this purpose. In short, it is critical that the purpose of the evaluation, (whether formative or summative), be clear-cut. The way to ensure this is to check that the purpose, type of data, status of system, and decision-maker correspond to those shown in Figure 8-1. If characteristics from both columns are involved, then both formative and summative evaluation is needed (hopefully, not at the same time).

	FORMATIVE	SUMMATIVE
PURPOSE	Improve System/ Instruction	Adoption of System
TYPE OF DATA	Course Performance	Comparative, Validation, Cost/Benefits
STATUS OF SYSTEM	Prototype	Operational
EVALUATOR	Usually Internal	Usually External
DECISION MAKER	Instructional Specialists	Management

Figure 8-1   Comparison of Formative and Summative Evaluation

In general, evaluation of CBT systems is based on the same methodology used for any educational evaluation (e.g., Popham 1975; Tuckman 1979). However, because of the capability of the computer to automatically and un-obtrusively collect detailed response data during CBT activities, evaluation can be much more sophisticated. For formative evaluation, this means that instructors have a great wealth of course and test data available to analyze. Likewise, in summative evaluation, data on alternative approaches, job performance, or costs can be collected much more systematically and objectively. Of course, such capabilities may not be utilized or appreciated.

FORMATIVE EVALUATION

Figure 8-2 outlines three major activities in formative evaluation: development of a prototype system or lesson(s), pilot tests, and field tests. Based on the system or lesson specifications, a prototype of the hardware, software, and/or courseware should be developed. The purpose of such a prototype is to

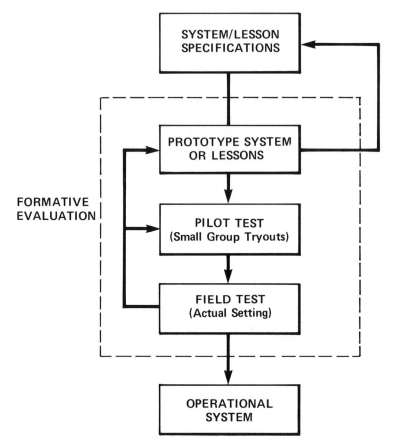

Figure 8-2 Major Activities in Formative Evaluation

determine if the design of the system or lesson is appropriate or usable before expending resources to develop the entire system or training program. Thus, a prototype represents some small portion of the system or curriculum, usually selected as exemplary of the full-scale effort. This may involve the use of "mock-up" equipment or lessons, e.g., the use of hardcopy illustrations instead of screen displays or a much simpler hardware configuration than is actually intended. The use of mock-ups is similar to what engineers or architects do when they create scale models of equipment or buildings. The intent is to create a concrete representation of the specifications before proceeding with further development. This happens to be a very important aspect of successful project management since it allows the decision-maker(s) to provide feedback on, and input to, the acceptability of the design before it is finalized.

The prototype stage can also serve the purpose of choosing between alternative designs for hardware, software, or courseware. Thus, multiple prototypes might be developed and subjected to pilot or field tests in order to select the superior design. While this obviously costs more than simply developing a single design, in those cases where a great deal of money will be invested in the training system, or where operational failures due to poor training cannot be tolerated (e.g., space or military missions), the funding of multiple prototypes is seen as worthwhile. For example, the U.S. Navy funded the development of a number of designers for the prototype of an Electronic Equipment Maintenance Trainer (EEMT). The best design was selected on the basis of cost effectiveness considerations (e.g., Pine, Koch, and Malec 1981). It is often the case that different instructional methodologies will result in different lesson designs. The best way of selecting among alternative designs is to develop prototypes and try them out in pilot or field tests.

The second stage of a formative evaluation is a pilot test. This involves trying out system or lesson prototypes (and later full-scale versions) with a small group of simulated students. Often pilot tests will be conducted with single individuals with the evaluator(s) noting all problems that occur. Typically the "students" are colleagues or subject matter experts who are not directly involved in the development of the system. The purpose of the pilot test is to detect any major problems in the hardware, software, and courseware. Another purpose is to try out data collection instruments (both online and offline) that will be used subsequently.

The availability of an online comment or mailbox capability is very helpful during pilot testing of a system. A comment feature allows a student to send a short note at any place in the course, with the system affixing the exact location (i.e., nearest label) to the message automatically. These comments are accumulated in a file which the instructional developer is then able to examine and make corrections from. The comment feature is also very helpful during instruction when it can be used by students to ask questions about things they do not understand and allow the instructor to provide a response. A mailbox feature provides the same kind of communication capability, although it usually cannot be used inside lessons and hence is used for more general feedback.

After all problems identified in pilot testing have been corrected, the next stage of formative evaluation is field testing in which the system or lesson prototypes are tried out in the actual training setting they are being designed for. If multiple locations are involved, it is essential to field test at more than one site since there are usually differences due to geography or local administration that should be accounted for. During the field test, the student response data collected should be the same as that to be collected in the operational system—although much more data may be collected during the field test. This allows evaluation of how well the data provided can be used by instructors or training managers to track student performance or by instructional developers to revise the courseware.

During the formative evaluation, it is important to continue with the existing instructional approaches and methods of assessing student performance to prevent the system from being perceived as an operational system, in which case it ceases to be a formative evaluation. In order to properly conduct a formative evaluation, it will be necessary to continually make revisions to the system or the instructional materials. This constant change makes it impossible to evaluate in a summative fashion.

As the arrows in Figure 8–2 show, the data collected in the pilot and field test stages of formative evaluation will lead to changes in the system or lesson prototype. It is not uncommon for such changes to the prototype to force modifications in the system or lesson design. At some point, time and money will run out and the prototype must be turned into the first version of an operational system. Alternatively, a set of system or training performance criteria may have been established (e.g., specifying average training duration or maximum student errors) and the system goes to operational phase when these are met. Since the formative evaluation cycle can go on almost indefinitely, it is important that there exist some termination rule (even if it is an arbitrary date).

The critical tools provided by a CBT system for formative and summative evaluation are analyses and reports of student response data. Figures 1–1 and 2–6 in previous chapters have illustrated student progress reports used in CMI systems. Figures 8–3 and 8–4 illustrate the kind of response analysis data needed to make detailed evaluation of courseware.

Figure 8–3 shows the data associated with a particular question frame in a statistics course. At the top of the figure is the exact location of the question (IP IDENTIFICATION) in the course STAT1, Segment 019. Below this is a representation of the statistics problem the student saw on the screen. Underneath this are the responses allowed for the question: timed out (ot), the correct answer (c1), two wrong answers (w1,w2) each with different feedback messages, and three unanticipated answers (u1,u2,u3) which have feedback messages that try to help the student calculate the correct answer. (These feedback messages are not shown in the figure.)

Beside these response options is a frequency matrix that shows the number of students who gave each of the various responses and on which attempt at the question. Of thirty-seven students who had gone through that question, eighteen provided the correct answer (c1) on their first attempt, ten on the second attempt (i.e., they provided some other answer on the first response), and one each on the third and fourth attempts. Thus, by the fourth attempt, all students had gotten the correct answer. Only one student gave an incorrect response (w1); the other five responses were unexpected answers.

IP IDENTIFICATION - 190175-004   STAT1-019

CRT DISPLAY:

$$f_{ij} = f_{row(i)} \times f_{col(j)}$$ ATTEMPTS UNTIL AND INCLUDING FIRST CORRECT

$$F_{12} =$$

MAID	DESCRIPTION OF STUDENT RESPONSE	ATTEMPT:	1	2	3	4	>4	SUB
ot			0	0	0	0	0	0
c1	45 ≤ NUMERICAL ANSWER ≥ 45.5		18	10	1	1	0	30
v1	45.5 ≤ NUMERICAL ANSWER ≥ 46		1	0	0	0	0	1
v2	50 ≤ NUMERICAL ANSWER ≥ 50		0	0	0	0	0	0
u1			3	0	0	0	0	3
u2			0	2	0	0	0	2
u3			0	0	1	0	0	1
		TOTALS:	22	12	2	1	0	37

KEYBOARD RESPONSES TO MAID 'U1', 'U2', 'U3'

k410(1)	1.
k411 (1)	2.
k412(1)	3.
k413(2)	4.
k415(2)	5.
k420(3)	6.

Figure 8-3   Student Responses for Specific Lesson Frame

As the listing of unexpected answers at the bottom of the figure shows, these were all empty returns—an easy way of getting a hint. If this question had required a word response instead of a numerical answer, this listing of unexpected answers would list all the words not explicitly matched in the correct and incorrect answers. Beside each unexpected response in the list is the student number in case there is a need to check with the student regarding why a particular response was made. All answers could be listed so that the exact response of every student is available. In the case of pointing input, the answer identified is the location of the screen the student pointed to.

Figure 8-4 is another data report corresponding to a series of questions identified by their labels in the left-hand column (i.e., BCA32A-BC118A). Each column represents the response of a student (S181-S199) to each of the questions. These data indicate correct answers (0), incorrect answers (1), unanticipated answers ($), blank responses (9), help responses (?), and unattempted questions (blanks). The matrix shows the percentage correct for each question across all students and for each student across all questions.

How would such reports be used for formative evaluation? Figure 8-3 would be used to determine if the instruction associated with that question frame is working and what kinds of errors are made in attempting to answer the question. In this particular case, most students get the answer correct on their first attempt, suggesting that the instruction is satisfactory. Furthermore,

STUDENT RESPONSE MATRIX   GROUP—TRIO   TOPIC BC

CODES: 0 = COR. ANS., 1 = INCOR. ANS., $ = UNANTIC. ANS., 9 = BLANK ANS., ? = ? IN ANS., BLANK = UNATTEMTED QU.

	S181	S182	S183	S184	S185	S186	S187	S188	S189	S190	S191	S192	S193	S194	S195	S196	S197	S198	S199	% COR.
BCA32A	1	0	0	0	0	0	0	0	0	0	0	0	0	9	0	0	1	0	0	83.3
BCA42A	0	0	0	0	0	0	0	0	0	0	0	0	0	0	0	0	0	0	0	100.0
BCA52A	0	0	0	0	1	0	0	0	0	0	0	0	1	1	1	1	0	0	0	88.9
BCA54A	1	1	1	1	1	1	1	1	1	$	1	1	1	1	1	1	1	1	1	18.8
BCA58A	0	0	0	0	0	1	1	0	1	1	0	0	0	0	1	1	1	0	1	46.2
BCA62A	0	0	0	0	0	0	0	0	0	0	0	1	0	0	0	0	0	0	0	84.6
BCA66A	0	0	0	0	0	0	0	0	0	0	0	1	0	0	0	0	0	0	0	84.6
BCA70A	0			0	0	0	0	0	0	0	0	1	0	0	0	0	1	0	0	84.6
BCA82A	1			0	0	0	0			0	1		0	0	0	0	0	0	0	76.9
BCA82B	0			0	0	0	0			0	0		0	1	0	0	0	0	?	83.3
BCA84A	0			0	0	0	0			1	0		0	0	0	0	0	0	0	91.7
BCA86A	1			0	0	0	0			0	0		0	0	0	0	0	0	0	83.3
BCA86B	0			0	0	0	0			0	0		0	0	0	0	0	0	0	81.8
BCA88A	0			0	0	0	0	1		1	1		0	0	1	0	1	0	0	72.7
BCA88B	0			1	0	0	0	1		0	0		0	1	0	0	1	0	1	57.1
BCA90A	0			0	0	0	0	0		0	0		0	1	0	1	1	0	?	64.3
BCA92A	0							1		1	1		0	1	0				1	0.0
BC108A																				
BC114A	1	?	1	0	0	1	0	1	1	0	0	0	0	1	0	1	1	1	0	50.0
BC118A	1	?	1	0	0	1	0	0	0	0	0	0	0	1	0	0	0	0	0	72.2
% COR.	76	100	100	82	88	89	80	90	0	83	65	80	81	54	71	75	35	94	71	

Figure 8–4   Student Response Matrix

those who do not get the question correct at first appear able to get it correct on their second attempt when given a hint. However, if most students were getting the question incorrect on their first attempt or taking many attempts to get it correct, the corresponding instruction (or the question) would need to be revised. Since the incorrect or unanticipated answers can be listed, the instructional developer would examine these responses for clues as to the nature of the problem.

Similarly, the data provided in Figure 8–4 would be used to identify problems in an entire lesson. For example, question BCA52A and BC108A resulted in 18.8 and 0.0 percent, respectively. This suggests a problem with the instruction associated with the questions or the questions themselves. Since everyone got question BCA42A correct, it might be that this item (or the instruction) is not needed. Finally, student S197 only scored 35 percent on the lesson—it would be important to check with this student to discover why.

Note that the emphasis in using these reports is to identify problems with the instruction, not track student progress. While they could be used for analyzing student performance, they are designed primarily for analysis of instructional effectiveness. Student listings (such as those shown in Figures 1–1 and 2–6) are more suitable for tracking student progress.

Most mature CBT systems provide data collection software and reports such as the two we have just looked at in either offline (i.e., printouts) or online (screen display) form. In order to do formative evaluation properly, this kind of response data analysis is needed. Furthermore, these same reports are needed to revise courseware after it has achieved operational status. As new instructional lessons or materials (or a new system capability) are added, it becomes necessary to use student response data to evaluate the new instruction.

The methods of formative evaluation described so far have focused on improving the hardware, software, or courseware. As has been pointed out in previous chapters, however, major obstacles in successful implementation of a CBT system are frequently organizational or political in nature, i.e., humanware problems. What is needed is a methodology for examining the attitudes and perceptions of individuals affected by CBT.

Transactional evaluation (TE) is a technique that accomplishes this and has been used in CBT projects (Wagner and Seidel 1978). TE provides a way of getting project participants and those affected by CBT to voice their perceptions and concerns about a project. The method involves having an outside evaluator who asks participants to list the goals, obstacles, and potential solutions of the project as they see them. These responses are then organized into an attitude survey with a four- or five-point rating scale (agree-disagree). This survey is then administered to the original participants and the data analyzed. Of particular interest are items that show polarization, consensus, and ambiguity. Once the data are analyzed, it is presented to the participants. The ensuing discussion is used to focus on strategies for implementing viable solutions to major obstacles identified. TE can be repeated throughout the course of a project to diagnose and correct humanware problems.

SUMMATIVE EVALUATION

In contrast to the purpose of formative evaluation, which is to improve the efficiency or effectiveness of a system or training program, the purpose of summative evaluation is to determine the efficiency or effectiveness and to make decisions based on this assessment. There are three kinds of summative evaluation that will be discussed in this section: comparative, validation, and cost/benefits. Each type corresponds to a particular type of decision to be made.

Comparative Studies

Comparative evaluation involves the comparison of CBT with existing training or some other training approach. The purpose is to determine whether CBT is more efficient or effective than the alternative to which it is compared. In many cases, it is sufficient to show that CBT is at least as good as other alternatives, since CBT may offer significant cost savings or other benefits (discussed later).

There are four principal dimensions that are typically compared: achievement, training duration, attrition, and attitudes. *Achievement* refers to some measure of course performance, whether final tests or overall course progress. Generally pre- and post-test scores between two or more matched groups receiving different instructional methods are compared. *Training duration* involves the time it takes students to complete a specified training course or program. *Attrition* refers to the number of students who fail to complete a course or training program (for academic reasons). *Attitudes* involve measures of student and instructor satisfaction/dissatisfaction with the training.

Over the past decade, many CBT comparison studies have been conducted by the military with a variety of systems and in many different training settings. Normally, the comparison is between CBT and conventional instruction (i.e., classroom lecture method), although comparisons have been made between various kinds of manual and automated individualized instruction.

One of the most comprehensive analyses is reported by Orlansky and String (1981a). They reviewed the results of forty-eight studies and found that CBT (CMI or CAI) resulted in the same levels of student achievement in thirty-two cases and superior achievement in fifteen cases.[1] The most clear-cut finding was that CBT (particularly CMI) reliably decreased training durations. The average student time saved over conventional instruction was 30 percent;

[1]The systems included PLATO, TICCIT, and AIS.

however, the data showed that when CBT was compared to some other form of individualized instruction, there were only slight gains. In other words, the significant time savings produced by CBT are basically due to the individualized instruction, not the use of the computer. On the other hand, in a large training system, individualized instruction is seldom possible without the use of the computer.

The data on attrition are much more equivocal. In the Orlansky and String review, they suggest that attrition may increase slightly over courses taught in conventional mode. They also point out the many other factors that can affect attrition in a military training environment, i.e., changes in recruitment standards and student throughput requirements. It is well known that student completion is a major concern in individualized instruction and that special steps must be taken in terms of providing intrinsic and extrinsic motivation; therefore, increases in attrition in CBT courses without such steps is not unexpected.

The attitude data reviewed by Orlansky and String indicated that students are generally very positive toward CBT. Of the thirty-nine studies that collected student attitude data, twenty-nine reported more favorable attitudes toward CBT than conventional instruction. In contrast, of the nine studies that collected instructor attitude data, instructors were more negative toward CBT in eight of the nine cases. These data suggest a clear-cut interpretation: resistance to CBT is much more likely to come from instructors rather than students.

The data presented by Orlansky and String are very similar to the results of many comparative studies that have been conducted in the educational domain (e.g., Edwards et al. 1975; Jamison, Suppes, and Wells 1974; Kulik, Kulik, and Cohen 1980; Thomas 1979; Vinsonhaler and Bass 1972). In general, computer-based instruction has been shown to be at least as good or slightly better in terms of student achievement scores. Student attitudes are almost always very positive toward the use of computers. Since reducing student time is of relatively little interest in education, it has not been measured as often.

One particularly important comparative study in the educational domain is the evaluation studies of PLATO and TICCIT in community colleges conducted by the Educational Testing Service (Aldermen, Appel, and Murphy 1978). The evaluation of TICCIT involved over 5,000 students in two community colleges using three algebra courses and two in English composition. The PLATO evaluation involved approximately 4,000 students in five community colleges with courseware in five subject areas: accounting, biology, chemistry, English, and mathematics.

There were significant differences in the way TICCIT and PLATO were implemented in the colleges. TICCIT was introduced primarily as mainline instruction with the instructor role as either supervision or supplementary assistance when requested. All TICCIT courseware utilized the learner control framework built into the system. In contrast, with PLATO the course instructor determined how PLATO was to be used. This resulted in substantial variation in how much exposure students had to the system. Overall, it was estimated that less than one-third of instruction utilized PLATO. In both TICCIT and PLATO, instructors were involved in the development of the courseware used.

The results of the evaluation showed important differences between PLATO and TICCIT. The findings with regard to attrition and achievement using PLATO showed no significant effects compared to conventional classes. Student and instructor attitudes toward PLATO were quite positive. One interesting finding was that a large number of instructors felt that PLATO increased their contact with students rather than decreasing it. Indeed, the majority of instructors (78 percent) did not perceive PLATO as decreasing their overall workload because of this increased contact. Even though the achievement data showed no effects for PLATO, the majority of instructors (80 percent) judged PLATO to have a positive effect on student performance.

TICCIT showed different results. There were positive effects in terms of increased student achievement over conventional classes, particularly in mathematics. There were also negative effects on student completion rates: in both courses fewer students completed the courses than in conventional classes. Clearly, learner control as implemented in the usual college setting did not work well without additional attention to motivational considerations. The results also showed that while student reactions to TICCIT were generally favorable, they were not as positive as reactions to PLATO. This seemed to be a function of the class size and the amount of instructor attention received. In the smaller classes, students were more favorable toward TICCIT than students who used TICCIT as part of a very large class.

The evaluation of PLATO and TICCIT produced many interesting results and outcomes beyond these broad conclusions. It is clear from this evaluation that the way a computer instructional system is introduced into a learning setting and the role played by instructors will significantly affect student achievement, attrition, and attitude outcomes. The guidelines provided in the previous chapter regarding implementation and management of a CBT project will help move results in the direction of favoring CBT.

Validation Studies

In contrast to comparative studies, the purpose of validation studies is to show that CBT materials or courses actually achieve their training goals in terms of job performance and outcomes. In order to carry out a validation study, it is necessary to correlate CBT measures with job measures. Because it is difficult to collect job performance data, few training courses or programs (CBT or otherwise) are ever validated. This is very unfortunate since it represents the most meaningful data that can be collected about the effects of CBT.

There are many kinds of job performance data that could be used for a validation study. This includes the number of transactions processed; the number of customers served; the number of units produced, serviced, or sold; and the number of machines or workers in operation (i.e., maintenance or safety records). Time measures can also be used, as in the average amount of time required to serve a customer, process a transaction, produce a unit, make a sale, service equipment, and so on. In those job activities where performance cannot be easily measured in quantitative terms, ratings of qualitative dimensions can be made by managers, supervisors, or co-workers. For example, management or flying skills can be rated using task checklists with objectively scored criteria.

In order to relate changes in job performance measures to CBT it is usually necessary to collect baseline data (scores on measures prior to the use of CBT). The objective is to show that the use of CBT positively affects the job in terms of the measures identified. Thus, the use of a CBT course on product knowledge or sales techniques could be shown to increase the total monthly sales of a group of salespersons relative to before the training or relative to another group that did not receive the training. A particularly powerful test of effectiveness is to suspend or remove the training some time after it has already been shown to have an effect. If the performance measures drop back to their original baseline levels and then go back to the improved levels when CBT is reintroduced, this clearly demonstrates that the effects are due to CBT and not other changes that may have happened when CBT was originally introduced.

Figure 8-5 illustrates the kinds of results such a validation study might produce. A manufacturing plant develops an online safety course that all new employees are required to take. Data are collected on the number of total injuries in the plant for the four months prior to the introduction of the CBT course. As the figure shows, once CBT is introduced, the number of injuries drops. To prove that the results are really due to CBT rather than some other

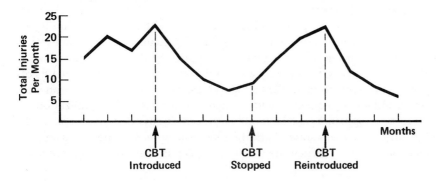

Figure 8-5   Results of CBT Validation Study

factor, the CBT course is stopped for three months. The number of injuries in-creases back to the baseline level. Once CBT is reintroduced, the injuries are reduced again.

Instead of this research design (called a time-series method), it would have been possible to compare two matched groups: one getting CBT and the other not (a control group). Alternatively, a number of different safety training pro-grams could be compared in addition to CBT. While the comparison of treat-ments with a control group is a more definitive design, it is often very difficult to conduct this kind of research in "real world" training settings. The time-se-ries method is usually more practical since it simply involves the introduction and suspension of a training program rather than running and testing multiple groups.[2]

Despite the importance of conducting validation studies in CBT, very few have been done. The one exception to this is in the area of simulators for mili-tary training. The military has been quite interested in measuring the transfer of training that results from the use of training devices compared to the use of actual equipment, particularly in terms of cost-effectiveness. Consequently, a number of studies have compared job performance after actual equipment and simulator training (e.g., Orlansky and String 1981b). In addition, there has been considerable interest in the military in comparing performance with CAL simulation to training using more expensive simulators. For example, Craw-ford and Crawford (1978) compared the use of PLATO to simulate an avionics console with workbook instruction in terms of simulator performance. The re-sults showed that not only was the simulation more effective than the work-book instruction, but that it could also replace practice on the simulator as well. (Unfortunately this study did not go on to collect actual job performance data.)

There are many reasons why validation studies are not conducted as they should be. While in theory, the responsibility of the training organization should extend out to the workplace and job performance, in practice it often goes only as far as the door of the training center. Responsibility for monitor-ing and changing job performance is usually in the hands of operational super-visors, managers, or the personnel department, and basically "off limits" to training. Even if this is not the case, it is often difficult to collect data in the work environment because it is given lower priority than operational tasks. Finally, many trainers do not truly believe that they could show real effects on job performance due to their training activities. This is part of the reason why training groups are frequently held in such low esteem in an organization.

Two developments that have already been discussed in this book could significantly change this state of affairs. One development is the increasing use of embedded training. When the training is given in the actual work environ-

---

[2]The details of using time series designs are discussed in Campbell and Stanley (1963).

ment on the same equipment or system to be used for the job, it becomes relatively easy to continue collecting performance data after the initial training is completed. For example, suppose the users of a billing system are taught how to use the system via online tutorials in their work setting. After they have finished their tutorial, response data on the number or duration of transactions processed on the job can be collected. These data can be related to the use of the tutorials and also to revisions and changes made in the tutorials (i.e., formative evaluation).[3]

The other significant development is an increasing trend toward decentralized training in the workplace rather than at centralized training centers (Kearsley 1981a). Clearly the availability of distributed computer systems and embedded training contribute toward this trend. The significance of this development is that it forces training organizations to think about designing and carrying out training activities on the job. Along with this comes the collection of evaluation data based on job performance measures instead of only training achievement scores.

This capability to collect job performance data and hence validate CBT materials and courses creates the possibility of a training assurance network. Without feedback from the job on the effectiveness of their efforts, trainers are typically unable to convince themselves or their managers about the value of their training activities. Clearly, validation of training programs has a great deal of importance beyond CBT. The use of CBT offers considerable potential in increasing the likelihood of validation. To date, however, this has not occurred often since most of the attention has been focused on comparative and cost/benefits studies.

Cost/Benefits Studies

Primarily because of the large start-up costs associated with CBT, many cost/benefits studies of CBT have been conducted, particularly in the military domain. In general, these studies have focused on the potential cost savings due to reduced training durations or fewer training resources (i.e., instructors, equipment, facilities). For example, Buchanan (1979) was able to show cost savings of over $40,000 annually by using PLATO for CMI in one pilot training program at United Airlines. CMI resulted in a reduction of training duration from fifteen days to under ten days and the replacement of three flight instructors with learning center coordinators. Buck and Beardsley (1980) describe the cost/benefits analysis conducted for the FAA CBT system. They examined four alternatives (manual individualized instruction, centralized CMI, centralized CMI/CAI, and remote CMI/CAI) in terms of start-up and recurring costs. They calculated total savings in the range of 4.9 to 6.7 million dollars based on reductions in student salaries, student training, and number

---

[3]Of course such automatic and unobtrusive monitoring of job performance raises serious concerns for privacy. Employees must be aware of and voluntarily agree to such monitoring.

of instructors required. Even though start-up costs for CBT were between 4.9 and 8.8 million dollars, their analysis showed breakeven periods of under two years when student salaries were taken into account.

In the domain of military training, Orlansky and String (1981b) reviewed twelve studies done on the cost effectiveness of maintenance simulators. They concluded that since achievement was the same or better than training using actual equipment and simulators cost approximately 60 percent less than actual equipment, simulators were cost effective over the use of actual equipment. In the study conducted by Crawford and Crawford (1978) described in the previous section, it was estimated that the use of the simulation could save approximately $43,000 per year for 200 pilots. In addition, this would only utilize 600 of the 8,000 hours available on the CBT system.

A number of assumptions and variables affect CBT cost/benefit analyses.[4] Three major categories of assumptions are: components included, degree of usage anticipated, and projected life span of system components. *Components included* refers to the extent to which the costs of all hardware components have been taken into account in the cost analysis. This includes initial and ongoing costs associated with each component. Figure 8-6 provides

Figure 8-6   CBT Cost Checklist

	Yes	No
DEVELOPMENT PHASE		
I Equipment (Acquisition)		
1. Processing units	[ ]	[ ]
2. Terminals	[ ]	[ ]
3. Multimedia devices	[ ]	[ ]
4. Peripherals (printers, disk drives)	[ ]	[ ]
5. Communications	[ ]	[ ]
6. Power or air conditioning	[ ]	[ ]
7. Carrels or furniture	[ ]	[ ]
II Facilities		
1. Offices	[ ]	[ ]
2. Production space	[ ]	[ ]
III Software		
1. System programs	[ ]	[ ]
2. Application programs	[ ]	[ ]
3. Diagnostic/Utility programs	[ ]	[ ]
4. Documentation	[ ]	[ ]
IV Instructional Development		
1. Analysis	[ ]	[ ]
2. Design	[ ]	[ ]
3. Development	[ ]	[ ]

[4]The following discussion is based on Kearsley (1982b), Chapter 11.

Figure 8-6   CBT Cost Checklist (continued)

	Yes	No
V Instructional Materials		
1. Printed text	[ ]	[ ]
2. Multimedia (slides, tapes, video)	[ ]	[ ]
3. Lecture/Group Discussion	[ ]	[ ]
4. Online (CAI, CAL, CAT, etc.)	[ ]	[ ]
VI Management/Administration		
1. Project administration	[ ]	[ ]
2. System integration and test	[ ]	[ ]
3. Procurement	[ ]	[ ]
VII Other Direct Costs		
1. Travel	[ ]	[ ]
2. Consultants	[ ]	[ ]
3. Supplies	[ ]	[ ]

OPERATIONAL PHASE

	Yes	No
I Equipment		
1. Maintenance	[ ]	[ ]
2. Space and replacement parts	[ ]	[ ]
II Facilities		
1. Classrooms	[ ]	[ ]
2. Laboratories	[ ]	[ ]
3. Learning centers	[ ]	[ ]
4. Libraries	[ ]	[ ]
5. Restrooms/Lounges	[ ]	[ ]
III Software		
1. Maintenance/Revision	[ ]	[ ]
IV Instructional Development		
1. Implementation		
a. Initial and ongoing training	[ ]	[ ]
b. Instructors, managers, proctors	[ ]	[ ]
2. Evaluation (includes revision)	[ ]	[ ]
VI Instructional Materials		
1. Reproduction/Duplication	[ ]	[ ]
2. Distribution	[ ]	[ ]
VII Management/Administration		
1. Project administration	[ ]	[ ]
VIII Other Direct Costs		
1. Travel	[ ]	[ ]
2. Consultants	[ ]	[ ]
3. Supplies	[ ]	[ ]

a comprehensive checklist of cost components that may apply to the development and operational phases of a CBT project (based on the specification of Seidel and Wagner 1979). Note that most components in categories II through VII involve labor costs (salaries) emphasizing the labor-intensive aspects of CBT. Since the equipment is the visible part of a CBT project, it tends to get most of the attention in cost analyses; however, the real costs lie in the humanware required for software and courseware development.

Degree of usage is another major assumption that must be carefully examined. The number of students who use a CBT system is a function of its availability and the number of terminals. Availability is a function of the number of hours and days a system can be used. For example, if it is assumed that a system is used six hours a day, five days a week, and eight months a year, the availability is :

$$6 \times 20 \times 8 = 960 \text{ hours/year.}$$

However, if it is assumed that the system is used eight hours a day, six days a week, for ten months, the availability is:

$$8 \times 24 \times 10 = 1920 \text{ hours/year.}$$

If the cost of a terminal is $3,000, the cost per student hour in the first case will be $3,000 ÷ 960 = $3.12, whereas in the second case it will be $3,000 ÷ 1,920 = $1.56. Thus, by making different assumptions about system availability, the cost per student hour can be dramatically altered.

A useful formula developed by Buck and Beardsley (1980) for computing the number of terminals needed is:

$$T = \frac{(\text{CBT hours/student}) \times (\text{Number students/year})}{(\text{Total training days/year}) \times (\text{Total hours training/day}) \times (\text{Utilization})}$$

The utilization factor is a percentage reflecting the actual level of usage of the system (accounting for hardware failures and poor scheduling). It is usually between 50 to 70 percent. In order to use this formula, it is necessary to estimate the total number of hours of CBT contact a student will have.

A third major assumption made in the costing of CBT systems is the *lifespan* of the hardware, software, and courseware. Since these costs are usually amortized over their anticipated lifespan, the period selected is important. Often the lifespans used are not realistic. For example, hardware is often amortized over five or more years, but with the rapid pace of computer technology, any lifespan over four years is probably unreasonable in practical terms. Except in unusual cases, most software and courseware have an even shorter lifespan—typically two or three years. Even relatively stable curriculum such as equipment, sales, safety, or maintenance training will need to be changed due to changes in organizational or government policies/procedures, or training philosophies. This means that, in most cases, CBT systems that cannot be shown to reach a breakeven point earlier than two or three years are not likely to be cost effective.

In addition to these three major assumptions that affect cost/benefit analyses, there are three basic variables that will affect CBT costs: type of system, type of CBT, and instructional sophistication. The major *types of CBT systems* were discussed in Chapter 4. Figure 8-7 shows how costs differ between timeshared and standalone systems in terms of number of terminals. With standalone terminals, the cost of each machine is relatively small so entry costs are much lower than with a timesharing system; however, since the cost of each standalone terminal is about the same, buying a lot of terminals quickly gets expensive. Since the terminals for the timesharing system can be simple (since central resources are shared), the cost per terminal is much less than the standalone terminals. Distributed systems would show a cost curve between the timesharing and standalone systems.

For example, suppose a timeshared system costs $40,000 and each terminal costs $1,000. The cost of a one-terminal system is $40,000 + $1,000 = $41,000. The cost of a ten-terminal system would be $40,000 + $10,000 = $50,000, and the cost of a twenty-terminal system would be $40,000 + $20,000 = $60,000. Now consider a standalone system in which complete terminals cost $5,000. A one-terminal system is $5,000; a ten-terminal system would cost $50,000; and a twenty-terminal system would be $100,000. Thus, under ten terminals, the standalone system is less expensive; over ten terminals, the timesharing system is more cost effective.

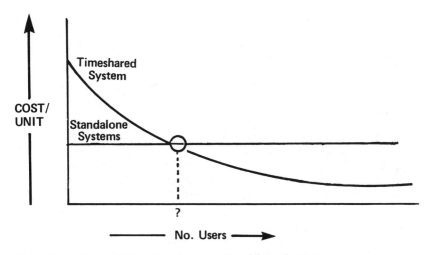

Figure 8-7   Costs of Timeshared versus Standalone Systems

The *type of CBT* involved (see Chapter 2) affects the hardware, software, and courseware development costs. For example, CAT and CMI do not generally require sophisticated display capabilities and involve fewer terminals to the extent that offline testing or training materials are used. On the other hand, CAI and CAL require terminals with full capabilities and involve significant courseware development efforts. As Figure 8-8 shows, system costs are generally lowest for CAT and highest for CAL, primarily due to the hardware and development costs. There is considerable overlap, however. As the figure shows, certain types of CAT (e.g., adaptive testing) might be more expensive than the simpler forms of CAL.

Instructional sophistication refers to the complexity of the programming and instructional strategies associated with the software and courseware. For example, CAI drills can be based on very simple linear logic in which items are randomly generated and a fixed number of tries is given, or based on more complex branching logic in which mistakes lead to specific types of remedial items. Similarly CAT, CMI, or CAL can involve relatively simple or quite complex logics that account for variations in development costs.

The degree of instructional sophistication is also a function of the nature of interaction involved. The simplest kind of interaction involves single key presses from a keyboard/keypad and output on a monochrome, alphanumeric display. The use of more complex input modes (e.g., touch panels, joysticks, graphic tablets) and output capabilities (e.g., color, graphics, audio, video) increases hardware, software, and courseware development costs. Speech input/output adds further costs. Thus, the costs of CBT increases with degree of CBT sophistication, as depicted in Figure 8-9.

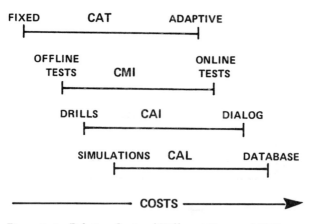

Figure 8-8   Relative Costs of Different Types of CBT

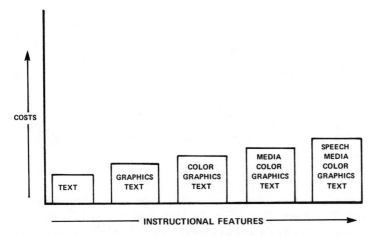

Figure 8-9   Effects of Instructional Sophistication on Costs

CASE STUDY: PRODUCT TRAINING AT ACME MACHINE COMPANY

Acme Machine Company is an industrial supplier of small motors that are used by other manufacturers to build a large variety of products. Because of the large number of different models of motors that Acme makes (more than 200), product training for new employees and new product training for all employees is a significant problem. Employees must understand how the features of each model fit certain customer needs and customer applications in order to make sales. Since the small motor business is highly competitive, having knowledgeable salespersons is an important business advantage.

The current training system involves the use of product manuals. Microfiche is used at the order desks to look up model numbers and prices. Orders are sent in by mail or phoned in if urgent. Acme has about 300 salespersons who work in 100 offices across the United States. Almost all orders are taken via phone by the salespersons at their desks. Lack of good product knowledge slows down the ordering process and essentially limits the number of orders which can be made.

The manager of training for Acme thinks that CBT might be a good way of improving product training for Acme salespersons. All product training could be done by terminals located in the workplace. Furthermore, the same system could be used for order entry and tracking instead of the manual system currently used. The training manager enlists the support of the data-processing manager since such a system will clearly involve this department.

To test out the idea, the training manager arranges a small pilot project in which a prototype CBT system for product knowledge is tried out. New salespersons trained via the prototype CBT system are able to consistently make more orders in comparison with the old system. Based on the pilot test data, the training manager estimates that a full-scale implementation of the system would allow each salesperson to make an average of four extra orders per day. Since the average value of each order to the company is $25, the value of these additional orders is:

$$4 \times \$25 \times 220 \text{ days/year} = \$22,000/\text{year}.$$

Since there are 300 salespersons in the company, the total value of the increased orders is:

$$\$22,000 \times 300 = \$6,600,000 \text{ per year}.$$

In order to produce these results, each salesperson must have a terminal on his or her desk. The terminal must have high resolution graphics to display product illustrations and a keyboard to enter orders. To allow orders to be processed and quick revisions to prices and product information, centralized databases are needed. To avoid the reliability problems of a timeshared system, standalone terminals are desired. Thus, a distributed system that allows downloading of sales orders and uploading of product information is the desired configuration.

Each terminal will cost about $4,000 plus $1,000 for a printer to be located in each office; a total of ($4,000 × 300) + ($1,000 × 100) = $1.3 million will be required for remote equipment. Another $500,000 will be required for the central system processor, system software, and all telecommunications equipment. Thus, $1.8 million is required for the initial hardware and software acquisition. In addition, there will be annual maintenance and operating costs of approximately $200,000 per year, including telecommunications charges.

These figures do not include the costs of the courseware needed for CBT. Approximately fifty hours of product training are needed. Because this is highly technical and graphic material, it will cost about $10,000 per hour to develop. The fifty hours of courseware will require $500,000. It is estimated that this courseware will have to be revised completely every two years; the annual revision cost is $250,000. In addition to these courseware costs, the software needed to make the system work (both for CBT and order processing) is estimated to cost $150,000 to develop, with annual revision costs of $50,000. So the initial development costs of the courseware and software are $650,000 with annual revision/maintenance costs of $300,000.

In total, the major costs associated with the CBT system are $1.8 million + $650,000 = $2.45 million for initial hardware, software, and courseware, plus $200,000 + $300,000 = $500,000 per year in operational costs. Other costs for facilities, management, and so on are included in the budgets of the training or data processing departments.

The total start-up costs for the first year are $2.45 million, plus $500,000, or approximately $3 million. Since the anticipated value of the system in terms of increased sales is over $6 million per year, the system has better than a 2:1 return on investment. Furthermore, the system would pay for itself within the first six months. The cost justification for CBT seems quite robust.

There are many additional benefits that have not been quantified. Because this system is an embedded training application, it will be possible to capture job performance data and relate it to changes in the CBT courseware and training program. In addition, all orders can be processed within twenty-four hours, and the status of any order can be displayed for a customer inquiry. Both of these capabilities will undoubtedly improve customer satisfaction with Acme. Furthermore, the system can also be used for electronic mail between offices, reducing the costs of and time delays associated with mail correspondence.

This case study raises the problem of "tolerable" costs (Seidel 1980). Although CBT promises to save Acme $6 million per year, $3 million must be spent to establish the system, plus $500,000 each year for operational costs. If Acme cannot raise the money needed for implementation of the system, it does not matter how great the potential savings are. Sometimes the start-up or ongoing costs of a CBT system are greater than an organization can afford. Under these circumstances, the scope of the CBT effort must be scaled down by selecting a less expensive type of CBT (e.g., CAT/CMI instead of CAI/CAL) or simply starting with a smaller effort.

As you know from the previous chapter, there are many implementation and management factors that could turn this case study into a successful or unsuccessful CBT application. Good evaluation can also significantly affect the success of a CBT project. In this case study, we saw the use of a pilot study and prototype system to try out the idea. Such a pilot test should identify the critical system (hardware, software, courseware, humanware) parameters that must be taken into account in the full-scale implementation. Furthermore, the pilot study identified the important benefit of CBT (increased orders) that could be used to justify the system. If this benefit had not been identified, it is unlikely that the high costs of the CBT system would be perceived as acceptable. Finally, the availability of job performance data will allow the training manager to show the direct effects of training on job productivity as well as making meaningful changes to the training program.

9

The Limits and
Potential of CBT

This final chapter discusses the current limits and future potentials of CBT. It tries to present a balanced view of the pros and cons of computer use in training.

TRAINING NEEDS AND PROBLEMS

Before specifically examining the limits and potential of CBT, let's consider how CBT relates to a set of typical training needs and problems found in most organizations.

Training Does Not Meet Job Needs

This represents one of the most common failings of training programs. No matter how good the training materials or the instructional delivery (computer or otherwise), if the right skills or knowledge are not taught, training will produce little positive effect on job performance. For example, suppose a sales training program focuses almost entirely on selling techniques with minimum attention to product knowledge; however, it turns out that many salespersons are seriously deficient in their product knowledge which prevents them from making their sales quotas. No matter how effective the existing sales training program is, it cannot help the sales force improve until it also addresses product knowledge. As another example, consider a training course for maintenance technicians that is based on a "cookbook" approach to troubleshooting, stressing the use of manuals and automated test equipment over understanding basic theory. Job performance data suggests that technicians trained by this course are able to deal with the most common and frequently occurring problems, but almost always have difficulty with the more difficult and unusual problems. The kind of knowledge required to deal with such "tough nut" troubleshooting is not part of the training program.

Probably more common than gross oversight in training programs is the presence of a lot of irrelevant and out-of-date material. Training programs often grow like topsy, with new materials simply being added to the existing materials with no integration or synthesis. Pruning irrelevant or out-of-date information is a task that seems to happen infrequently in most training programs. (It is much more common to simply create a new training program.) The need to keep changing training programs to prevent obsolescence and irrelevance is the reason why training development must be looked upon as an iterative activity.[1]

The tools that prevent these problems are needs analysis and job/task analysis. By carefully studying the desired goals of the training and the performance requirements of the job or task, it is possible to specify what skills and knowledge should be taught and in what manner. Instead of having subject matter experts define the topics and content of a training course, the content should be determined on the basis of instructional objectives derived from the skills and knowledge required to do the job. This approach forms the foundation for all ISD activities.

Without the use of proper analysis techniques in the development of a course, CBT is unlikely to have any significant effect on job performance. If the training is irrelevant or obsolete, computers cannot change this, but computers can play a role in reducing the problem. To the extent that needs assessment and job/task analysis procedures are automated, they may be done with less effort and time. In cases where computers are used to deliver instruction (i.e., CAI, CAL, simulators), the possibility for quick and relatively easy revision of training materials exists. Changes can be made to the central database and the revised materials made available to all users immediately.[2] Finally, jobs that involve interaction with computer systems are much more likely to involve well-defined skills and knowledge and be relatively easy to analyze.

Still, the solution to the problem of irrelevant training lies primarily in the use of proper ISD procedures, not the computer. In fact, in many cases it is the use of ISD methods in the context of implementing CBT that really deserves the credit for resulting improvements in training efficiency or effectiveness.

[1] A pretty good analogy can be made between training and farming in terms of the regular seasonal cycles of tilling, fertilizing, sowing, spraying, and harvesting versus the repeated activities of analysis, design, development, implementation, and evaluation. One should not conclude from this metaphor, however, that trainers are misguided farmers.

[2] Assuming a distributed or timeshared network. The problem of updating courseware/software for standalone terminals with no communications capabilities is basically the same as for print or other offline media.

Training Is Too Long or Too Expensive

These two problems are often interrelated since training duration usually affects training expenditures in terms of student or instructor salaries, or the amount of equipment or facilities required. Clearly, the problem of training irrelevance just discussed could be a factor affecting training time and costs. Training programs may be unduly expensive due to unnecessary content or activities; however, the major factor influencing the duration of training programs is the need to teach classes at the level of the slowest learners. This is the reason why any type of individualized instruction (i.e., CMI, CAI, CAL, simulators) can reliably produce decreases of 30 to 40 percent in the amount of total training time required.

As far as training expenditures are concerned, it is frequently the case that the majority of costs for training are not direct instructional costs but secondary expenses associated with travel, facilities, or equipment operation and management/administration. Thus, anything that reduces these secondary costs is likely to have a significant impact on overall training expenses. Distributed computer systems capable of delivering decentralized training can dramatically cut travel costs and the amount of training facilities needed. The use of simulation and simulators to reduce the costs of actual equipment in training has been discussed in previous chapters. The use of computers for training management and administration tasks has also been discussed.

While CBT has reduced costs by decreasing the number of training staff needed in some applications, this is not a typical outcome. For example, when CBT is implemented, it is almost always the case that instructors' roles change significantly but rarely that they are no longer needed. Instructors may spend their time tutoring, managing, or developing rather than teaching in the traditional sense. CBT sometimes allows instructors to handle a larger number of students without any negative effects, or allows instructors to be replaced by less experienced (and less expensive) assistants, but they are not to be eliminated (e.g., Van Matre et al. 1981). Of course, many existing training staff may lack the appropriate skills to work in a CBT setting and need retraining or replacement.

Another major factor affecting training time and expense is the instructional management system. The scheduling of students and training resources (i.e., instructors, equipment, facilities) will affect the amount of time required for training and costs. For example, if completion of training requires use of a simulator or training media (i.e., video, slide/tapes), scheduling these resources efficiently via CMI will likely affect training durations. In many training systems, students are expected to complete "preschool" courses on their own before attending a training center. By using CAT in the field to determine when students have mastered the preschool materials, it is possible to ensure that all students have essentially the same level of preparation, thereby allowing training to be shorter and to proceed more quickly.

Training Is Not Effective

Sometimes the concern is not with the efficiency of the training but its effectiveness in terms of producing the desired job performance. There are certain types of training (e.g., aircrew, medical, nuclear) where the consequences of inadequate training can be very serious in terms of loss of life. In other areas, inadequate training may result in lost revenue (e.g., sales, management, customer service) or lost production capacity (e.g., equipment operation, supervision).

There are many causes of ineffective training. A common one is that it does not meet job needs as already discussed. A second common cause is lack of adequate feedback and practice during learning. In classroom training, it is not unusual for a student to get feedback and practice only once or twice in a course when tests are given. Worse yet, the kind of practice exercises provided are often not very meaningful. For example, sales or management trainees are given paper and pencil tests rather than actual role-playing exercises. Even in cases where "hands-on" practice is available, it typically provides only a very limited sample of the kind of experiences that will be found on the job. There are only a small number of training areas where students usually get a reasonable degree of realistic practice during training (e.g., aircrew training, emergency services).

As has been discussed considerably in this book, CBT can have a major impact on improving training effectiveness because it can provide a very high level of feedback and practice. The feedback ensures that students understand what they are learning; the practice increases the skill levels and improves retention. While all types of CBT can increase the degree of feedback and practice in a training program, CAI, CAL, and simulators are particularly important in this respect. Simulations can provide the kind of realistic practice needed by students. This could be practice in equipment operation or maintenance, making management or marketing decisions, dealing with customers or employees, and so on.

A third major cause of ineffective training is poor teaching. This includes the use of inappropriate instructional strategies, the failure to motivate students or focus their attention on the learning tasks, and lack of creativity or enthusiasm. All of these factors can result in training courses that are perceived as boring and a waste of time by students. The extent to which students actively participate in learning activities is usually a significant indicator of how effective training will be. Active participation means that the student is getting practice and feedback during learning.

Clearly, CBT has some inherent advantages in terms of producing more effective teaching. These include the capability to be highly interactive, the capability to be visually stimulating (through the use of color, graphics, dynamic displays), and the existence of a large number of relatively well-defined instructional strategies (as discussed in Chapters 2 and 5). CBT can easily produce ineffective training, however. It is possible to develop lessons with minimal or trivial interaction and to use an inappropriate strategy (e.g., a CAI tutorial where a CAL simulation is needed). And it is certainly possible to develop boring and unimaginative CBT courseware. If an instructional developer lacks interest and enthusiasm for the subject, this will show in the resulting training materials regardless of what delivery system is involved.

So CBT is not likely to improve the effectiveness of teaching if the necessary enthusiasm, creativity, and understanding of the subject matter are lacking. CBT can help to minimize one important aspect which affects teaching effectiveness: variability. It is well accepted that one of the great drawbacks of conventional classroom instruction is the high degree of variability in outcomes due to different instructors (and even the same instructors at different times). The identical set of training materials can be used by one instructor with good results whereas another instructor may do poorly. Once CBT courseware is adequately tested and "tuned," its effects are generally reliable. If the courseware is effective, it will be consistently effective across all students (with allowances for individual differences, which are discussed in the next section). This is one of the major rationales for putting a lot of instructional development effort into CBT courseware; it should represent the best possible training. CBT can be looked at as a means of consistently replicating the best instructional resources of an organization.

Training Does Not Meet Individual Needs

Many training problems are created because training courses or programs are not responsive to individual needs. The most common problem is that the materials or instruction are at the wrong level of difficulty for an individual. In most training courses, a high level of heterogeneity is normal.[3] This means that there will be a wide variation in the educational backgrounds and work experiences of the students. Given this fact, it is almost ludicrous to use classroom/lecture instruction in most training settings. Yet classroom/lecture instruction dominates training because it is relatively inexpensive, involves minimal preparation effort, and is administratively simple in terms of scheduling and organization. It represents a compromise between something that is easy to do and something that works.

Under most circumstances, CBT can provide training that meets individual needs. This includes the rate of learning (i.e., self-paced) and what is learned. Being able to skip material that is already understood or to spend a lot of time on new topics is the primary way in which CBT allows individualized instruction. Some CAI systems (such as TICCIT) allow students to develop

---

[3]This is in contrast to public education (at least up to the end of high school) where students at any given age will have relatively similar entry level skills—although socio-economic status affects this significantly.

their own instructional strategies and adjust the level of difficulty of the material. In most simulations and simulators, students can set parameters affecting the complexity of the underlying model. In some CMI systems, students have a choice of alternate learning activities or media. Adaptive testing (discussed in Chapter 2) allows tests to be uniquely tailored to each student.

From a humanistic perspective, individuals expect training to improve their self-worth and self-esteem in terms of newly acquired skills or knowledge. Without adequate feedback on their learning progress, it is difficult for individuals to derive any satisfaction from training activities. One of the great ironies of CBT is that it can be much more satisfying (i.e., more humanistic) than most training programs involving human instructors by virtue of the high degree of feedback and interaction involved. This is amply shown by the consistently positive attitudes that students show toward the use of CBT.

Obviously, CBT can address individual needs in ways that classroom instruction cannot; however, it is more expensive, takes longer to prepare, and is more administratively complex. It also tends to be more efficient and effective, as we saw in the previous chapter. For organizations that genuinely care about improving the quality of training, particularly in terms of meeting individual needs, CBT seems to be a clear-cut choice.

There are many ways, however, in which the level of individualization possible with current CBT systems is inadequate. We cannot match differences in learning styles very well, nor are current systems able to diagnose learning problems in any sophisticated fashion. Research is being conducted on intelligent tutoring systems that will change this situation considerably (discussed later in this chapter). While the current CBT capabilities do not begin to touch the capabilities of a good instructor in meeting the needs of a student, they are able to provide much more individualization than most students now receive in the context of classroom training.

Training Is Not Flexible Enough

A constant complaint voiced by many managers and students is that training programs are not flexible enough in terms of when, where, or how they are offered. Training classes are normally offered at fixed times in specific locations and in a single form. The workplace, however, demands continuous training activities, preferably at or close to the job site, and in different forms to meet the varying needs of different groups or individuals. In many cases, employees must wait some period of time before they can take training necessary to begin a job or receive a promotion. There are many jobs where it is not only expensive but impractical to send someone from the field to a training center. Consider, for example, a sailor on duty at sea, an oil company employee in a remote drilling location, or a busy executive who travels constantly. Clearly, CBT can minimize this problem by providing training "on demand" (i.e., whenever and wherever needed).

As far as form is concerned, different levels or kinds of employees often require different presentations of the same material. For example, skills and knowledge associated with implementing an automated office system will be different for a word-processing supervisor, director of administration, or a systems analyst in the data-processing division, even though the same content is involved. Each person has a different perspective and training need as a consequence of his or her job function. In conventional classroom instruction, however, the tendency is to try and meet all needs with the same course (or perhaps develop three separate courses). With CBT, it is possible to present the same content in different ways to suit the needs of different levels or types of employees. Alternatively, users can be provided with powerful software interfaces that allow them to tailor presentations to their own needs.

Another problem in certain training systems is large fluctuations in student loads, which cause staffing or scheduling difficulties. Most traditional training programs are designed around an average class size or an average yearly student load. Too many or too few students cannot be easily accommodated since this means adding or dropping resources (i.e., instructors, facilities, etc.). Often a new product or piece of equipment will involve a large number of people to be trained over a short time, followed by a small number of people to be trained over a long time period (i.e., the life of the product or equipment). CBT can provide a great deal of flexibility in handling such load fluctuations since it is primarily a matter of more or fewer terminals. Once a course is available on the system, it can be used daily by hundreds of students or once a year by one student.

Despite the capabilities of CBT to provide certain kinds of flexibility, few current systems offer the level of flexibility possible with a human instructor or manager. A good instructor can change delivery strategies in the middle of a lecture based on feedback from students. Instructors and print media can be used in virtually any training domain and in any physical environment. Before CBT can match the full flexibility possible with conventional training methods (i.e., lecture and print), a number of major developments are needed. These developments are discussed later in this chapter.

SOME CURRENT LIMITATIONS OF CBT

As will have become clear in the previous section, CBT will not necessarily be the answer to all training problems. Even in those cases where CBT has significant potential, there are often drawbacks. In addition, CBT introduces some special considerations that can negatively affect training programs. Such considerations include reliability, usability, courseware development, hardware availability, transportability/compatibility, and learning/teaching strategies.

Reliability

Reliability is a major factor affecting the success of a CBT system. In many systems, reliability is sufficiently poor that use of the system is discouraged. This may be hardware, software, or courseware reliability. Acceptable levels of reliability are only achieved through deliberate measures: redundant hardware components, fault tolerant system design, thorough testing and debugging of software and courseware, proper preventive maintenance, and adequate training of operating personnel. Furthermore, it is important to be able to minimize problems when they do occur by means of adequate backup and recovery measures. Today, there is no excuse for unreliable CBT systems other than inexperience or incompetence on the part of system or project managers. Online training systems should be as reliable as online reservation, banking, or electronic mail systems.

Usability

A great deal of effort is now being expended by computer manufacturers to make their systems more usable. This means improving the hardware and software interfaces so that systems are easier and simpler to use. For example, signing-on should only require turning on a terminal and typing in a user name or ID. Getting a print of the screen should be possible by pressing a button. Terminals should be equipped with a variety of different input modes (e.g., touch, cursor control, function keys). Most importantly, systems should be designed to minimize the possibility of errors by users. For example, the original model of a well known microcomputer had the reset key located just above the return key making it easy for the user to inadvertently destroy the active program. By using menus to control branching in a program rather than some kind of control language, the memory load on the user is decreased and the possibility of syntax errors eliminated.

As an example of how terminals can be designed to be more usable, Figure 9-1 illustrates the accessory module found at the rear of the Bell & Howell microcomputer. This module features jacks for headphones and external speakers, adjustable audio volume, external jacks for paddles or joysticks, video output jacks (for use with multiple monitors), multiple power outlets (for external peripherals such as video players or printers), a cover lock/power interlock (which turns off power automatically when the cover is opened), and a built-in carrying handle. While none of these features by themselves is very critical, the presence of all of them together makes the terminal much more versatile and very convenient to use for multimedia interactive training.

A broad spectrum of usability considerations are covered under the rubric of human factors (also called ergonomics). Much work has been done in

Figure 9-1 Accessory Module of Bell & Howell Microcomputer (Courtesy, Bell & Howell Corp.)

the past few years to improve both hardware and software. Some of this work as it applies to CBT is reviewed by Kearsley and Hillelsohn (1982). Despite a lot of progress, many CBT systems are still not easy to use. The hardware or software may be cumbersome (e.g., loading/unloading diskettes, finding and loading programs or data files). The most natural ways of interacting with a computer, namely speech and language, are still not feasible for widespread use (see discussion in next section).

Courseware Development

The problems associated with courseware development have already been discussed in detail in Chapter 5. They need to be mentioned again here since they represent major limitations to the use of CBT. Although the process of developing courseware is not really much more laborious than developing a textbook, it requires a set of skills not widely available. Thus, while many people have the requisite writing skills (in addition to subject matter expertise) to create a text, few have the necessary combination of instructional design and programming skills needed to develop CBT. This is likely to change as more individuals become "computer literate" and gain experience with CBT. In addition, the emergence of powerful authoring systems minimizes the amount of instructional and programming background required.

Difficulty in finding CBT designers/developers is one aspect of the problem; the length of time required to develop effective CBT materials is another. Even with experienced staff, courseware can often take four to six months for initial development and many more months for proper "tuning" (i.e., formative evaluation). In many business and industrial settings, such development times are not considered very acceptable or responsive to operational needs. In a typical development project, most of the time is spent in doing the necessary analysis and design activities, i.e., identifying tasks, objectives, lesson specifications. ISD procedures need to be streamlined in order to fit within the time constraints and budgets of most training settings.[4] Authoring systems which automate various ISD and production steps can help significantly (e.g., Brecke and Blaiwes 1981; O'Neal and O'Neal 1979).

Hardware Availability

For CBT to be a practical reality, sufficient terminals must be available wherever and whenever needed. This means not only in training centers or job settings, but all of the other locations where people are likely to study: homes, libraries, in airplanes, at the beach, and so on. In order to make terminals and CBT this ubiquitous, there are a number of conditions that must be met: affordability, portability, and networking. In order to have terminals literally everywhere, they must become so inexpensive that cost becomes essentially unimportant. With some terminals in the $100 to $300 price range we are close to meeting this criterion today; however, the necessary peripherals such as printers, disk drives, and communications modems must also be equally inexpensive (a condition not true at present).

Terminals must be portable. Until terminals can be carried around easily and are self-contained (like books), electronic learning will be restricted to certain environments (e.g., training centers). A great deal of studying is done in informal settings which current terminals (even compact microcomputers) are not suitable for. As we shall discuss shortly, progress in hand-held computers promises to change this situation within a few years.

Finally, many more communication and information networks will be needed to support large-scale terminal usage (CBT or otherwise). At present, only about a few dozen public networks exist (these are described later).[5] While these networks all utilize a common communications interface (RS–232), making it possible for the same terminal to access all of them, it is often confusing and cumbersome. Accessing different communication networks should be as simple as changing channels on a radio or TV.

[4]For an example, see Bunderson et al. (1981) in which the concept of "work models" is proposed to streamline task analysis in the context of interactive videodisc.

[5]There are, however, hundreds of private networks: most large organizations have their own internal data networks.

Transportability/Compatibility

Lack of transportability and incompatibility of software and courseware across different systems has been one of the major limitations of CBT since the field's inception. Relative to the amount of courseware and software developed, very little has been shared or used on multiple systems. There are many reasons for this beyond the obvious fact that most major CBT systems (e.g., PLATO, IIS, TICCIT, etc.) are software incompatible. One major factor has been the lack of outstanding software: only a handful of programs have been sufficiently valuable to be widely available on many different machines.[6] There is a strong tendency in the software world to "reinvent the wheel," i.e., create a program from scratch instead of modifying an existing program that might be suitable. In the training domain, there is a similar tendency not to use courseware developed elsewhere. In many cases this is because it does not match the philosophy or style of an organization (even though the content may be appropriate).

Despite these objections, there are many cases where courseware would be shared within an organization or across an industry if it could be transported easily from one system to another. Communications networks promise to make this possible. Even though two systems may be physically incompatible, it may be possible to transfer courseware from another system via communications. Since the program is being executed by the host system, the communicating terminal simply has to be able to properly display the transmissions.

As a consequence of the lack of common standards within the computer industry and especially CBT, it is particularly important to anticipate and allow for future growth during system design or selection. Since you may effectively be locked into a single type of CBT system for many years, it is important to be sure that the system selected will be able to expand in any direction that your CBT activities could take.

Learning/Teaching Strategies

One of the important theoretical contributions that CBT has made to the field of instruction is explicit identification of the many different kinds of learning and teaching strategies possible. By representing such strategies in the form of programs, they are operationally defined and replicable. Furthermore, since very detailed data can be collected on their effectiveness, it is possible to compare such strategies on an empirical basis. None of these things are really possible in conventional instructional modes.

The capability to make our learning and teaching strategies explicit in this way has made us realize how little we know about effective instructional strat-

---

[6]The "VisiCalc" program (originally developed by Personal Software Inc.) and subsequent imitations is probably the best known example.

egies. Even though CBT has resulted in a great deal of research into such strategies (e.g., O'Neil 1978), there is a tremendous amount we do not understand about how to use computers in training, which limits the utility of CBT. For example, social learning (particularly role modeling) is known to be very important in many training domains, yet it has not really been addressed by CBT. With the advent of interactive videodisc, we may see the development of strategies for role modeling. Similarly, we do not know much about how to trade-off the use of visual and spoken instruction when both capabilities are available. In fact there are literally dozens of significant issues that await further research before we can more effectively utilize computers for training.

FUTURE DEVELOPMENTS IN CBT

Balancing the current limitations of CBT are a number of future developments, some of which will likely affect these limitations. Future developments include interactive videodisc, hand-held computers, intelligent tutoring systems, speech, communications networks, and authoring systems.

Interactive Videodisc

Interactive (computer-controlled) videodisc provides a very important capability for CBT: multimedia presentations (i.e., photographs, video, audio). While randomly accessed multimedia capabilities have been available in some CBT systems for many years, videodisc provides a much more compact, useable, and reliable technology. Videodisc is proving to be particularly significant in two areas of CBT: simulation and interpersonal skills. The capability to design sequences involving photographs and sounds of actual equipment greatly increases the realism of simulation. The capability to show the reactions of people (e.g., employees, customers) to actions taken makes interactive videodisc ideal for management, sales, customer relations, or medical training (see Figure 9–2).

A large number of prototype projects have been completed that demonstrate the potential of videodisc for training (e.g., Kearsley 1981b). At the present time, a great deal of effort is being devoted to the exploration of different design/development strategies (e.g., Bunderson 1980; Kribs 1980; Lipson 1981; Nugent and Stone 1980). The length of time required for mastering (often three to four weeks) and the cost of videodisc players (suitable for interactive use) represent current limitations to the widespread use of videodisc. Schneider and Bennion (1981) and Sigel, Schubin, and Merrill (1980) provide introductions to current videodisc technology.

Videodisc is likely to be an important component of many future CBT systems. There are many ways in which videodisc can be used for CBT. For example, videodisc can be used to provide multimedia databases to be used in training. One of the most advanced applications employing videodisc is Spa-

Figure 9-2   Interactive Videodisc System (Courtesy, WICAT Systems)

tial Data Management Systems (SDMS) in which information is organized visually in hierarchial planes and accessed via a joystick. The user (student) can move across planes and "zoom" in and out to other levels. SDMS provides a very "friendly" interface since there are few errors possible in accessing information. An evaluation of SDMS for basic skills education is described in Hum-RRO (1982).

Hand-held Computers

The emergence of hand-held computers in the early 1980s represents the logical consequence of increased miniaturization of computers due to VLSI (Very Large Scale Integration) circuit technology. The technology underlying calculators, electronic toys, televisions, watches, telephones, and other consumer items has quickly been converging toward the various components needed for hand-held computers.

The first generation of hand-held computers offered for sale featured full keyboards, reasonable amounts of computing power, printer and communication interfaces, all for prices in the $100 to $500 price range (Williams 1981). These commercially available hand-helds all feature very limited single-line displays, however. Hand-helds designed for military applications have multi-line graphics displays (Felling 1980) and we can expect commercially available handhelds to also have full displays within a few years.

The current training applications being explored for hand-held computers are maintenance and product training, particularly as job aids. Hand-helds allow maintenance technicians to receive help and instruction while trouble-shooting and repairing equipment in the field. Hand-helds can be used to provide salespeople with latest information on both their own products and their competitors'. For example, while making a customer visit, a salesperson could enter pertinent information and obtain detailed sales quotes or selling advice.

A basic limiting factor in hand-helds is the size of the display and keyboard (Francis 1982); however, with sufficiently high resolution, displays as small as four or five inches square can be quite functional. By minimizing the use of keyed input, disadvantages due to the smallness of the keyboard can be reduced. The use of speech input/output will ultimately eliminate problems due to display or keyboard size (discussed later).

The impact of hand-helds on making computers more portable and less expensive is likely to be dramatic; they will play an important role in future CBT.

Intelligent Tutoring Systems

One of the most important future development areas in CBT is intelligent tutoring systems (Sleeman and Brown 1982). "Intelligent" refers to programs which are capable of understanding what they are teaching and what the student is/is not learning. Such software is based upon research and techniques developed in the field of Artificial Intelligence.

A number of demonstration programs have been developed that illustrate the power of intelligent tutoring systems. One of the most significant is SOPHIE, a tutor for electronics troubleshooting. Figure 2–8 in Chapter 2 showed a fragment of a dialog between SOPHIE and a student. The dialog is *mixed-initiative*, i.e., either the student or program could initiate a question. The dialog is also conversational—the program understands English in the context of this task domain. Most importantly, notice that the program is able to reason about the student's progress and take appropriate remedial actions when it diagnoses a student misunderstanding. SOPHIE is described in detail in Brown, Burton, and deKleer (1982).

STEAMER (Williams, Hollan, and Stevens 1981) is another intelligent tutoring system developed to teach the operation of steam propulsion plants. The program incorporates a very detailed model of how such plants operate, which allows it to "coach" students during simulations. A number of such tutors have been developed to teach students how to program (e.g., Barr, Beard, and Atkinson 1975; Gentner 1979; Miller 1979).

The structure of intelligent tutoring programs is much different from the CBT software and courseware discussed in this book. Such systems are usually written in a dialect of the LISP programming language and involve building a knowledge representation of the subject matter domain being taught. The program constructs a model of the student's understanding as learning progresses and uses tutoring rules to try and match the student model with its "expert" model of the subject. All instructional interactions and sequences are generated rather than being prespecified. A new generation of very powerful standalone computers that run LISP are being developed for use with intelligent tutoring systems. It seems likely that during the current decade, intelligent tutoring will replace our current "dumb" CBT systems.

Speech

Closely related to intelligent tutoring systems is the use of speech input and output in CBT. The reason for the relationship is that most research and development on speech processing also comes from the field of Artificial Intelligence. In fact, understanding natural language is a problem domain underlying both speech processing and intelligent tutoring systems.

Of the two parts to speech processing, the generation (synthesis) of speech is by far the easier problem than speech recognition. Speech synthesis is important in CBT because it is not always possible to prerecord responses. For example, suppose a simulation involves the use of randomly generated parameters. If speech output is involved, it is necessary to generate novel words or phrases each time the simulation is run. In some cases, speech synthesis eliminates the need to store a large number of responses; however, there is a problem getting good quality synthesized speech (particularly when continuous) and so it has received limited use in CBT. There are some projects that have demonstrated its feasibility, however (e.g., Sanders, Benbassat, and Smith 1976; Martin 1977).

Speech recognition is a more difficult problem since it requires understanding what the person is saying in order to accurately recognize utterances. Under certain conditions (e.g., limited vocabulary, single words or phrases, trained speakers), it is possible to use speech input in current training applications. For example, speech input/output has been successfully demonstrated in ground controller simulators where speech is the usual mode of communication on the job (Grady et al. 1978). It has also been explored in the domain of maintenance training where the student frequently has hands and eyes on equipment but can listen and talk.

There seems little doubt that speech input/output will one day be our major method for interacting with computer systems, just as with other people. This will make computer systems very usable and natural. However, it appears that it will take a number of years before our understanding of speech input is sufficiently far along to make general conversation with computers possible. In the meantime, there are a number of training applications where speech input/output is feasible and can be used effectively.

Communications Networks

Another extremely important development area for CBT is the increasing proliferation of communications networks. At present, only the PLATO system features a large network exclusively for CBT purposes. Two other large educational networks exist: CONDUIT and EDUCOM. Both of these networks exist primarily for exchange of courseware at the college and university level.

A number of large public networks have emerged in recent years to provide information utilities, electronic mail, or information retrieval services. For example, the Source℠ operated by Source Telecomputing Corporation (a subsidiary of *Reader's Digest*) offers access to thousands of programs and databases as well as electronic mail and shopping. The Source can be used by almost any type of terminal and is relatively inexpensive to use (i.e., $10 to $20 per hour). DIALOG is an information retrieval service that provides access to over 150 databases in all major disciplines. Typical costs for searches are in the $10 to $20 range per database. As with the Source, almost any type of terminal can be used.

The significance of such communications networks to CBT is that courseware developed on such systems can be shared broadly. Equally important is the easy availability of hundreds of databases and programs that might be used as part of CBT activities. For example, senior managers might use financial or resource databases to learn economic forecasting and decision making. Engineers could use various analysis routines to study design parameters or construct their own simulation models. Salespeople can construct account profiles and analyze sales prospects while learning about new products or product lines. The number of potential applications is enormous. One of the important benefits of using such computer tools during training is that they tend to be used on the job, usually increasing the employee's productivity.

Current public information networks such as the Source and DIALOG are limited to alphanumeric (i.e., text) data only; however, with the eventual acceptance of videotex in North America (it is already widely used in Europe), information networks will offer full color graphics. This will make their use for CBT even more likely and worthwhile. In fact, it is entirely possible that videotex will eventually provide the medium for widespread dissemination of CBT courseware independent of particular systems.[7]

---

[7]Current videotex developments are described in Sigel (1980) and Tydeman (1982).

Authoring Systems

Although authoring systems have already been discussed a number of times in this book, it is important to point out that considerable progress is being made in their development. For example, work is underway to develop authoring capabilities specifically suited for the creation of simulations (e.g., Montgomery 1982). Authoring systems are also being developed to help create and produce offline text or audiovisual materials (e.g., Braby and Kincaid 1981) as well as manage the instructional development process (e.g., O'Neal and O'Neal 1979). Thus, we are seeing a large variety of tools being developed to make authoring easier and faster.

Authoring systems may also help reduce the problems associated with courseware transportability. It is possible to develop an authoring system in which the program is represented in the form of a generalized design language. This design language can be automatically translated into any specified author or programming language for a particular CBT system or machine. Thus, courseware is not directly authored for any specific system but can be produced to run on any system desired (e.g., Schuyler 1976).

Development of authoring systems in CBT is quite consistent with the general trends in the computer world toward the creation of high-level programming environments in which programs are created either by English-like statements or by assembling already existing building blocks.[8] Both approaches essentially eliminate the need for the user to learn a formal programming language, although procedural thinking is still necessary.

SUMMING UP

In this final chapter, the relationship of CBT to common training problems, current limitations of CBT, and future developments in CBT have been discussed. It was emphasized that CBT will not automatically solve all training problems. In fact, some training problems, such as training being irrelevant to job needs, are not likely to be affected by CBT. On the other hand, CBT has the potential to significantly affect many training problems, such as training being too long or expensive, not effective, or not meeting individual needs.

Current CBT systems can present a number of limitations that reduce their potential to improve training. Systems are often not reliable enough, hardware or software is not very usable, courseware development is too lengthy or expensive, the amount or type of hardware (i.e., terminals) needed is not available, software and courseware is not transportable or compatible, and the appropriate learning/teaching strategies are not known or used. There are many training applications where none of these limitations will apply; there are some where they prevent CBT from being successful.

[8]The "tool-kits" provided in Smalltalk systems are the best available examples of this building block approach (e.g., Tesler 1981).

A number of future developments promise to alter the nature of CBT significantly. This includes interactive videodisc, hand-held computers, intelligent tutoring systems, speech input/output, communications networks, and authoring systems. Figure 9–3 indicates how these developments will likely impact the current limitations.

None of these developments is likely to have any effect on the reliability of CBT systems since this is largely a factor of good system design, testing, and management. The presence of hand-helds, intelligent tutors, speech input/output, and communications networks are all likely to make CBT more usable. Advances in networks and authoring systems are likely to reduce the costs of courseware development and improve the transportability/compatibility of CBT materials. Hand-helds will undoubtedly eliminate problems associated with hardware availability (due to low cost and portability). Finally, videodisc, intelligent tutors, and speech input/output are likely to broaden the range of CBT learning/teaching strategies possible. Figure 9–3 suggests that we can expect to see CBT systems become a lot more usable, courseware and hardware more available, and a wider range of strategies in use. It also suggests that reliability may continue to remain a problem area for CBT systems (although, ironically, one well within the state of the art to solve).

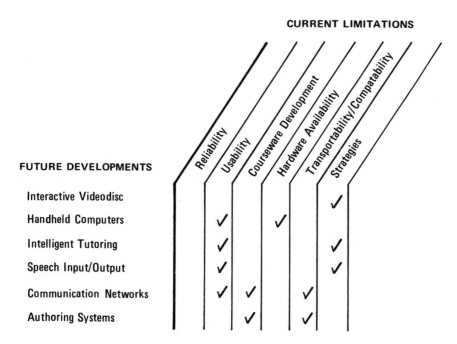

Figure 9-3   Comparison of Current Limitations and Future Developments in CBT

As computers become ever more ubiquitous in workplaces, homes, and equipment, their use for instruction will become common place. Interactive and individualized instruction is likely to become accepted as the norm, not as a special case. Authoring of courseware is likely to be done by single individuals (the textbook model) as well as by large multidisciplinary teams (the television/film model). A large repertoire of learning/teaching strategies will be used, ranging from drills and tutorials to simulations and games. Students will more often be taught how to use the computer than be taught by it.

During the present decade, we can expect to see CBT increase substantially in the scope and nature of applications. Hopefully, this book has provided some insight into the current CBT practices and uses which will provide the foundation for these future efforts.

Appendix:
Further Resources

This Appendix provides some guidance in terms of access to further CBT resources. This includes professional societies, publications, and commercial vendors. Note that addresses and phone numbers are likely to change.

PROFESSIONAL SOCIETIES

There are a number of major professional societies that are active in instructional computing, although not necessarily CBT. They hold conferences, publish journals or newsletters, and represent one of the best sources of help for CBT information.

- Association for the Development of Computer Based Instructional Systems (ADCIS)

  Gordon Hayes, Executive Secretary
  158 Bond Hall
  Western Washington University
  Bellingham, WA 98225
  (206) 676-2860

  ADCIS holds annual conferences, has a special interest group in CBT, publishes a newsletter, and the *Journal of Computer Based Instruction*.

- Association for Educational Data Systems (AEDS)

  1201 16th Street, NW
  Washington, DC 20036

AEDS holds annual conferences and publishes the AEDS *Monitor* and *AEDS Journal.*

■ Society of Applied Learning Technology (SALT)

> 50 Culpeper Street
> Warrenton, VA 22186
> (703) 347-0055

SALT holds numerous conferences and workshops on topics relevant to CBT and sponsors the *Journal Educational Technology Systems.*

■ Association for Educational Communications and Technology (AECT)

> 1126 16th Street, NW
> Washington, DC 20036
> (202) 466-4780

AECT holds annual conferences and publishes *Educational Communications Technology Journal, Journal of Instructional Development,* and *Instructional Innovator.*

■ National Society for Performance and Instruction (NSPI)

> 1126 16th Street, NW
> Suite 315
> Washington, DC 20036
> (202) 861-0777

NSPI holds annual conferences and publishes the *Performance & Instruction Journal.*

■ Association for Computing Machinery Special Interest Group on Computer Uses in Education (ACM/SIGCUE)

> ACM
> 11 West 42nd Street
> New York, NY 10036

ACM/SIGCUE sponsors sessions at annual ACM conferences and publishes the *SIGCUE Bulletin.*

PUBLICATIONS

In addition to the publications of the professional societies just described, the following periodicals feature articles relevant to CBT:

■ *Educational Technology*
140 Sylvan Avenue
Englewood Cliffs, NJ 07632

■ *T.H.E. (Technological Horizons in Education) Journal*
Box 992
Acton, MA 01720

- *Training and Development Journal*
  American Society for Training and Development (ASTD)
  600 Maryland Avenue, SW
  Suite 305
  Washington, DC 20024

- *Training*
  731 Hennepin Avenue
  Minneapolis, MN 55403

- *Electronic Learning*
  902 Sylvan Avenue
  Englewood Cliffs, NJ 07632

- *Computers & Education*
  Pergamon Press
  Maxwell House
  Fairview Park
  Elmsford, NY 10523

COMMERCIAL VENDORS

The following companies market CBT systems:

- Control Data Corporation (PLATO)
  PLATO Marketing HQAO20
  Box 0
  Minneapolis, MN 55440

- IBM Corporation (IIAS/IIPS)
  1133 Westchester Avenue
  White Plains, NY 10604

- McDonnell Douglas Astronautics Co. (AIS)
  Computer Based Training Systems Group
  700 Broadway, Suite 617
  Denver, CO 80203

- Hazeltine Corp. (TICCIT)
  7680 Old Springhouse Road
  McLean, VA 22102

- Boeing Computer Services Company (Scholar/Teach 3)
  Education & Training Division
  Box 24346
  Seattle, WA 98124

- Honeywell Information Systems, Inc. (CAN/8, NATAL)
  200 Smith Street. MS 440
  Waltham, MA 02154

- Digital Equipment Corp. (GIGI)
  Education Computer Systems
  129 Parker Street, PK3-2/M94
  Maynard, MA 01754

- Bell & Howell (PASS)
  AV Products Division
  7100 N. McCormick Road
  Chicago, IL 60645

- WICAT Systems (WISE)
  Box 539
  1875 South State Street
  Orem, UT 84057

- Primarius Inc.
  4186J Sorrento Valley Blvd.
  San Diego, CA 92121

- KEE Inc.
  8994 Seminole Blvd.
  Seminole, FL 33540

- Regency Systems Inc.
  Box 3590
  1610 Interstate Drive
  Champaign, IL 61820

- Goal Systems International (Phoenix)
  Box 29481
  Columbus, OH 43229

- Global Information Systems Technology (Simpler)
  201 West Springfield
  Suite 410
  Champaign, IL 61820

In addition, the following companies provide CBT consulting services:

- Instructional Communications, Inc. (ICOM)
  Box 6312
  Cherry Creek Station
  Denver, CO 80206
  (301) 321-7407

- Courseware Applications, Inc. (CAPP)
  1489 Fairmount Avenue
  St. Paul, MN 55105
  (612) 690-3834

- Computer Based Education Systems
  13 Acorn Drive
  Hawthorn Woods, Il 60047
  (312) 438-8271

- Systems in Education, Ltd.
  3485 West 11th Avenue
  Vancouver, B.C.
  (604) 731-3937

- InterCom
  302 East John Street
  Champaign, IL 61820
  (217) 384-0112

- Design Ware Inc.
  185 Berry Street
  San Francisco, CA
  (415) 546-1866

- HOMECOM, Ltd.
  91 Glencameron Road
  Thornhill, Ontario, Canada
  (416) 223-1652

- HumRRO
  300 North Washington Street
  Alexandria, VA 22314
  (703) 549-3611

Bibliography

Adams, J. A. "On the Evaluation of Training Devices." *Human Factors* 21 (1979): 711–720.

Al-Awar, J.; Chapanis, A.; and Ford, W. R. "Tutorials for the First-Time Computer User." *IEEE Transactions on Professional Communication* 24, no. 1 (March 1981): 30–36.

Alderman, D. L.; Appel, L. R.; and Murphy, R. T. "PLATO and TICCIT: An Evaluation of CAI in the Community College." *Educational Technology* 18, no. 4 (1978): 40–45.

Anderson, R. H. *Selecting and Developing Media for Instruction.* New York: Van Nostrand Reinhold, 1976.

Avner, R. A. "Production of Computer-Based Instructional Materials." In *Issues in Instructional Systems Development*, edited by H. F. O'Neil, Jr. New York: Academic Press, 1979.

Baker, F. B. *Computer-Managed Instruction: Theory and Practice.* Englewood Cliffs, N.J.: Educational Technology Publications, 1978.

Baker, F. B. "Computer-Managed Instruction: A Context for Computer-based Instruction." In *Computer Based Instruction*, edited by H. F. O'Neil. New York: Academic Press, 1981.

Baker, J. C. "Corporate Involvement in CAI." *Educational Technology* (1978): 12–16.

Barr, A.; Beard, M.; and Atkinson, R. C. "A Rationale and Description of a CAI Program to Teach the BASIC Programming Language." *Instructional Science* 4 (1975): 1–31.

Barry, S. T. "A Play within a Play: Using the Computer to Teach about Itself." *T.H.E. Journal* (February 1982): 56–58.

Blake, D. C. I. "Visual Flight Rules (VFR) Control Tower Simulator." *Journal Educational Technology Systems* 7, no. 1 (1979): 79–89.

Bork, A. "Learning through Graphics." In *Computers and Communications*, edited by R. J. Seidel and M. L. Rubin. New York: Academic Press, 1977.

Bork, A. *Learning with Computers*. Bedford, Mass.: Digital Press, 1981.

Boucher, B. G. *Handbook and Catalog for Instructional Media Selection*. Englewood Cliffs, N.J.: Educational Technology Publications, 1973.

Braby, R., and Kincaid, J. P. "Computer Aided Authoring and Editing." *Journal Educational Technology Systems* 10, no. 2 (1981): 109–124.

Branscomb, L. M. "CBT at IBM." *ADCIS SIGCBT Newsletter* 2, no. 3 (January 1980): 1–2.

Branson, R. K. "Implementation Issues in Instructional Systems Development: Three Case Studies." In *Issues in Instructional Systems Development*, edited by H. F. O'Neil. New York: Academic Press, 1979.

Bregar, W. S., and Farley, A. M. "Artificial Intelligence Approaches to CBI." *Journal of Computer Based Instruction* 6, no. 4 (May 1980): 106–114.

Brenner, L. P., and Coe Agee, C. "The Symbiosis of PLATO and Microcomputers." *Educational Technology* (October 1980): 45.

Brecke, F., and Blaiwes, A. "CASDAT: An Innovative Approach to More Efficient ISD." *Journal Educational Technology Systems* 10, no. 3 (1981): 271–283.

Bretz, R. *A Taxonomy of Communication Media*. Englewood Cliffs, N.J.: Educational Technology Publications, 1971.

Brigham, C. R. "Programming Languages." In *Information Technology in Health Education*, edited by E. C. Deland. New York: Plenum Press, 1978.

Brown, J. S., and Burton, R. R. "Diagnostic Models for Procedural Bugs in Basic Mathematical Skills." *Cognitive Science* 2 (1978): 155–191.

Brown, J. S.; Burton, R. R.; and deKleer, J. "Pedagogical, Natural Language and Knowledge Engineering Techniques in SOPHIE I, II, and III." In *Intelligent Authoring Systems*, edited by D. Sleeman and J. S. Brown. New York: Academic Press, 1982.

Buchanan, C. "Results of One Year of Computer Based Instruction at the United Airlines Flight Operations Training Center." *ADCIS Proceedings*. San Diego, Calif., 1979.

Buck, J. A., and Beardsley, P. S. "How CBI Was Cost-Justified in the FAA." *ADCIS Proceedings*. Washington, D.C., 1980.

Buck, J. A.; Bullar, D. R.; and Fagan, T. B. "Requirements Analysis and Feasibility Study of Computer-Based Instruction for the FAA Department of Transportation." *ADCIS Proceedings*. San Diego, Calif., 1979.

Bunderson, C. V. "The Design and Production of Learner Controlled Courseware for the TICCIT System: A Progress Report." *International Journal of Man-Machine Studies* 6 (1974): 479–491.

Bunderson, C. V. "Instructional Strategies for Videodisc Courseware: The McGraw-Hill Disc." *Journal Educational Technology Systems* 8, no. 3 (1980): 207–229.

Bunderson, C. V. "Courseware." In *Computer Based Instruction,* edited by H. F. O'Neil. New York: Academic Press, 1981.

Bunderson, C. V., and Faust, G. W. "Programmed and Computer-Assisted Instruction." In *Seventy-fifth yearbook of the National Society for the Study of Education.* Chicago: University of Chicago Press, 1976.

Bunderson, C. V.; Gibbons, A. S.; Olsen, J. B.; and Kearsley, G. "Work Models: Beyond Instructional Objectives." *Instructional Science* 10 (1981): 1–11.

Burke, R. L. *CAI Sourcebook.* Englewood Cliffs, N.J.: Prentice-Hall, 1982.

Burton, R. R., and Brown, J. S. "Toward a Natural Language Capability for Computer-Assisted Instruction." In *Procedures for Instructional Systems Development,* edited by H. F. O'Neil. New York: Academic Press, 1979.

Butler, F. C. *Instructional Systems Development for Vocational and Technical Training.* Englewood Cliffs, N.J.: Educational Technology Publications, 1972.

Caldwell, R. M. "Guidelines for Developing Basic Skills Instructional Materials for Use with Microcomputer Technology." *Educational Technology* (October 1980): 7–12.

Campbell, D. T., and Stanley, J. C. *Experimental and Quasi-Experimental Designs for Research.* Chicago: Rand McNally, 1963.

Carbonell, J. R. "AI in CAI: An Artificial Intelligence Approach to Computer-Assisted Instruction." *IEEE Transactions on Man-machine Systems* 11 (1970): 190–202.

Carbonell, J. R.; Elkind, J. I.; and Nickerson, R. S. "On the Psychological Importance of Time in a Timesharing System." *Human Factors* 10, no. 2 (1968): 135–142.

Clogston, T. "CBI for a High-Tech Industry." *Instructional Innovator* (September 1980): 22–24.

Collins, A. "Processes in Acquiring Knowledge." In *Schooling and the Acquisition of Knowledge.* edited by R. C. Anderson, R. J. Spiro, and W. E. Montague. Hillsdale, N.J.: Earlbaum Associates, 1977.

Crawford, A. M., and Crawford, K. S. "Simulation of Operational Equipment with a Computer-Based Instructional System: A Low Cost Training Technology." *Human Factors* 20 (1978): 215–224.

Cream, B. W.; Eggemeier, F. T.; and Klein, G. A. "A Strategy for the Development of Training Devices." *Human Factors* 20 (1978): 145–158.

Davis, J. D. "The Navy CMI System: A Brief Overview." *Journal Educational Technology Systems* 6, no. 2 (1978): 143–150.

Davis, R. W. "Approaches to CBI Effectiveness: Activity in the Bell System." *T.H.E. Journal* 8, no. 3 (March 1981): 43–45.

Davis, R. H.; Alexander, L. T.; and Yelon, S. L. *Learning Systems Design.* New York: McGraw-Hill, 1974.

Diem, R. A., and Fairweather, P. G. "An Evaluation of a Computer Assisted Education System in an Untraditional Academic Setting: A County Jail." *AEDS Journal* (Spring 1980): 204–212.

Duc Quy, N., and Covington, J. "The Microcomputer in Industry Training." *T.H.E. Journal* (March 1982): 65–68.

Edwards, J.; Norton, S.; Taylor, S.; Weiss, M.; and Dusseldorp, R. "How Effective is CAI? A Review of the Research." *Educational Leadership* 33 (1975): 147–153.

Farrow, D. R. "Reducing the Risks of Military Aircrew Training through Simulation Technology." *NSPI Journal* (March 1982): 13–18.

Feingold, S. W. "PLANIT: A Language for CAI." *Datamation* 14, no. 9 (September 1968): 41–47.

Felling, R. L. "Hand-held Tactical Terminals." *Military Electronics/Countermeasures* (April 1980).

Feurzeig, W., and Lukas, G. "LOGO: A Programming Language for Mathemathics." *Educational Technology* 12, no. 3 (March 1972): 39–46.

Francis, L. "Five Phases in the Life of CBE Sites: II. Staff Selection and Retention." *ADCIS Proceedings*. San Diego, Calif., 1979.

Francis, L. "Hand-held Computers—For CBI?" *ADCIS Proceedings*. Vancouver, B. C., June 1982.

Frye, C. H. "CAI Languages: Capabilities and Applications." *Datamation* 14, no. 9 (September 1968): 34–37.

Gagne, R. M., and Briggs, L. J. *Principles of Instructional Design.*" New York: Holt, Rinehart and Winston, 1981.

Gaines, B. R. "The Learning of Perceptual Motor Skills by Men and Machine and Its Relationship to Training." *Instructional Science* 2 (1972): 263–312.

Gentner, D. R. "Toward an Intelligent Computer Tutor." In *Procedures for Instructional Systems Development*, edited by H. F. O'Neil. New York: Academic Press, 1979.

Grady, M. W.; Porter, J. E.; Satzer, W. J.; and Sprouse, B. D. *Speech Understanding in Air Intercept Controller Training System Design*. Technical Report NAVTRAEQUIPCEN 78-C-0044-1, 1978.

Gunwaldsen, R. L. *CHARGE Image Generator: Theory of Operation and Author Language Support*. TR-75-3. Alexandria, Va.: HumRRO, May 1975.

Halley, R., and Kearsley, G. "It Sure Ain't HAL: Using Computer Automated Speech in CBI Systems." *Third Canadian Symposium on Instructional Technology*. Vancouver, B. C., February 1980.

Hamovitch, M., and Van Matre, N. *Computer Managed Instruction in the Navy, III. Automated Performance Testing in the Radioman A School*. NPRDC TR-81-7. San Diego, Calif., March 1981.

Heines, J. "The Use of Computer-Managed Instruction to Control On-site, Self Instructional Training in a Small Systems Customer Environment." *ADCIS Proceedings*. Dallas, Texas, 1978.

Heines, J. "Evaluating the Use of Interactive, Computer-Managed Instruction to Control the Quality of Self-Paced Training without the Presence of an Instructor." *ADCIS Proceedings*, San Diego, Calif., 1979.

Hillelsohn, M. J., and Kearsley, G. *Evaluating the Feasibility of Using CBI for DELPRO Training.* SR 81-9. Alexandria, Va.: HumRRO, December 1981.

HumRRO. "Instructional Applications of Spatial Data Management." *Videodisc/ Videotext* (Spring 1982).

Jamison, D.; Suppes, P.; and Wells, S. "The Effectiveness of Alternative Instructional Media: A Survey." *Review of Educational Research* 44 (1974): 1–61.

Kearsley, G. "The Relevance of AI Research to CAI." *Journal Educational Technology Systems* 6, no. 3 (1978): 229–250.

Kearsley, G. "Designing and Developing Distributed Education." *Training and Development Journal* (December 1981a).

Kearsley, G. "Videodiscs in Education and Training: The Idea Becomes Reality." *Videodisc/Videotext* (Fall 1981b): 268–220.

Kearsley, G. "Authoring Systems in Computer Based Education." *Communications of the ACM* (July 1982a): 429–437.

Kearsley, G. *Costs, Benefits and Productivity in Training Systems.* Reading, Mass.: Addison-Wesley, 1982b.

Kearsley, G., and Hillelsohn, M. J. "Human Factors Considerations for CBT Systems." *Journal of Computer Based Instruction,* (May 1982).

Kearsley, G.; Hillelsohn, M. J.; and Hunter, B. "Computer Literacy in Business and Industry: Three Microcomputer Examples." *Educational Technology* (July 1982): 9–14.

Kearsley, G.; Hillelsohn, M. J.; and Seidel, R. J. "The Use of Microcomputers for Training: Business and Industry." *Journal Educational Technology Systems* 10, no. 2 (1981): 101–108.

Kearsley, G., and Hunka, S. "Copyright and CAI." *ACM SIGCUE Bulletin* 11 (1977): 2–12.

Kearsley, G., and Hunka, S. "Documentation in CBI." *ACM SIGCUE Bulletin* 13, no. 1 (1979): 3–13.

Kearsley, G., and O'Neal, A. F. "The Dialectics of Artist and Technologist in Instructional Systems Development." *Proceedings of 17th Annual AEDS Conference.* Detroit, Mich., 1979.

Kemp, J. E. *Instructional Design.* Belmont, Calif.: Fearon/Lear Seigler, 1971.

Ketner, W. B. "The Videodisc/Microcomputer for Training." *Training and Development Journal* (May 1981).

Kingman, J. C. "Designing Good Educational Software." *Creative Computing* (October 1981): 72–81.

Kling, R. "Social Analyses of Computing: Theoretical Perspectives in Recent Empirical Research." *ACM Computing Surveys* 12, no. 1 (March 1980): 61–110.

Kribs, D. H. "Authoring Techniques for Interactive Videodisc." *Journal Educational Technology Systems* 8, no. 3 (1980): 211.

Kulik, J. A.; Kulik, C. C.; and Cohen, P. A. "Effectiveness of Computer-Based College Teaching: A Meta-Analysis of Findings." *Review of Educational Research* 50, no. 4 (Winter 1980): 525–544.

Lippey, G. *Computer Assisted Test Construction*. Englewood Cliffs, N.J.: Educational Technology Publications, 1974.

Lipson, J. "Design and Development of Programs for Videodisc." *Journal Educational Technology Systems* 9, no. 3 (1981): 277.

Lockhart, K.; Sturges, P.; Van Matre, N.; and Zachai, J. *Computer Managed Instruction in the Navy: IV. The Effects of Test Item Format on Learning and Retention*. NPRDC TR 81-8. San Diego, Calif., March 1981.

Logan, R. S. "Assessment of Instructional Systems Development." In *Issues in Instructional Systems Development*, edited by H. F. O'Neil. New York: Academic Press, 1979.

Lowe, N. "A Committment to Education: Basic Math and CAI at the Aetna Life and Casualty." *ADCIS Proceedings*. San Diego, Calif., 1979.

McKnight, L. R.; Waters, B. K.; and Lamos, J. P. "Development and Evaluation of a Microcomputer Testing Terminal for Testing and Instruction." *Behavior Research Methods & Instrumentation* 10, no. 2 (1978): 340-344.

Mager, R. F. *Preparing Instructional Objectives*. Belmont, Calif.: Fearon Publishers, 1975.

Malone, T. W. "Heuristics for Designing Enjoyable User Interfaces: Lessons from Computer Games." In proceedings, *Human Factors in Computer Systems*. Gaithersburg, Md.: National Bureau of Standards, March 1982.

Marti, H., and Vogel, J. S. "The Value of a Top Management Game in the Education of Production Engineers." In *Computers in Education*, edited by R. Lewis and D. Tagg. Amsterdam: North Holland Publishers, 1981.

Martin, J. *Future Developments in Telecommunications*. Englewood Cliffs, N.J.: Prentice-Hall, 1977.

Martin, T. B. "A Practical Voice Input System." In *Computers and Communications*, edited by R. Seidel and M. Rubin. New York: Academic Press, 1977.

Merrill, M. D. *Instructional Design: Readings*. Englewood Cliffs, N.J.: Prentice-Hall, 1971.

Merrill, M. D. "Learner Control: Beyond Aptitude-Treatment Interactions." *Audiovisual Communications Review* 23 (1975): 217-226.

Merrill, M. D.; Schneider, E. W.; and Fletcher, K. A. *TICCIT*. Englewood Cliffs, N.J.: Educational Technology Publications, 1980.

Merrill, P. F. "Displaying Text on Microcomputers." In *The Technology of Text*, edited by D. H. Johassen. Englewood Cliffs, N.J.: Educational Technology Publishers, 1982.

Miller, M. L. "A Structured Planning and Debugging Environment for Elementary Programming." *Journal of Man-Machine Studies* 11 (1979): 79-95.

Misselt, A.; Francis, L.; Call-Himwich, E.; Himwich, H.; and Avner, R. A. *Implementation and Operation of Computer Based Instruction*. CERL, University of Illinois. MTC Report 25, August 1980.

Modesitt, K. L. "Training and Education at Texas Instruments: Coming of Age in Corporate Life." *ADCIS Proceedings*. Atlanta, Ga., 1981.

Montgomery, A. "An Editor for the Automated Generation of Graphics Simulations." *ADCIS Proceedings*. Vancouver, B. C., June 1982.

Nugent, G. C., and Stone, C. "Videodisc Instructional Design." *Educational Technology* (May 1980).

O'Neal, H. L.; Faust, G. W.; and O'Neal, A. F. "An Author Training Course." In *Procedures for Instructional Systems Design*, edited by H. F. O'Neil. New York: Academic Press, 1979.

O'Neal, A. F., and O'Neal, H. L. "Author Management Systems." In *Issues in Instructional Systems Design*, edited by H. F. O'Neil. New York: Academic Press, 1979.

O'Neil, H. F. *Learning Strategies*. New York: Academic Press, 1978.

O'Neil, H. F. *Procedures for Instructional Systems Design*. New York: Academic Press, 1979a.

O'Neil, H. F. *Issues in Instructional Systems Design*. New York: Academic Press, 1979b.

Orlansky, J., and String, J. *Cost-Effectiveness of Computer-Based Instruction in Military Training*. IDA P-1375. Arlington, Va.: Institute for Defense Analyses, April 1979.

Orlansky, J., and String, J. "Computer-Based Instruction for Military Training." *Defense Management Journal* (2nd quarter 1981a): 46–54.

Orlansky, J., and String, J. *"Cost-Effectiveness of Maintenance Simulators for Military Training*. IDA P-1568. Arlington, Va.: Institute for Defense Analyses, August 1981b.

Paine, T. G. S. "Transport Canada's Air Traffic Services Simulation and Evaluation Program. *Journal Educational Technology Systems* 7, no. 1 (1979): 69–77.

Parsons, H. M. *The Design of Man-Machine Systems Experiments*. Baltimore, Md.: Johns Hopkins Press, 1970.

Pask, G., and Scott, B. C. E. "Learning Strategies and Individual Competence." *International Journal of Man-Machine Studies* 4 (1972): 217–253.

Pflasterer, D., and Montgomery, A. "CAMIL and the Effective Implementation of Instructional Software for a Large Scale CMI/CAI System. *Proceedings 17th Annual AEDS Conference*. Detroit, Mich., May 1979.

Pine, S. M.; Koch, C. G.; and Malec, V. M. *Electronic Equipment Maintenance Training (EEMT) System: System Definition Phase*. NPRDC TR 81-11. San Diego, Calif., May 1981.

Polcyn, K. A. "The U.S. Navy CMI Satellite Demonstration." *Educational Technology* (December 1976): 21–25.

Popham, W. J. *Educational Evaluation*. Englewood Cliffs, N.J.: Prentice-Hall, 1975.

Rahmlow, H. F. *Computer Based Education within Insurance and Related Financial Services*. Bryn Mayr, Penn.: American College, December 1978.

Rahmlow, H. F. "Outstanding Large-Scale Projects in Business and Education." *ADCIS Proceedings*. San Diego, Calif., 1979.

Rahmlow, H. F.; Fratini, R. C.; and Ghesquiere, J. R. *PLATO*. Englewood Cliffs, N.J.: Educational Technology Publications, 1980.

Rebstock, T. C. "CBT Breaks Ground in the Oilfield." *ADCIS Proceedings*. Washington, D.C., 1980.

Rebstock, T. C., and Harkey, J. C. "PLATO Simulation for Process Operator Training. *ADCIS Proceedings*. San Diego, Calif., 1979.

Reid, J. B.; Palmer, R.; Whitlock, J.; and Jones, J. "Computer Assisted Instruction: Performance of Student Pairs Related to Individual Differences." *Journal of Educational Psychology* 65 (1973): 65–73.

Reigeluth, C. M. "TICCIT to the Future: Advances in Instructional Theory for CBI." *Journal of Computer Based Instruction* 6 (1979): 40–46.

Rockway, M. R., and Yasatuke, J. Y. "The Evolution of the Air Force Advanced Instructional System." *Journal Educational Technology Systems* (Winter 1974).

Roid, G. "The Technology of Test-Item Writing. In *Procedures for Instructional Systems Development*, edited by H. F. O'Neil. New York: Academic Press, 1979.

Saal, H. J. "Local Area Networks." *Byte* (October 1981): 92–112.

Sanders, W. R.; Benbassat, G. V.; and Smith, R. L. Speech Synthesis for CAI: The MISS System and Its Applications." *ACM SIGCUE Bulletin* 8 (1976): 200–211.

Schneider, E. W., and Bennion, J. L. *Videodiscs*. Englewood Cliffs, N.J.: Educational Technology Publications, 1981.

Schultz, R. E. "Computer Aids for Developing Tests and Instruction." In *Procedures for Instructional Systems Development*, edited by H. F. O'Neil. New York: Academic Press, 1979.

Schuyler, J. A. "Computer Augmentation of the CAI Courseware Authoring Process: The CAI Design System." *Journal of Computer Based Instruction* 3, no. 2 (1976): 59–67.

Seaman, J. "Microcomputers Invade the Executive Suite." *Computer Decisions* (February 1981): 68–174.

Seidel, R. J. "Transactional Evaluation: Assessing Human Interactions during Program Development." *ACM SIGCUE Bulletin* (December 1978).

Seidel, R. J. "It's 1980: Do You Know Where Your Computer Is?" *Phi Delta Kappan* (March 1980): 481–485.

Seidel, R. J., and Wagner, H. "A Cost Effectiveness Specification." In *Procedures for Instructional Systems Development*, edited by H. F. O'Neil. New York: Academic Press, 1979.

Seidel, R. J., and Wagner, H. "Management." In *Computer Based Instruction*, edited by H. F. O'Neil. New York: Academic Press, 1981.

Seidel, R. J.; Wagner, H.; Rosenblatt, R. D.; Hillelsohn, M. J.; and Stelzer, J. "Learner Control of Instructional Sequencing within an Adaptive Tutorial Environment." *Instructional Science* 7 (1978): 37–80.

Shelley, C. B., and Groom, V. "The Apollo Flight Controller Training System Concept and Its Educational Implications." In *Computer Assisted Instruction, Testing and Guidance*, edited by W. Holtzman. New York: Harper and Row, 1970.

Siegel, M. A. "Computer-Based Education in Prison Schools." *Journal Educational Technology Systems* 7, no. 3 (1979): 239–256.

Siegel, M. A., and Simutis, Z. M. "CAI for Adult Basic Skills Training: Two Applications." *ADCIS Proceedings*. San Diego, Calif., 1979.

Sigel, E. *Videotext*. New York: Harmony Books, 1980.

Sigel, E.; Schubin, M.; and Merrill, P. F. *Videodiscs*. White Plains, N.Y.: Knowledge Industry Publications, 1980.

Sleeman, D., and Brown, J. S. *Intelligent Tutoring Systems*. New York: Academic Press, 1982.

Smith, S. L., and Duggan, B. C. "Do Large Shared Displays Facilitate Group Effort?" *Human Factors* 7 (1965): 237–244.

Starkweather, J. "A Common Language for a Variety of Programming Needs." In *Computer Assisted Instruction: A Book of Readings*, edited by R. Atkinson and H. Wilson. New York: Academic Press, 1969.

Steinberg, E. "Review of Student Control in Computer Assisted Instruction." *Journal of Computer Based Instruction* 3 (1977): 84–90.

Suppes, P., and Macken, E. "The Historical Path from Research and Development to Operational Use of CAI." *Educational Technology* (April 1978): 9–12.

Suppes, P., and Morningstar, M. *Computer Assisted Instruction at Stanford, 1968–1968; Data, Models and Evaluation of the Arithmetic Programs*. New York: Academic Press, 1972.

Tanenbaum, A. S. *Computer Networks*. Englewood Cliffs, N.J.: Prentice-Hall, 1981.

Taylor, S. S. "CREATE: A Computer-Based Authoring Curriculum." In *Issues in Instructional Systems Development*, edited by H. F. O'Neil. New York: Academic Press, 1979.

Tesler, L. "The Smalltalk Environment." *Byte* 6, no. 8 (August 1981): 90–147.

Thiagarajan, S., and Stolovitch, H. D. *Instructional Simulation Games*. Englewood Cliffs, N.J.: Educational Technology Publications, 1978.

Thomas, D. B. "The Effectiveness of CAI in Secondary Schools." *AEDS Journal* 12, no. 3 (Spring 1979): 103–116.

Tosti, D. T., and Ball, J. R. "A Behavioral Approach to Instructional Design and Media Selection." *Audiovisual Communications Review* 1 (1969): 5–25.

Trollip, S. R. "The Evaluation of a Complex Computer-Base Flight Procedures Trainer." *Human Factors* 21 (1979): 47–54.

Tuckman, B. W. *Evaluating Instructional Programs*. Boston: Allyn and Bacon, 1979.

Tydeman, J. "Videotex." *The Futurist* (February 1982).

Van Matre, N. "The Many Uses of the Evaluation in the Navy's CMI System." *ADCIS Proceedings*. Dallas, Texas, 1978.

Van Matre, N. *Computer Managed Instruction in the Navy, I. Research Background and Status*. NPRDC TR 80-33. San Diego, Calif., September 1980.

Van Matre, N.; Hamovitch, M.; Lockhart, K; and Squire, L. *Computer Managed Instruction in the Navy, II. A Comparison of Two Student/Instructor Ratios in CMI Learning Centers*. NPRDC TR 81-6. San Diego, Calif., February 1981.

Van Matre, N.; Pennypacker, H. S.; Hartman W. M.; Brett, B. E.; and Ward, L. O. "The Instructional Effects of Charting Student Performance during CMI." *ADCIS Proceedings*. San Diego, Calif., 1979.

Visonhaler, J., and Bass, R. "A Summary of Ten Major Studies of CAI Drill and Practice." *Educational Technology* 12, no. 2 (1972): 29–32.

Wagner, H., and Seidel, R. J. "Program Evaluation." In *Learning Strategies*, edited by H. F. O'Neil. New York: Academic Press, 1978.

Wagner, H.; Trexler, R. C.; Hillelsohn, M. J.; and Seidel, M. J. *Automated Instructional Development System: Validation Study*. RP-ED-78-6. Alexandria, Va.: HumRRO, March 1978.

Warner, S. S. "The Sales Call Simulator: A System for Rapid Production of Specialized Training Courseware." *ADCIS Proceedings*. San Diego, Calif., 1979.

Weiss, D. J. "Computerized Adaptive Achievement Testing." In *Procedures for Instructional Systems Development*, edited by H. F. O'Neil. New York: Academic Press, 1979.

Williams, G. "The Panasonic and Quasar Hand-Held Computers." *Byte* (January 1981).

Williams, M.; Hollan, J.; and Stevens, A. "An Overview of STEAMER: An Advanced Computer-Assisted Instruction System for Propulsion Engineering." *Behavioral Research Methods & Instrumentation* 13, no. 2 (1981): 85–90.

Zinn, K. "Instructional Programming Languages." *Educational Technology* (March 1970): 43–46.

Index